COMPLETE YEAR 3

Weekly Learning Activities

MW01130460

Thinking Kids™
Carson-Dellosa Publishing LLC
Greensboro, North Carolina

Thinking Kids
An imprint of Carson-Dellosa Publishing LLC
P.O. Box 35665
Greensboro, NC 27425 USA

© 2014 Carson-Dellosa Publishing LLC. Except as permitted under the United States Copyright Act, no part of this publication may be reproduced, stored, or distributed in any form or by any means (mechanically, electronically, recording, etc.) without the prior written consent of Carson-Dellosa Publishing LLC. Thinking Kids is an imprint of Carson-Dellosa Publishing LLC.

Printed in the USA • All rights reserved.   ISBN 978-1-48380-193-3
02-209147784

Table of Contents

Table of Contents

Table of Contents

The *Complete Year* series has been designed by educators to provide an entire school year's worth of practice pages, teaching suggestions, and multi-sensory activities to support your child's learning at home. Handy organizers are included to help students and parents stay on track and to let you see at a glance the important skills for each quarter and each week of the academic year.

A variety of resources are included to help you provide high-quality learning experiences during this important year of your child's development.

Suggested Calendar (Page 7)

Use this recommended timetable to plan learning activities for your child during all 36 weeks of the school year.

A Guide to School Skills and Subject Areas for Third Grade: Reading and Language Arts, Math, Science, Social Studies (Page 8)

Refer to this useful guide for information about what your child will be learning this school year, what to expect from your third grader, and how to help your child develop skills in each subject area.

Quarter Introductions (Pages 14, 108, 202, 296)

Four brief introductions outline the skills covered in practice pages for each nine-week grading period of the school year. In addition, they include a variety of ideas for multi-sensory learning activities in each subject area. These active, hands-on projects are fun for parents and children to do together and emphasize real-world applications for school skills.

Weekly Skill Summaries (Example: Page 17)

Thirty-six handy charts precede the practice pages for each week and give a snapshot of the skills covered. In addition, they provide ideas for fun, multi-sensory learning activities for each subject area.

Practice Pages (Example: Page 18)

Nine practice pages are provided each week for a total of over 300 skill-building activities to help your child succeed this year.

Quarter Check-Ups (Pages 107, 201, 295, 389)

Four informal assessment pages allow students to do a quick self-check of the important skills emphasized during the previous nine weeks. Parents can use these pages to see at a glance the skills their children have mastered.

Suggested *Complete Year* Calendar*

First Quarter: Weeks 1–9
(First nine-week grading period of the school year, usually August–October)

Second Quarter: Weeks 10–18
(Second nine-week grading period of the school year, usually October–December)

Third Quarter: Weeks 19–27
(Third nine-week grading period of the school year, usually January–March)

Fourth Quarter: Weeks 28–36
(Fourth nine-week grading period of the school year, usually April–June)

During Each Nine-Week Quarter:

- Read the **Quarter Introduction** to get an overview of the skills and subject areas emphasized. Choose several multi-sensory learning activities you plan to do with your child this quarter.

- Each week, glance at the **Weekly Skill Summary** to see targeted skills. Make a quick plan for the practice pages and multi-sensory learning activities your child will complete.

- Choose **Practice Pages** that emphasize skills your child needs to work on. Each page should take 10 minutes or less to complete.

- Ask your child to check the boxes on the **Quarter Check-Up** to show what skills he or she has mastered. Praise your child's progress and take note of what he or she still needs to work on.

* This calendar provides a schedule for using *Complete Year* during a typical nine-month academic calendar. If your child attends a year-round school or a school with a different schedule, you can easily adapt this calendar by counting the weeks your child attends school and dividing by four.

A Guide to School Skills for Third Grade

This guide provides background information about the skills and subject areas that are important for success in third grade. Tips are provided for helping your child develop in each curricular area.

Complete Year supports skills included in the Grade 3 Common Core State Standards for English Language Arts and Mathematics, which have been adopted by most U.S. states. A complete guide to these standards may be found at www.corestandards.org.

In addition, activities in *Complete Year* support the study of science and social studies topics appropriate for third grade.

 Reading and Language Arts

Reading

In third grade, your child will enjoy reading a wide variety of teacher-selected and self-selected texts. By this time, many children have mastered basic information about the alphabet, phonics, and sight words. They are able to read longer texts with greater speed and fluency. Your third grader will read stories, poems, chapter books, and nonfiction texts for learning in content areas such as science and social studies.

- Guided Reading
  Take the opportunity to teach and reinforce a variety of skills based on what your child is reading. Skills may include building vocabulary, understanding grammar, listening, following directions, reading comprehension, recognizing the main idea, recognizing details, sequencing, character analysis, cause and effect, distinguishing between fact and fiction, comparing and contrasting, predicting outcomes, classifying, making inferences, drawing conclusions, and critical thinking. The mastery of these skills will provide your child with the tools needed for being an independent reader.

- Independent Reading
  Provide 15–30 minutes each day for your child to read a book of his or her own choosing. Encourage your child to explore different genres such as historical fiction, fantasy, adventure, science fiction, fables and folktales, biography, poetry, and nonfiction.

- Reading Aloud
Even though your child is becoming an independent reader, taking time to read aloud together provides many benefits. Listening to stories promotes increased attention span, vocabulary development, reading comprehension, critical thinking, general knowledge about the world, and a deeper understanding of grammar and language. As your child matures, he or she may be interested in listening to longer and more complex chapter books. If your child enjoys it, consider trading the book back and forth as you read aloud, making up dramatic voices for the characters. A list of read-alouds for third graders is found on page 394.

- Suggested Activities Before, During, and After Reading
Before reading, encourage your child to…
-Talk about his or her purpose for reading the book. Is it primarily for enjoyment? To practice specific skills?
-Look at the book's cover and predict what the story will be about. If possible, relate the subject to personal experiences.
-Preview the book and choose several new vocabulary words. Write these on an index card to be used as a bookmark.

During reading, encourage your child to…
-Monitor comprehension by frequently asking "Does this make sense?"
-Look back at previously read passages to answer questions. Reread confusing parts.
-Make predictions by asking "What do I think will happen next? Why?"
-Make inferences by asking questions such as "What kind of person is this character? How do I know?"
-Create mental images to help visualize the author's descriptions.
-Consider taking notes when reading nonfiction.
-Use strategies to find the meaning of an unknown word: use context clues, ask a knowledgeable person for the meaning, or look up the definition in a dictionary.

After reading, encourage your child to…
-Practice a specific skill such as understanding adjectives or recalling details. Look for examples in the book.
-Think of questions that remain about the story. Go back and reread specific passages to help answer questions.
-Summarize the book orally or in writing.

-Do a creative project about the book's theme, setting, characters, or events. Some ideas for projects are found below.

- Book Projects
  After reading a book, your child might enjoy planning and carrying out one or more of these projects.
  -Write an interview with a character.
  -Illustrate a favorite scene.
  -Create a commercial to promote the book.
  -Write an anonymous review of the book at an online bookstore.
  -Write to the author.
  -Design a book jacket.
  -Write a new ending.
  -Invent a slogan that states the theme of the book.
  -Create a Venn diagram that compares and contrasts events, characters, or settings.
  -Keep a journal of books you have read. Write the date and the title of the book you read. Keep track of your thoughts and feelings as you read.

Language Skills

Your third grader will study a wide range of grammar and language skills, often in the context of reading, writing, and speaking.

- Spelling
  Spelling is a skill that requires practice, but it does not have to be a chore. Never overemphasize the need for correct spelling to the point where it discourages your child from writing freely. Instead, teach your child that spelling is an interesting study of words and word patterns. Use multi-sensory activities for helping your child practice spelling words. For example, sing the letters that make up each word or spell words while jumping, clapping, or marching. Show your child how to do "rainbow writing," or writing a spelling word at a large size and then tracing it with several crayon colors for reinforcement. Provide a notebook where your child can write personal "spelling demons," or tricky words such as **beautiful**, **friendly**, and **surprise**.

- Grammar and Usage
  This year, your child will work with parts of speech (nouns, pronouns, verbs, adjectives, adverbs, etc.), verb tenses, writing complete sentences, punctuation, and other grammar and usage skills.

  Help your child develop these skills by closely examining sentences from a favorite book, pointing out capital letters, punctuation marks, subject-verb agreement, and other features. Avoid emphasizing too many skills at once. If your child's writing shows several types of language errors, choose just one or two to emphasize during rewriting.

- Vocabulary Development
  Your child's vocabulary will grow by leaps and bounds as he or she reads new books, participates in classroom discussions, and investigates new science and social studies topics. During third grade, your child will study homophones (words that sound alike but have different spellings and meanings), word parts (including word roots, prefixes, and suffixes), context clues, and words from reading.

Writing

In third grade, your child will write fiction and nonfiction stories, book reports and other pieces that express an opinion, and reports and other pieces that provide information. He or she will draw on personal experiences and on research from the Internet and other sources. Your son or daughter will learn to use the writing process to plan, draft, revise, and proofread.

Math

Math is an integral part of your child's world. Everyday experiences such as preparing meals, shopping, and playing games provide rich opportunities to explore numbers, shapes, quantities, and patterns. As you go about routines at home with your child, make sure to include discussions about numbers. Let your child see that you use math when you pay bills, make home repairs, or keep a calendar. During third grade, your child will review and master skills taught in earlier grades (such as addition and subtraction) and begin to explore multiplication and division, fractions, geometry, and other new concepts.

- Using the Four Operations (Addition, Subtraction, Multiplication, Division)
Your third grader will practice using addition and subtraction to solve problems with multi-digit numbers. A deeper understanding of place value (see below) will help your child with addition that requires regrouping (or "carrying" to the next place column) and subtraction that requires regrouping (or "borrowing" from the next place column).

  This year, your child will learn that multiplication takes the place of repeated addition (for example, $2 + 2 + 2 = 2 \times 3$) and that division splits a number into equal shares (for example, $6 \div 3$ divides 6 into 3 equal shares of 2). Your child will practice multiplication and division facts.

  Use a variety of strategies to help your child solve problems using the four operations. Flash cards and practice pages like the ones found in this book will help with speed, accuracy, and memorization of facts. Use manipulatives such as coins, beads, craft sticks, and dry pasta shapes for hands-on practice with regrouping and other abstract concepts. Finally, relate math problems to your child's interests and everyday experiences.

- Place Value
In third grade, your child will continue to work with place value to develop the understanding that a number such as **2,873** is made up of three ones, seven tens, eight hundreds, and two thousands. Your child will use this knowledge to round numbers to a given place value and to solve multi-digit problems using the four operations. To help with place value, use manipulatives (such as stacks of interlocking blocks) or a multi-column chart like the one described on page 15.

- Fractions
This year, your child will learn that fractions are parts of whole numbers. He or she will represent fractions on a number line and recognize that some fractions, such as $\frac{1}{2}$ and $\frac{2}{4}$, are equivalent. Help your child with fractions by cutting paper shapes into equal parts and by marking the position of fractions on a number line. Use a standard ruler to show how one whole inch can be divided into halves, fourths, eighths, and sixteenths.

- Measurement and Geometry

  Third graders will work with telling time, counting money, measuring length, measuring volume, finding the perimeter and area of a shape, and creating graphs. To help with these skills, make sure your child has access to materials and tools including real or pretend coins and dollar bills, an analog and a digital clock, rulers in inches and centimeters, and graph paper.

  Whenever possible, involve your child with everyday measuring tasks. Ask him or her to weigh produce at the grocery store, decide how many minutes are left before it is time to go somewhere, count out money at the store, or measure dimensions when helping with home repairs.

Science

Your third grader will enjoy reading and learning about animals, ecosystems, space, rocks and minerals, plants, the human body, vehicles, inventions, technology, and a myriad of other fascinating science topics. Encourage your child to satisfy his or her curiosity by reading nonfiction books from the library, exploring science Web sites for kids, and conducting supervised, hands-on experiments. Activity suggestions in this book will get you started.

Social Studies

Third-grade social studies will expand your child's knowledge about communities and communication, world history and geography, government, and famous Americans. Encourage your child to learn about current events by regularly reading a newspaper or Internet news site or by watching news programs on TV. Help your child gather information and make careful judgments. Take time to watch TV documentaries with your child and discuss the views presented. Provide a globe, world map, or atlas to help your child better understand his or her place in the world. Use the activity suggestions in this book as a springboard to exploring social studies with your child.

First Quarter Introduction

The first weeks of a new school year are an exciting and eventful time for your child. As he or she becomes accustomed to new routines during the school day, take time to establish routines at home, too. Set a regular bedtime, provide a good breakfast each day, and allow time for active play. Make sure that reading is part of your child's daily routine, too. Supporting your child's learning at home is a vital part of his or her academic success. Using the weekly resources and activities in this book will help.

First Quarter Skills

Practice pages in this book for Weeks 1–9 will help your child improve the following skills.

Reading and Language Arts
- Understand the difference between common and proper nouns
- Make words plural
- Understand pronouns
- Understand verbs, including helping verbs, linking verbs, and irregular verbs
- Understand verbs in the present, past, and future tenses
- Use correct subject-verb agreement
- Understand adjectives and adverbs
- Review types of sentences

Math
- Add numbers, including multi-digit numbers, with and without regrouping
- Subtract numbers, including multi-digit numbers, with and without regrouping
- Practice mental math
- Solve word problems

Multi-Sensory Learning Activities

Try these fun activities for enhancing your child's learning and development during the first quarter of the school year. Be sure to choose activities that include speaking, listening, touching, and active movement.

Reading and Language Arts

Give your child the subject of a sentence, such as **city lights**, **the proud peacock**, **an old friend**, or **noisy crowds**. Challenge your child to finish the sentence. Have your child write each sentence, circling the noun in the subject and one or more verbs in the predicate.

Brainstorm adjectives that can describe people and personalities such as **carefree**, **grumpy**, **anxious**, **lighthearted**, **curious**, or **jolly**. Then, ask your child to list adjectives to describe characters from a book or movie.

Play "Hangman." Explain that the secret word is a proper noun and tell whether it names a specific person (such as **Aunt Jennifer**), place (such as **Seattle**) or thing (such as the **Atlantic Ocean**). As a further clue, provide the first, capital letter of the word.

Encourage your child to write a funny poem, play, or illustrated book about irregular verbs. In it, he or she should explain that the past-tense forms of **run**, **grow**, **give**, **wear**, and similar verbs are **ran**, **grew**, **gave**, and **wore** (not **runned**, **growed**, **gived**, and **weared**!).

Print a short story or folktale from a free Web site. After your child reads the story, ask him or her to use a colored pen to circle each pronoun and draw an arrow from it to the noun the pronoun replaces.

Math

Create or purchase flash cards for addition and subtraction facts with answers from 0–20. Use the cards with your child for five minutes each day.

Use the flash cards from the previous activity. Spread the cards on the floor, problem side up. Call out a number from **1** to **20**. When you say "go," your child should run and collect all the cards whose problems have that number as their solution.

Make a place value board by dividing a sheet of poster board into three columns labeled **Hundreds**, **Tens**, and **Ones**. Then, give your child a box of cereal and 18 small zip-top bags. Ask your child to fill nine of the bags by placing 10 pieces of cereal in each bag. Ask your child to fill the other nine bags by counting out 100 pieces of cereal for each bag. Next, ask your child to use the board, the bags of cereal, and single pieces of

First Quarter Introduction, cont.

cereal to model numbers such as **46** or **123**. For **123**, your child would place one 100 bag in the Hundreds column, two 10 bags in the Tens column, and three single pieces of cereal in the Ones column. After your child is proficient with using the board to show numbers, ask him or her to use it to model addition and subtraction problems that require regrouping.

Make up story problems that relate to your child's interests. For example, say, "Your video game character had 18 bags of gold. He found 8 more bags of gold on his latest quest. How many bags of gold does he have all together?"

 **Science**

Have your child list plants and animals native to your area. Encourage him or her to choose one plant and one animal to research. For each species, investigate appearance, behavior, habitat, etc. Then, ask your child to create a booklet, poster, or diorama that shows what he or she learned.

 **Social Studies**

Encourage your child to learn about current events by reading an Internet news site, watching a TV newscast, or reading a newspaper. Then, ask him or her to write a brief summary of the most important and interesting news of the day. Listen as your child reads the summary at the dinner table or before bed. Choose one or more events from the summary to discuss together.

 Seasonal Fun

Show how to fold cardstock into tent-shaped place cards for a special meal. Ask your child to use his or her best handwriting to write each family member's name on a card first with pencil and then with pen. Use a hot glue gun to attach fall leaves, acorns, wildflowers, and other natural items to celebrate the season.

Make spiced cider with your child. For 12 servings, simmer these ingredients on the stove for 20 minutes: 1 quart cider, 3 c cranberry juice, 2T brown sugar, 2 cinnamon sticks, $\frac{1}{2}$ t whole cloves, 4 lemon slices. Strain and serve. Use addition and subtraction to modify the recipe for the number of people in your family.

Week 1 Skills

Subject	Skill	Multi-Sensory Learning Activities
Reading and Language Arts	Understand common and proper nouns.	• Complete Practice Pages 18–20. • Challenge your child to write limericks like this one, varying the name of the place in each poem: There was a young lady from Leeds Who swallowed a package of seeds. Now this sorry young lass Is quite covered in grass, But has all the tomatoes she needs! Challenge your child to write limericks that name people instead of places, too. Remind your child that the names of specific people and places are proper nouns, and always begin with capital letters.
	Add **s** or **es** to make nouns plural.	• Complete Practice Pages 21 and 22. • Write these words on index cards: **student, berry, story, baseball, family, house**. Then, write **s** and **ies** on self-sticking notes. Have your child add one of the sticky notes to each card to show how to make the word plural.
Math	Add single-digit and two-digit numbers.	• Complete Practice Pages 23–26. • Have your child write addition facts on index cards, then cut apart each problem and answer in puzzle-like pieces. Mix up the pieces and have your child match the problems and sums.

Common and Proper Nouns

Look at the list of nouns in the box. Write the common nouns under the kite. Write the proper nouns under the balloons. Remember to capitalize the first letter of each proper noun.

lisa smith

cats

shoelace

saturday

dr. martin

whistle

teddy bears

main street

may

boy

lawn chair

mary stewart

bird

florida

school

apples

washington, d.c.

pine cone

elizabeth jones

charley reynolds

Nouns in the Clouds

If a word is a common noun, write it in the cloud titled **Common Nouns**. If it is a proper noun, change its first letter to a capital letter and write it in the cloud titled **Proper Nouns**.

1. ohio

2. dr. simon

3. ocean

4. president lincoln

5. dog

6. jane

7. new york

8. ice cream

9. mount everest

10. columbus

11. teacher

12. second avenue

13. circus

14. sheriff

Common Nouns

Proper Nouns

Proper Nouns

Write about you! Write a proper noun for each category below. Capitalize the first letter of each proper noun.

1. Your first name: _____

2. Your last name: _____

3. Your street: _____

4. Your city: _____

5. Your state: _____

6. Your school: _____

7. Your best friend's name: _____

8. Your teacher: _____

9. Your favorite book character: _____

10. Your favorite vacation place: _____

Bright and Beautiful

Color the space yellow if you have to add an **s** to make the word plural.

Color the space orange if you have to add **es** to make the word plural.

Color the space blue if you have to change the last letter, then add **es** to make the word plural.

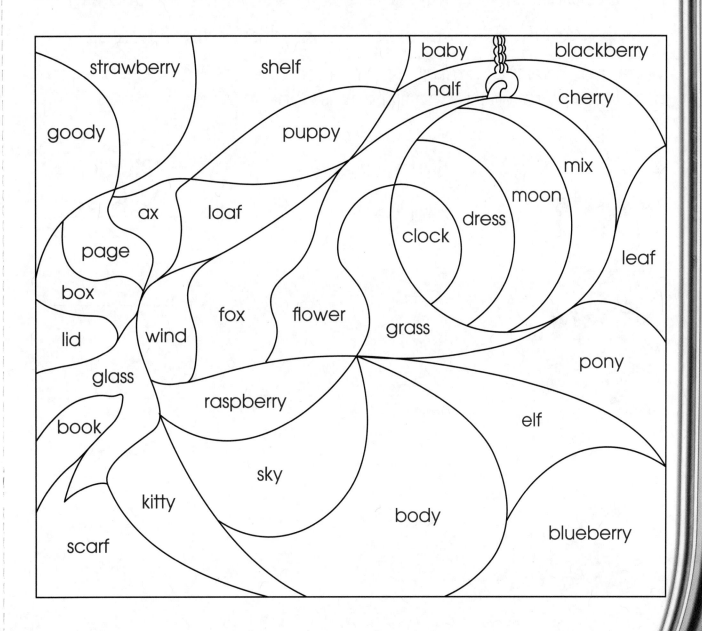

Plurals

A word that names one thing is **singular**, like **house**. A word that names more than one thing is **plural**, like **houses**.

To make a word plural, we usually add **s**.

Examples: one book — two book**s**   one tree — four tree**s**

To make plural words that end in **s**, **ss**, **x**, **sh** and **ch**, we add **es**.

Examples: one fox — two fox**es**   one bush — three bush**es**

Write the word that is missing from each pair below. Add **s** or **es** to make the plural words. The first one is done for you.

	Singular	Plural
	table	tables
	beach	_____
	class	_____
	_____	axes
	brush	_____
	_____	crashes

Add 'Em Up!

Addition is "putting together" or adding two or more numbers to find the sum.

Add the following problems as quickly and as accurately as you can.

```
   3        6        5        2
 + 2      + 4      + 4      + 9
```

```
   6        4        9        7        8        8
 + 2      + 1      + 6      + 6      + 7      + 9
```

```
   9        1        4        7        5        5
 + 4      + 8      + 7      + 9      + 6      + 3
```

```
            6        8        7        4
          + 6      + 8      + 7      + 4
```

```
            2        5        3        5
          + 8      + 2      + 6      + 8
```

How quickly did you complete this page? _____

Going in Circles

Where the circles meet, write the sum of the numbers from the circles on the right and left and above and below. The first row shows you what to do.

Magic Squares

Some of the number squares below are "magic" and some are not. Squares that add up to the same number horizontally, vertically and diagonally are "magic." Add the numbers horizontally and vertically in each square to discover which ones are "magic."

Example:

4	9	2
3	5	7
8	1	6

15
15
15

15 15 15 15

Magic? **yes**

1.

7	2	1
3	4	8
5	9	6

___ ___ ___

Magic? _____

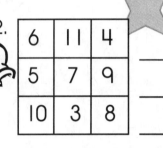

2.

6	11	4
5	7	9
10	3	8

___ ___ ___

Magic? _____

3.

3	8	1
2	4	6
7	0	5

___ ___ ___

Magic? _____

4.

2	7	0
1	3	5
6	9	4

___ ___ ___

Magic? _____

5.

5	10	3
4	6	8
9	2	7

___ ___ ___

Magic? _____

6.

7	12	5
6	8	10
11	4	9

___ ___ ___

Magic? _____

7.

1	2	3
4	5	6
7	8	9

___ ___ ___

Magic? _____

8.

6	7	4
1	5	9
8	3	2

___ ___ ___

Magic? _____

Challenge: Can you discover a pattern for number placement in the magic squares? Try to make a magic square of your own.

Addition

Add.

Example:

Add the ones.

26
+21
‾‾
7

Add the tens.

26
+21
‾‾
47

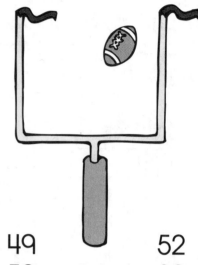

18
+11
‾‾

24
+35
‾‾

38
+21
‾‾

49
+50
‾‾

52
+33
‾‾

75
+12
‾‾

83
+16
‾‾

67
+32
‾‾

44
+25
‾‾

28
+41
‾‾

68 + 20 = _____   54 + 25 = _____   71 + 17 = _____

The Lions scored 42 points. The Clippers scored 21 points.
How many points were scored in all?   _____

Week 2 Skills

Subject	Skill	Multi-Sensory Learning Activities
Reading and Language Arts	Replace nouns with pronouns.	• Complete Practice Page 28. • Give your child clues to a person, thing, or group of people. Use a pronoun such as **he**, **she**, **they**, or **it** in each clue. Can your child guess the noun?
	Understand verbs.	• Complete Practice Pages 29 and 30. • Read *Thank You, Amelia Bedelia* by Peggy Parish (or any other Amelia Bedelia book). Ask your child to list the things that Amelia Bedelia was asked to do in the story. Emphasize that these words are verbs. Ask your child to use the verbs in different sentences, adding **–s** or **–ing** endings as needed.
	Distinguish between nouns and verbs.	• Complete Practice Pages 31 and 32. • Read *The Legend of the Indian Paintbrush* by Tomie dePaola. Then, take turns with your child acting out and guessing nouns from the story. Remind your child that a noun names a person, place, or thing.
Math	Add larger numbers with and without regrouping.	• Complete Practice Pages 33–36. • Write addition equations for your child to solve, putting a blank in different positions. Examples: 45 + _____ = 96, _____ + 18 = 72. • Ask your child to make a poster or digital presentation explaining how to use regrouping to "carry" a ten or hundred when adding problems like this one: 167 + 78.

Little Words Mean a Lot

A **pronoun** is a word that takes the place of a noun. These sentences are based on *The Littles* by John Peterson. Above each **bold** word below, write a pronoun that could replace it.

she	it	her	we	he	his	I	him	they	your

1. Uncle Nick shouted at Mus Mus as **Uncle Nick** walked to the kitchen.

2. **Lucy** ran to **Lucy's** mother in tears.

3. **The Littles** crowded up to the kitchen door.

4. Granny Little said, "**Granny Little** wouldn't believe it if **Granny Little** didn't see it with these old eyes."

5. Lucy said, "**Mus Mus**" is a cute name.

6. **Will and Tom** have gone to get some leftovers.

7. **Uncle Nick** kept on writing **Uncle Nick's** life story.

8. **Mrs. Little** whispered, "Don't bother **Uncle Nick**."

9. Granny Little turned **Granny Little's** back on **Uncle Nick**.

10. Tom told Uncle Nick, "**Lucy and Tom** want to read **Uncle Nick's** book."

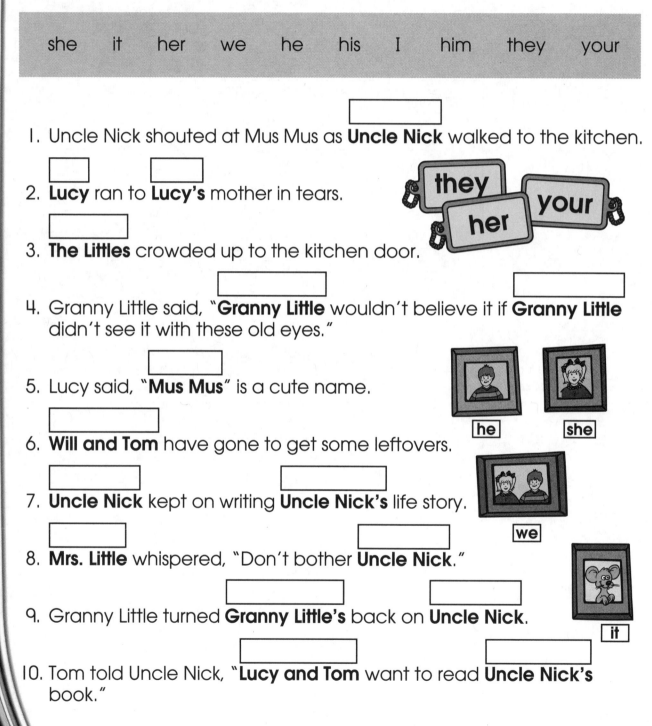

Verbs

Write the verb that answers each question. Write a sentence using that verb.

| stir | clap | drag | hug | plan | grab |

Which verb means to put your arms around someone?

_____

_____

Which verb means to mix something with a spoon?

_____

_____

Which verb means to pull something along the ground?

_____

_____

Which verb means to take something suddenly?

_____

_____

Now and Then

Match a verb from the box with each sentence. Write its letter in the blank.

A. made	C. gazed	E. broke	G. swallow	I. cross
B. tell	D. filled	F. ride	H. come	J. snipped

1. The Scarecrow told the Wizard he had _____ for his brains.
2. The Wizard _____ the Scarecrow's head with a mixture of bran and pins so he would be sharp.
3. To hold his heart, the Tin Woodman had his chest _____ open.
4. His heart was _____ of silk and sawdust.
5. Courage is inside you so the Lion had to _____ a green liquid.
6. The Lion was proud to _____ his friends of his new gift.

7. Oz told Dorothy she should _____ the desert first on her way home.
8. He invited her to _____ in his hot air balloon for the trip to Kansas.
9. The citizens of the Emerald City _____ up at the beautiful silk balloon.
10. Just as Dorothy reached the balloon, the ropes _____ and the balloon rose into the air without her.

Write each verb under past or present.

Past	Present
_____	_____
_____	_____
_____	_____
_____	_____
_____	_____

Nouns and Verbs

A **noun** names a person, place or thing. A **verb** tells what something does or what something is. Some words can be a noun one time and a verb another time.

Complete each pair of sentences with a word from the box. The word will be a noun in the first sentence and a verb in the second sentence.

mix	kiss	brush	crash

1. Did your dog ever give you a _____?
   (noun)

   I have a cold, so I can't _____ you today.
   (verb)

2. I brought my comb and my _____.
   (noun)

   I will _____ the leaves off your coat.
   (verb)

3. Was anyone hurt in the _____?
   (noun)

   If you aren't careful, you will _____ into me.
   (verb)

4. We bought a cake _____ at the store.
   (noun)

   I will _____ the eggs together.
   (verb)

Nouns and Verbs

Write the correct word in each sentence. Use each word once. Write **N** above the words that are used as nouns (people, places and things). Write **V** above the words that are used as verbs (what something does or what something is).

Example:

          N   V

I need a ___drink___. I will ___drink___ milk.

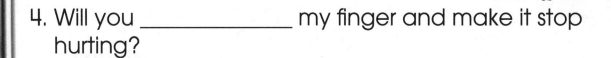

mix	beach	church	class	kiss	brush	crash

1. It's hot today, so let's go to the _____.

2. The _____ was crowded.

3. I can't find my paint _____.

4. Will you _____ my finger and make it stop hurting?

5. I will _____ the red and yellow paint to get orange.

6. The teacher asked our _____ to get in line.

7. If you move that bottom can, the rest will _____ to the floor.

Leafy Addition

Add, then color according to the code.

Code:

green — 79   orange — 35   red — 78

yellow — 87   purple — 56   brown — 94

57
+ 21

34
+ 22

23
+ 12

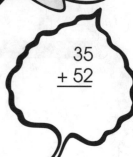
35
+ 52

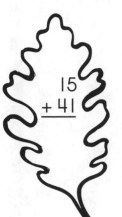
15
+ 41

62
+ 32

20
+ 74

34
+ 44

56
+ 23

47
+ 40

27
+ 8

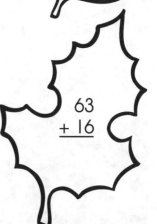
63
+ 16

Adding Larger Numbers

When adding two-, three- and four-digit numbers, add the ones first, then tens, hundreds, thousands, and so on.

Examples:

Tens	Ones
5	4
+ 2	5
	9

Tens	Ones
5	4
+ 2	5
7	9

Add the following numbers.

```
  81          67          34          730
+23         +22         +82         +265
```

```
  76        1,803         523          267
+73        +1,104       +476         + 12
```

```
                         4,254         111
                        + 545        + 82
```

```
                          164          727
                        +425         + 51
```

Addition: Regrouping

Regrouping uses 10 ones to form one 10, 10 tens to form one hundred, one 10 and 5 ones to form 15, and so on.

Add using regrouping. Color in all the boxes with a 5 in the answer to help the dog find its way home.

	63 + 22	5,268 4,910 + 1,683	248 + 463	291 + 543	2,934 + 112
1,736 + 5,367	2,946 + 7,384	3,245 1,239 + 981	738 + 692	896 + 728	594 + 738
2,603 + 5,004	4,507 + 289	1,483 + 6,753	1,258 + 6,301	27 469 + 6,002	4,637 + 7,531
782 + 65	485 + 276	3,421 + 8,064			
48 93 + 26	90 263 + 864	362 453 + 800			

Addition: Regrouping

Addition means "putting together" or adding two or more numbers to find the sum. For example, 3 + 5 = 8. To regroup is to use 10 ones to form 1 ten, 10 tens to form 1 hundred and so on.

Add using regrouping.

Example:

Add the ones.

$$\begin{array}{r} 88 \\ +21 \\ \hline 9 \end{array}$$

Add the tens with regrouping.

$$\begin{array}{r} 88 \\ +21 \\ \hline 109 \end{array}$$

$$\begin{array}{r} 37 \\ +72 \\ \hline \end{array} \qquad \begin{array}{r} 56 \\ +67 \\ \hline \end{array} \qquad \begin{array}{r} 51 \\ +88 \\ \hline \end{array} \qquad \begin{array}{r} 37 \\ +55 \\ \hline \end{array} \qquad \begin{array}{r} 70 \\ +68 \\ \hline \end{array}$$

$$\begin{array}{r} 93 \\ +54 \\ \hline \end{array} \qquad \begin{array}{r} 47 \\ +82 \\ \hline \end{array} \qquad \begin{array}{r} 81 \\ +77 \\ \hline \end{array} \qquad \begin{array}{r} 23 \\ +92 \\ \hline \end{array} \qquad \begin{array}{r} 36 \\ +71 \\ \hline \end{array}$$

92 + 13 = _____   73 + 83 = _____   54 + 61 = _____

The Blues scored 63 points. The Reds scored 44 points.
How many points were scored in all?   _____

Week 3 Skills

Subject	Skill	Multi-Sensory Learning Activities
Reading and Language Arts	Write complete sentences that include nouns and verbs.	• Complete Practice Page 38. • Ask your child to copy five sentences from a favorite book and underline the main noun and verb in each one.
	Understand that a helping verb often comes before the main verb in a sentence.	• Complete Practice Pages 39 and 40. • Watch a video clip of a rocket launch, storm, race, or other exciting event. Have your child write five sentences about the event, using one of the helping verbs listed on page 39 in each.
	Understand that a linking verb connects a noun with a word that describes it.	• Complete Practice Pages 41 and 42. • Print a short encyclopedia article from the Internet about one of your child's favorite topics. Provide a colored pen and ask your child to use it to underline each helping verb and circle each linking verb.
Math	Add with regrouping.	• Complete Practice Pages 43–45. • Provide a calendar and ask your child to use it to write 10 addition problems. He or she might add the number of days in each month leading up to a birthday or holiday or the number of days in each month of the school year. Have your child circle each problem that requires regrouping.
	Use mental math to add.	• Complete Practice Page 46. • Give an addition problem for your child to solve mentally, then have your child give one for you to solve. Keep going until someone misses an answer. Discuss types of problems that are easy to solve mentally and those that are more challenging.

Sentences

Every sentence must have two things: a **noun** that tells who or what is doing something and a **verb** that tells what the noun is doing.

Add a **noun** or a **verb** to complete each sentence. Be sure to begin your sentences with capital letters and end them with periods.

Example: reads after school (needs a noun)

Brandy reads after school.

1. brushes her dog every day

_____

2. at the beach, we

_____

3. hugs me too much

_____

4. in the morning, our class

_____

5. stopped with a crash

_____

Helping Verbs

A **helping verb** is a word used with an action verb.

Examples: might, shall and **are**

Write a helping verb from the box with each action verb.

can	could	must	might
may	would	should	will
shall	did	does	do
had	have	has	am
are	were	is	
be	being	been	

Example:

Tomorrow, I ____might____ play soccer.

1. Mom _____ buy my new soccer shoes tonight.

2. Yesterday, my old soccer shoes _____ ripped by the cat.

3. I _____ going to ask my brother to go to the game.

4. He usually _____ not like soccer.

5. But, he _____ go with me because I am his sister.

6. He _____ promised to watch the entire soccer game.

7. He has _____ helping me with my homework.

8. I _____ spell a lot better because of his help.

9. Maybe I _____ finish the semester at the top of my class.

Helping Verbs

A **verb phrase** contains a **main verb** and a **helping verb**. The helping verb usually comes before the main verb. **Has** and **have** can be used as helping verbs.

Example: We **have learned** about dental health.
              ↑   ↑
           helping main
           verb   verb

Underline the helping verb and circle the main verb in each sentence.

1. A dental hygienist has come to talk to our class.

2. We have written questions ahead of time to ask her.

3. I have wondered if it is really necessary to brush after every meal.

4. We have waited to be shown the proper way to floss our teeth.

5. We have learned the names of all the different kinds of teeth.

6. We have listed incisors, cuspids and molars as names of teeth.

7. Most of us have known the parts of a tooth for a long time.

8. The teacher has given us a list of snack foods that may cause cavities.

9. Nearly half the class has eaten too much sugar today.

10. I have experimented with different kinds of toothpaste to see which ones clean teeth best.

Linking Verbs

Linking verbs connect the noun to a descriptive word. Linking verbs are often forms of the verb **be**.

The linking verb is underlined in each sentence. Circle the two words that are being connected.

Example: The (cat) is (fat.)

1. My favorite food <u>is</u> pizza.

2. The car <u>was</u> red.

3. I <u>am</u> tired.

4. Books <u>are</u> fun!

5. The garden <u>is</u> beautiful.

6. Pears <u>taste</u> juicy.

7. The airplane <u>looks</u> large.

8. Rabbits <u>are</u> furry.

Linking Verbs

A **linking verb** does not show action. Instead, it links the subject of the sentence with a noun or adjective in the predicate. **Am**, **is**, **are**, **was** and **were** are linking verbs.

Example:
Thomas Jefferson **was** president of the United States.

Write a linking verb in each blank.

1. The class's writing assignment _____ a report on U.S. presidents.

2. The reports _____ due tomorrow.

3. I _____ glad I chose to write about Thomas Jefferson, the third president of our country.

4. Early in his life, he _____ the youngest delegate to the First Continental Congress.

5. The colonies _____ angry at England.

6. Thomas Jefferson _____ a great writer, so he was asked to help write the Declaration of Independence.

7. The signing of that document _____ a historical event.

8. Later, as president, Jefferson _____ responsible for the Louisiana Purchase.

9. He _____ the first president to live in the White House.

10. Americans _____ fortunate today for the part Thomas Jefferson played in our country's history.

Addition: Regrouping

Study the example. Add using regrouping.

Examples:

Add the ones. Regroup.		Add the tens. Regroup.		Add the hundreds.

$$\begin{array}{r} 1 \\ 156 \\ +267 \\ \hline 3 \end{array} \qquad \begin{array}{r} 6 \\ +7 \\ \hline 13 \end{array} \qquad \begin{array}{r} 1 \\ 5 \\ +6 \\ \hline 12 \end{array} \qquad \begin{array}{r} 11 \\ 156 \\ +267 \\ \hline 23 \end{array} \qquad \begin{array}{r} 1 \\ 156 \\ +267 \\ \hline 423 \end{array}$$

$$\begin{array}{r} 29 \\ 46 \\ +12 \\ \hline \end{array} \qquad \begin{array}{r} 81 \\ 78 \\ +33 \\ \hline \end{array} \qquad \begin{array}{r} 52 \\ 67 \\ +23 \\ \hline \end{array} \qquad \begin{array}{r} 49 \\ 37 \\ +19 \\ \hline \end{array} \qquad \begin{array}{r} 162 \\ +349 \\ \hline \end{array}$$

$$\begin{array}{r} 273 \\ +198 \\ \hline \end{array} \qquad \begin{array}{r} 655 \\ +297 \\ \hline \end{array} \qquad \begin{array}{r} 783 \\ +148 \\ \hline \end{array} \qquad \begin{array}{r} 385 \\ +169 \\ \hline \end{array} \qquad \begin{array}{r} 428 \\ +122 \\ \hline \end{array}$$

Sally went bowling. She had scores of 115, 129 and 103. What was her total score for three games? _____

Addition: Regrouping

Add using regrouping. Then, use the code to discover the name of a United States president.

$$
\begin{array}{r} 348 \\ +752 \\ \hline 1,100 \end{array}
\qquad
\begin{array}{r} 642 \\ +277 \\ \hline \end{array}
\qquad
\begin{array}{r} 386 \\ +787 \\ \hline \end{array}
\qquad
\begin{array}{r} 184 \\ +875 \\ \hline \end{array}
\qquad
\begin{array}{r} 578 \\ +874 \\ \hline \end{array}
$$

$$
\begin{array}{r} 653 \\ +768 \\ \hline \end{array}
\qquad
\begin{array}{r} 653 \\ +359 \\ \hline \end{array}
\qquad
\begin{array}{r} 946 \\ +239 \\ \hline \end{array}
\qquad
\begin{array}{r} 393 \\ +257 \\ \hline \end{array}
\qquad
\begin{array}{r} 199 \\ +843 \\ \hline \end{array}
$$

$$
\begin{array}{r} 721 \\ +679 \\ \hline \end{array}
$$

___. ___ ___ ___ ___ ___ ___ ___ ___ ___ ___

1012	1173	1059	1421	919	650	1452	1042	1100	1400	1185
N	A	S	I	W	T	H	O	G	N	G

Addition: Regrouping

Study the example. Add using regrouping.

Example:

	Steps:
5,356	1. Add the ones.
+3,976	2. Regroup the tens. Add the tens.
9,332	3. Regroup the hundreds. Add the hundreds.
	4. Add the thousands.

```
  6,849          1,846          9,221
+3,276         +8,384         +6,769
```

```
  2,758          5,299          7,932
+3,663         +8,764         +6,879
```

A plane flew 1,838 miles on the first day. It flew 2,347 miles on the second day. How many miles did it fly in all? _____

Addition: Mental Math

Try to do these addition problems in your head without using paper and pencil.

7 +4	6 +3	8 +1	10 +2	2 +9	6 +6

10 +20	40 +20	80 +100	60 +30	50 +70	100 +40

350 +150	300 +500	400 +800	450 +10	680 +100	900 +70

1,000 +200	4,000 400 +30	300 200 +80	8,000 500 +60	9,800 +150	7,000 300 +30

Week 4 Skills

Subject	Skill	Multi-Sensory Learning Activities
Reading and Language Arts	Understand that the past tense forms of irregular verbs such as **sing** (**sang**) do not end with **ed**.	• Complete Practice Pages 48–52. • Past-tense verbs that are not formed by adding **ed** are irregular verbs. Say an irregular verb such as **do**, **goes**, **know**, **fall**, **read**, **eat**, or **speaks** in the present tense. Ask your child to supply the past tense. Have him or her write the past tense beside the present tense. Compare the changes made to each word.
Math	Add numbers to four digits, regrouping when needed.	• Complete Practice Pages 53–56. • Explore population data on census.gov. Have your child use addition to find the number of people in your city and a nearby city or in several cities in one region of the state where you live. • Encourage your child to examine food labels in your kitchen or at the grocery store. Ask him or her to use addition to find out how many servings of different foods equal 1,000 calories. Two thousand calories?
Bonus: Science		• Explain that every person has a unique set of fingerprints. Have your child use a stamp pad to make a print of each fingertip. Provide a magnifying glass so he or she can study the prints and describe each design as a loop, a whorl, or an arch. Compare your child's fingerprints to those of other family members.

Irregular Verbs

Irregular verbs are verbs that do not change from the present tense to the past tense in the regular way with **d** or **ed**.

Example: sing, **sang**

Read the sentence and underline the verb. Choose the past-tense form from the box and write it next to the sentence.

blow — blew	fly — flew
come — came	give — gave
take — took	wear — wore
make — made	sing — sang
grow — grew	

Example:

　　Dad will <u>make</u> a cake tonight.　　　　　made

1. I will probably grow another inch this year. _____

2. I will blow out the candles. _____

3. Everyone will give me presents. _____

4. I will wear my favorite red shirt. _____

5. My cousins will come from out of town. _____

6. It will take them four hours. _____

7. My Aunt Betty will fly in from Cleveland. _____

8. She will sing me a song when she gets here. _____

Irregular Verbs

Circle the verb that completes each sentence.

1. Scientists will try to (find, found) the cure.

2. Eric (brings, brought) his lunch to school yesterday.

3. Every day, Betsy (sings, sang) all the way home.

4. Jason (breaks, broke) the vase last night.

5. The ice had (freezes, frozen) in the tray.

6. Mitzi has (swims, swum) in that pool before.

7. Now I (choose, chose) to exercise daily.

8. The teacher has (rings, rung) the bell.

9. The boss (speaks, spoke) to us yesterday.

10. She (says, said) it twice already.

Irregular Verbs

The verb **be** is different from all other verbs. The present-tense forms of **be** are **am**, **is** and **are**. The past-tense forms of **be** are **was** and **were**. The verb **to be** is written in the following ways:

singular: I am, you are, he is, she is, it is
plural: we are, you are, they are

Choose the correct form of **be** from the words in the box and write it in each sentence.

are	am	is	was

Example:

I _____ am _____ feeling good at this moment.

1. My sister _____ a good singer.

2. You _____ going to the store with me.

3. Sandy _____ at the movies last week.

4. Rick and Tom _____ best friends.

5. He _____ happy about the surprise.

6. The cat _____ hungry.

7. I _____ going to the ball game.

8. They _____ silly.

9. I _____ glad to help my mother.

Irregular Verbs

Past-tense verbs that are not formed by adding **ed** are called **irregular verbs**.

Example:

Present	Past
sing	sang

Circle the present-tense verb in each pair of irregular verbs.

1. won   win
2. feel   felt
3. built   build

4. tell   told
5. eat   ate
6. blew   blow

7. say   said
8. came   come
9. grew   grow

Write the past tense of each irregular verb.

1. throw _____
2. wear _____
3. hold _____

4. sing _____
5. lose _____
6. fly _____

7. swim _____
8. sit _____
9. sell _____

In each blank, write the past tense of the irregular verb in parentheses.

1. I _____ my library book to my sister. (give)

2. She _____ for school before I did. (leave)

3. She _____ the bus at the corner. (catch)

4. My sister _____ my book on the way to school. (lose)

5. My sister _____ back to find it. (go)

Irregular Verbs: Past Tense

Irregular verbs change completely in the past tense. Unlike regular verbs, past-tense forms of irregular verbs are not formed by adding **ed**.

Example: The past tense of **go** is **went**.

Other verbs change some letters to form the past tense.
Example: The past tense of **break** is **broke**.

A **helping verb** helps to tell about the past. **Has**, **have** and **had** are helping verbs used with action verbs to show the action occurred in the past. The past-tense form of the irregular verb sometimes changes when a helping verb is added.

Present Tense Irregular Verb	Past Tense Irregular Verb	Past Tense Irregular Verb With Helper
go	went	have/has/had gone
see	saw	have/has/had seen
do	did	have/has/had done
bring	brought	have/has/had brought
sing	sang	have/has/had sung
drive	drove	have/has/had driven
swim	swam	have/has/had swum
sleep	slept	have/has/had slept

Choose four words from the chart. Write one sentence using the past-tense form of the verb without a helping verb. Write another sentence using the past-tense form with a helping verb.

1. _____

_____

2. _____

_____

3. _____

_____

4. _____

_____

Fishy Addition

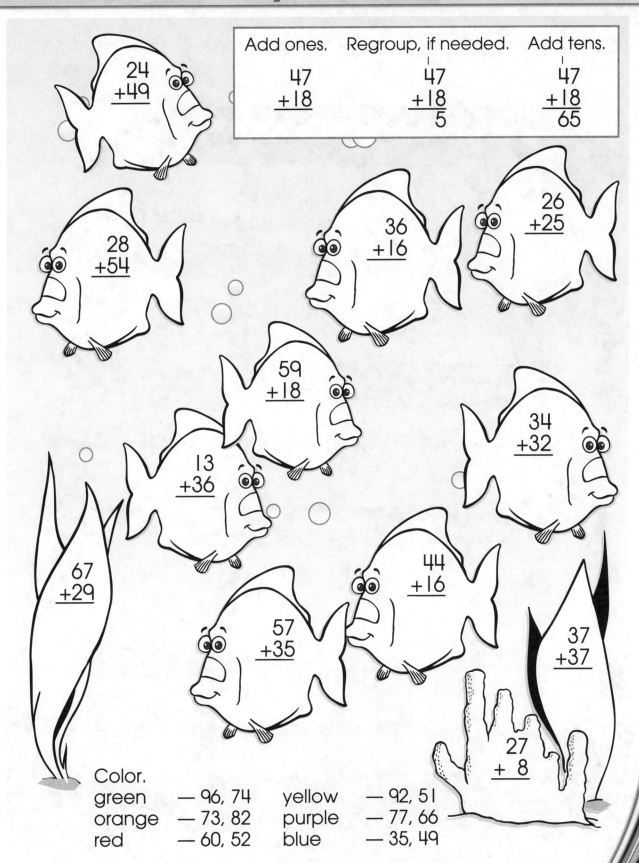

Add ones.	Regroup, if needed.	Add tens.
47 +18	47 +18 5	47 +18 65

24
+49

28
+54

36
+16

26
+25

59
+18

13
+36

34
+32

67
+29

57
+35

44
+16

37
+37

27
+ 8

Color.
green — 96, 74   yellow — 92, 51
orange — 73, 82   purple — 77, 66
red — 60, 52   blue — 35, 49

Make the Windows Shine!

Add. Each problem you complete makes the window "squeaky" clean.

$$479 + 319$$

$$248 + 629$$

$$327 + 544$$

$$572 + 318$$

$$815 + 177$$

$$527 + 144$$

$$429 + 343$$

$$262 + 319$$

$$462 + 529$$

$$648 + 238$$

$$756 + 127$$

$$563 + 208$$

$$646 + 248$$

$$924 + 66$$

$$628 + 259$$

$$526 + 347$$

$$927 + 46$$

$$765 + 218$$

Four-Digit Addition: Regrouping

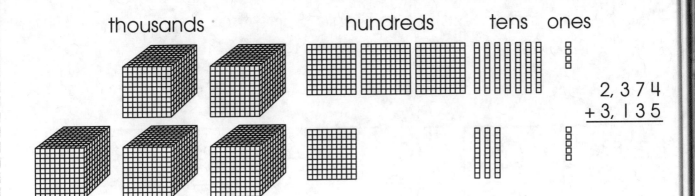

thousands   hundreds   tens   ones

$$
\begin{array}{r}
2,374 \\
+\,3,135 \\
\end{array}
$$

1. | Add ones. Ask: Do I need to regroup?

$$
\begin{array}{r}
2,374 \\
+\,3,135 \\
\hline
9
\end{array}
$$

2. | Add tens. Ask: Do I need to regroup?

$$
\begin{array}{r}
2,\overset{1}{3}74 \\
+\,3,135 \\
\hline
09
\end{array}
$$

3. | Add hundreds. Ask: Do I need to regroup?

$$
\begin{array}{r}
2,\overset{1}{3}74 \\
+\,3,135 \\
\hline
509
\end{array}
$$

4. | Add thousands. Ask: Do I need to regroup?

$$
\begin{array}{r}
2,\overset{1}{3}74 \\
+\,3,135 \\
\hline
5509
\end{array}
$$

Add. Regroup when needed.

$$
\begin{array}{r}
6,208 \\
+\,1,913 \\
\end{array}
\qquad
\begin{array}{r}
5,416 \\
+\,5,298 \\
\end{array}
\qquad
\begin{array}{r}
7,526 \\
+\,2,484 \\
\end{array}
$$

$$
\begin{array}{r}
2,352 \\
+\,1,292 \\
\end{array}
\qquad
\begin{array}{r}
2,671 \\
+\,3,619 \\
\end{array}
\qquad
\begin{array}{r}
3,614 \\
+\,2,902 \\
\end{array}
$$

Picnic Problems

Help the ant find a path to the picnic. Solve the problems. Shade the box if an answer has a **9** in it.

836 + 90	536 + 248	952 + 8	362 + 47	486 + 293	368 + 529
789 526 + 214	2846 +6478	932 + 365	374 + 299	835 + 552	956 874 + 65
4768 +2894	38 456 +3894	4507 +2743	404 + 289	1843 +6752	4367 +3571
639 + 77	587 342 + 679	5379 1865 +2348	450 + 145	594 + 278	459 + 367
29 875 +2341	387 29 +5614	462 379 + 248			

Week 5 Skills

Subject	Skill	Multi-Sensory Learning Activities
Reading and Language Arts	Understand that present-tense verbs tell what is happening now.	• Complete Practice Pages 58 and 59. • Challenge your child to write the nursery rhyme "Mary Had a Little Lamb," changing all of the verbs into present-tense form. Encourage your child to have fun changing the verbs in other well-known rhymes, too.
	Understand that past-tense verbs tell what already happened.	• Complete Practice Pages 60–62. • Ask your child to write a short story about something that happened yesterday. Remind him or her that all the verbs should be in the past-tense form. Read the story aloud and thank your child for sharing it with you!
Math	Subtract numbers up to three digits, with and without regrouping.	• Complete Practice Pages 63–66. • Roll three dice and have your child do the same. Write the numbers rolled in any order to make a three-digit number. Whose number is larger? That player must subtract the other player's number from the larger number and submit the answer to be checked. Keep playing for five rounds. • Ask your child to make a poster or digital presentation explaining how to use regrouping to "borrow" a ten or hundred when subtracting problems like this one: 887 – 598.

Present-Tense Verbs

The **present tense** of a verb tells about something that is happening now, happens often or is about to happen. These verbs can be written two ways: The bird sing**s**. The bird is sing**ing**.

Write each sentence again, using the verb **is** and writing the **ing** form of the verb.

Example: He cooks the cheeseburgers.

He is cooking the cheeseburgers.

1. Sharon dances to that song.

_____

2. Frank washed the car.

_____

3. Mr. Benson smiles at me.

_____

Write a verb for the sentences below that tells something that is happening now. Be sure to use the verb **is** and the **ing** form of the verb.

Example: The big, brown dog   is barking   .

1. The little baby _____ .

2. Most nine-year-olds _____ .

3. The monster on television _____ .

Present-Tense Verbs

When something is happening right now, it is in the **present tense**. There are two ways to write verbs in the present tense:

Examples: The dog **walks**.   The cats **play**.
          The dog **is walking**.   The cats **are playing**.

Write each sentence again, writing the verb a different way.

Example:

He lists the numbers.

He is listing the numbers.

1. She is pounding the nail.

_____

2. My brother toasts the bread.

_____

3. They search for the robber.

_____

4. The teacher lists the pages.

_____

5. They are spilling the water.

_____

6. Ken and Amy load the packages.

_____

Past-Tense Verbs

The past tense of a verb tells that something already happened. To tell about something that already happened, add **ed** to most verbs. If the verb already ends in **e**, just add **d**.

Examples:

We enter**ed** the contest last week.
I fold**ed** the paper wrong.
He add**ed** two boxes to the pile.

We tast**ed** the cupcakes.
They decid**ed** quickly.
She shar**ed** her cupcake.

Use the verb from the first sentence to complete the second sentence. Add **d** or **ed** to show that something already happened.

Example:

My mom looks fine today. Yesterday, she ____looked____ tired.

1. You enter through the middle door.

    We _____ that way last week.

2. Please add this for me. I already _____ it twice.

3. Will you share your cookie with me?

    I _____ my apple with you yesterday.

4. It's your turn to fold the clothes. I _____ them yesterday.

5. May I taste another one? I already _____ one.

6. You need to decide. We _____ this morning.

Past-Tense Verbs

When you write about something that already happened, you add **ed** to most verbs. For some verbs that have a short vowel and end in one consonant, you double the consonant before adding **ed**.

Examples:

He hug**ged** his pillow.   The dog grab**bed** the stick.
She stir**red** the carrots.   We plan**ned** to go tomorrow.
They clap**ped** for me.   They drag**ged** their bags on the ground.

Use the verb from the first sentence to complete the second sentence. Change the verb in the second part to the past tense. Double the consonant and add **ed**.

Example:

We skip to school. Yesterday, we _____*skipped*_____ the whole way.

1. It's not nice to grab things. When you _____ my cookie, I felt angry.

2. Did anyone hug you today? Dad _____ me this morning.

3. We plan our vacations every year. Last year, we _____ to go to the beach.

4. Is it my turn to stir the pot? You _____ it last time.

5. Let's clap for Andy, just like we _____ for Amy.

6. My sister used to drag her blanket everywhere.

    Once, she _____ it to the store.

Past-Tense Verbs

When you write about something that already happened, you add **ed** to most verbs. Here is another way to write about something in the past tense.

Examples: The dog **walked**.   The dog **was walking**.
            The cats **played**.   The cats **were playing**.

Write each sentence again, writing the verb a different way.

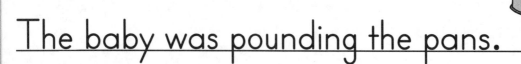

Example: The baby pounded the pans.

<u>The baby was pounding the pans.</u>

1. Gary loaded the car by himself.

_____

2. They searched for a long time.

_____

3. The water spilled over the edge.

_____

4. Dad toasted the rolls.

_____

Subtraction

Subtraction means "taking away" or subtracting one number from another to find the difference. For example, 10 – 3 = 7.

Subtract.

Example: Subtract the ones.   Subtract the tens.

$$\begin{array}{r} 39 \\ -24 \\ \hline 5 \end{array} \qquad \begin{array}{r} 39 \\ -24 \\ \hline 15 \end{array}$$

$$\begin{array}{r} 48 \\ -35 \\ \hline \end{array} \qquad \begin{array}{r} 95 \\ -22 \\ \hline \end{array} \qquad \begin{array}{r} 87 \\ -16 \\ \hline \end{array} \qquad \begin{array}{r} 55 \\ -43 \\ \hline \end{array}$$

$$\begin{array}{r} 37 \\ -14 \\ \hline \end{array} \qquad \begin{array}{r} 69 \\ -57 \\ \hline \end{array} \qquad \begin{array}{r} 44 \\ -23 \\ \hline \end{array} \qquad \begin{array}{r} 99 \\ -78 \\ \hline \end{array}$$

66 - 44 = _____   57 - 33 = _____

The yellow car traveled 87 miles per hour. The orange car traveled 66 miles per hour. How much faster was the yellow car traveling?   _____

Subtraction: Regrouping

Subtraction means "taking away" or subtracting one number from another to find the difference. For example, 10 – 3 = 7. To regroup is to use 1 ten to form 10 ones, 1 hundred to form 10 tens and so on.

Study the example. Subtract using regrouping.

Example:

$$32 = 2 \text{ tens} + 12 \text{ ones}$$
$$-13 = 1 \text{ ten} + 3 \text{ ones}$$
$$19 = 1 \text{ ten} + 9 \text{ ones}$$

33 -28	86 -59	92 -37	71 -48

63 -47	45 -18	31 -22	55 -39

82 - 69 = ____   73 - 36 = ____

The Yankees won 85 games.
The Cubs won 69 games.
How many more games
did the Yankees win?   _____

Subtraction: Regrouping

Regrouping for subtraction is the opposite of regrouping for addition. Study the example. Subtract using regrouping. Then, use the code to color the flowers.

Example:

$$\begin{array}{r} 647 \\ -453 \\ \hline 194 \end{array}$$

Steps:
1. Subtract ones.
2. Subtract tens. Five tens cannot be subtracted from 4 tens.
3. Regroup tens by regrouping 6 hundreds (5 hundreds + 10 tens).
4. Add the 10 tens to the 4 tens.
5. Subtract 5 tens from 14 tens.
6. Subtract the hundreds.

If the answer has:
1 one, color it red;
8 ones, color it pink;
5 ones, color it yellow.

428
−397

368
−173

943
−652

637
−242

726
−331

549
−361

749
−568

528
−270

Subtraction: Regrouping

Study the example. Follow the steps. Subtract using regrouping.

Example:

$$\begin{array}{r} 634 \\ -\ 455 \\ \hline 179 \end{array}$$

Steps:

1. Subtract ones. You cannot subtract 5 ones from 4 ones.
2. Regroup ones by regrouping 3 tens to 2 tens + 10 ones.
3. Subtract 5 ones from 14 ones.
4. Regroup tens by regrouping hundreds (5 hundreds + 10 tens).
5. Subtract 5 tens from 12 tens.
6. Subtract hundreds.

635 -169	553 -174	832 - 563	944 - 578
423 - 268	941 - 872	733 - 498	266 - 197
387 - 198	594 - 385	960 - 759	887 - 598

Sue goes to school 185 days a year. Yoko goes to school 313 days a year. How many more days of school does Yoko attend each year?

_____

Week 6 Skills

Subject	Skill	Multi-Sensory Learning Activities
Reading and Language Arts	Use past-tense verbs in sentences.	• Complete Practice Pages 68 and 69. • Help your child search for a recent news story in the newspaper or on the Internet. Read the story, noting each past-tense verb used.
	Understand that future-tense verbs tell what will happen.	• Complete Practice Page 70. • Ask your child to write five sentences describing things he or she plans to do someday. All verbs should be in the future tense.
	Review verb tenses.	• Complete Practice Page 71. • Ask your child to have fun writing three short stories about the adventures of Yolanda Yesterday (with verbs in the past tense), Peggy Present (with verbs in the present tense), and Tommy Tomorrow (with verbs in the future tense).
	Use correct subject-verb agreement.	• Complete Practice Page 72. • Help your child develop a "good ear" for detecting errors in subject-verb agreement. Say incorrect sentences such as "You goes to school on Mondays" and have your child correct you.
Math	Use regrouping to subtract numbers.	• Complete Practice Pages 73–75. • Ask your child to find the height of each family member in inches and subtract to find out how much shorter each person is than a 96-inch tall ceiling. Have your child circle each problem that required regrouping.
	Use mental math to subtract.	• Complete Practice Page 76. • Give your child mental subtraction problems about money. For example, ask, "A piece of candy costs 40 cents. You pay with a dollar. What is your change?"

Past-Tense Verbs

Write sentences that tell about each picture using the words **was** and **were**. Use words from the box as either nouns or verbs.

pound	spill	toast	list	load	search

_____

_____

_____

_____

_____

_____

_____

_____

_____

Past-Tense Verbs

The **past tense** of a verb tells about something that has already happened. We add a **d** or an **ed** to most verbs to show that something has already happened.

Use the verb from the first sentence to complete the second sentence.

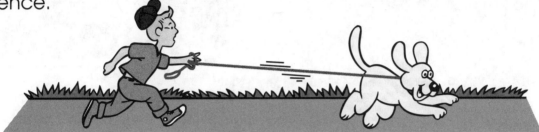

Example:

Please **walk** the dog.   I already __walked__ her.

1. The flowers look good.   They _____ better yesterday.

2. Please accept my gift.   I _____ it for my sister.

3. I wonder who will win.   I _____ about it all night.

4. He will saw the wood.   He _____ some last week.

5. Fold the paper neatly.   She _____ her paper.

6. Let's cook outside tonight.   We _____ outside last night.

7. Do not block the way.   They _____ the entire street.

8. Form the clay this way.   He _____ it into a ball.

9. Follow my car.   We _____ them down the street.

10. Glue the pages like this.   She _____ the flowers on.

Future-Tense Verbs

The **future tense** of a verb tells about something that has not happened yet but will happen in the future. **Will** or **shall** are usually used with future tense.

Change the verb tense in each sentence to future tense.

Example: She cooks dinner.

_____ She will cook dinner.

1. He plays baseball.

_____

2. She walks to school.

_____

3. Bobby talks to the teacher.

_____

4. I remember to vote.

_____

5. Jack mows the lawn every week.

_____

6. We go on vacation soon.

_____

Verb Tenses

Verb tenses can be in the past, present or future.

Match each sentence with the correct verb tense.
(**Think:** When did each thing happen?)

It will rain tomorrow.   past   **Past**

He played golf.   present

Molly is sleeping.   future   **Present**

Jack is singing a song.   past

I shall buy a kite.   present

Dad worked hard today.   future   **Future**

Change the verb to the tense shown.

1. Jenny played with her new friend. (present)

_____

2. Bobby is talking to him. (future)

_____

3. Holly and Angie walk here. (past)

_____

Subject-Verb Agreement

The subject and verb in a sentence must agree in number.

Examples:

An adult **plant makes** seeds.

singular   singular
noun   verb

Adult **plants make** seeds.

plural   plural
noun   verb

If the subject and verb agree, circle the letter under **Yes** at the end of the sentence. If they do not, circle the letter under **No**.

		Yes	No
1.	Seeds travel in many ways.	A	R
2.	Sometimes, seeds falls in the water.	T	D
3.	Then, they may floats a long distance.	S	L
4.	Animals gather seeds in the fall.	O	E
5.	Squirrels digs holes to bury their seeds.	M	A
6.	Cardinals likes to eat sunflower seeds.	J	N
7.	The wind scatters seeds, too.	E	G
8.	Dogs carries seeds that are stuck in their fur.	L	N
9.	Some seeds stick to people's clothing.	I	T
10.	People plants seeds to grow baby plants.	R	D

Write the circled letters on the lines above the matching numbers to spell the answer to this question: *Which lion scatters seeds?*

___ ___ ___ ___ ___ ___ ___ ___ ___ ___!
 1   10 5   8   2   7   3   9   4   6

Subtraction: Regrouping

Study the example. Follow the steps. Subtract using regrouping. If you have to regroup to subtract ones and there are no tens, you must regroup twice.

Example:

```
  300
– 182
  118
```

Steps:
1. Subtract ones. You cannot subtract 2 ones from 0 ones.
2. Regroup. No tens. Regroup hundreds (2 hundreds + 10 tens).
3. Regroup tens (9 tens + 10 ones).
4. Subtract 2 ones from 10 ones.
5. Subtract 8 tens from 9 tens.
6. Subtract 1 hundred from 2 hundreds.

```
  602        306        600        807        703
 -423       -128       -263       -499       -328
```

```
  800        206        400        508        909
 -557       -137       -224       -379       -769
```

```
  207        604        308        700        900
 -138       -397       -199       -531       -278
```

Subtraction: Regrouping

Subtract. Regroup when necessary. The first one is done for you.

```
  7,354          4,214          8,437          6,837
 -5,295         -3,185         -5,338         -4,318
  2,059
```

```
  5,735          1,036          6,735          3,841
 -3,826         -  947         -6,646         -1,953
```

Columbus discovered America in 1492. The Pilgrims landed in America in 1620. How many years difference was there between these two events?

_____

Mountaintop Getaway

Solve the problems. Find a path to the cabin by shading in all the answers that have a **3** in them.

	98 − 52	46 − 12	68 − 17
79 − 53	65 − 23	63 − 31	86 − 32
59 − 45	75 − 64	67 − 24	97 − 54	55 − 43
87 − 65	44 − 32	57 − 24	69 − 25	75 − 61	48 − 26
88 − 25	48 − 13	95 − 24	58 − 16	35 − 13	39 − 17

SECRET PATHS

Subtraction: Mental Math

Try to do these subtraction problems in your head without using paper and pencil.

9 -3	12 -6	7 -6	5 -1	15 -5	2 -0
40 -20	90 -80	100 -50	20 -20	60 -10	70 -40
450 -250	500 -300	250 -20	690 -100	320 -20	900 -600
1,000 -400	8,000 -500	7,000 -900	4,000 $-2,000$	9,500 $-4,000$	5,000 $-2,000$

Week 7 Skills

Subject	Skill	Multi-Sensory Learning Activities
Reading and Language Arts	Understand that adjectives describe nouns.	• Complete Practice Pages 78–82. • Blindfold your child and hand him or her a scoop of ice cream sealed in a zip-top bag. Ask your child to describe how it feels and list the adjectives he or she uses. Remove the blindfold and have your child describe other objects such as a scented candle or a rough towel. For each item, add to the list of adjectives.
	Begin proper adjectives such as **American** with a capital letter.	• Complete Practice Page 83. • Read a news article with your child. Can you find three proper adjectives and mark them with a highlighter pen? Does each begin with a capital letter?
Math	Use regrouping to subtract numbers up to four digits.	• Complete Practice Pages 84–86. • Have your child find out in what year family members and friends were born. Subtract those years from the present year to determine each person's age. Circle each problem that required regrouping. • Show how to use a pencil to draw light vertical lines in a subtraction problem to divide the numbers into columns. This will help keep track of regrouping needed.
Bonus: Social Studies		• Attend a local festival, farmers' market, or other event with your child. Discuss the purpose of the event and why it is important to the community. Then, ask your child to write a journal entry that describes the day with sentences that include vivid adjectives.

Adjectives

Use the words in the box to answer the questions below. Use each word only once.

polite	careless	neat	shy	selfish	thoughtful

1. Someone who is quiet and needs some time to make new friends is _____.

2. A person who says "please" and "thank you" is _____.

3. Someone who always puts all the toys away is _____.

4. A person who won't share with others is being _____.

5. A person who leaves a bike out all night is being _____.

6. Someone who thinks of others is _____.

Adjectives

Use the adjectives in the box to answer the questions below.

polite   careless   neat   shy   selfish   thoughtful

1. Change a letter in each word to make an adjective.

    near   _____

    why   _____

2. Write the word that rhymes with each of these.

    fell dish   _____

    not full   _____

    hair mess   _____

3. Find these words in the adjectives. Write the adjective.

    at   _____

    are   _____

    it   _____

Adjectives: Explaining Sentences

Use a word from the box to tell about a person in each picture below. Then, write a sentence that explains why you chose that word.

| polite   neat   careless   shy   selfish   thoughtful |

The word I picked: _____

I think so because . . .

_____

The word I picked: _____

I think so because . . .

_____

The word I picked: _____

I think so because . . .

_____

Adjectives

Look at each picture. Then, add adjectives to the sentences. Use colors, numbers, words from the box and any other words you need to describe each picture.

polite	neat	careless
shy	selfish	thoughtful

Example:

The boy shared his pencil.

<u>The polite boy shared his red pencil.</u>

The girl dropped her coat.

_____

The boy played with cars.

_____

The boy put books away.

_____

Marvelous Modifiers

Words that describe are called **adjectives**.
Circle the adjectives in the sentences below.

1. Lucas stared at the cool white paint in the can.

2. The green grass was marked with bits of white paint.

3. The naughty twins needed a warm soapy bath.

4. The painters worked with large rollers.

5. Lucas thought it was a great joke.

For each noun below, write two descriptive adjectives. Then, write a sentence using all three words.

1. marshmallows _____   _____

_____

_____

2. airplane _____   _____

_____

_____

3. beach _____   _____

_____

_____

4. summer _____   _____

_____

_____

Proper Adjectives

A **proper adjective** is a word that describes a noun or a pronoun. A proper adjective always begins with a capital letter.

Example:
The **American** flag waves proudly over the **United States** capital.

Underline the proper adjective in each sentence.

1. Spanish music is beautiful.

2. Some Americans buy Japanese cars.

3. I saw the Canadian flag flying.

4. Have you ever eaten Irish stew?

5. The Russian language is hard to learn.

6. Did you say you like French fries?

7. My favorite dog is a German shepherd.

8. Dad fished for Alaskan salmon.

Rewrite each phrase, changing the proper noun into a proper adjective.

1. the mountains of Colorado _____

2. skyline of Chicago _____

Subtraction

REGROUP (1 ten = 10 ones)	Subtract ones.	Subtract tens.
$\begin{array}{r}\overset{4}{\cancel{5}}\overset{1}{8}\\-\ 2\ 9\\\hline\end{array}$	$\begin{array}{r}\overset{4}{\cancel{5}}\overset{1}{8}\\-\ 2\ 9\\\hline 9\end{array}$	$\begin{array}{r}\overset{4}{\cancel{5}}\overset{1}{8}\\-\ 2\ 9\\\hline 2\ 9\end{array}$

Solve these problems.

96 − 27	35 − 19	87 − 65	45 − 18	74 − 47

31 − 19	86 − 58	67 − 29	73 − 29	92 − 52

55 − 27	81 − 69	63 − 17	98 − 19	42 − 16

67 − 28 = _____   42 − 23 = _____

Round and Round She Goes...

Take a ride around this wheel. Solve the subtraction problems.

Four-Digit Subtraction: Regroup

The Windy Breeze Kite Co. made 3,426 kites to sell. After one week, they had 1,619 remaining. How many did they sell the first week?

1. | Subtract ones. Ask: Do I need to regroup? |

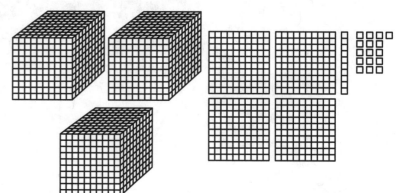

```
  3,426
- 1,619
      7
```

1 ten =
10 ones

2. | Subtract tens. Ask: Do I need to regroup? |

```
  3,4²⁶
- 1,619
    07
```

3. | Subtract hundreds. Ask: Do I need to regroup? |

```
  ³,4²⁶
- 1,619
   807
```

1 thousand =
10 hundreds

4. | Subtract thousands. |

```
²³,4²⁶
- 1,619
  1 807
```

Subtract. Regroup when needed.

```
  6,485          7,648          3,847
- 2,354        - 6,727        - 2,599
```

```
  8,104          9,463          5,847
- 6,043        - 4,825        - 2,498
```

Week 8 Skills

Subject	Skill	Multi-Sensory Learning Activities
Reading and Language Arts	Use adjectives such as **colder** and **coldest** to compare two or more things.	• Complete Practice Page 88. • Choose two objects, such as two stones, and challenge your child to make five comparisons between them using words such as **harder**, **bigger**, **rounder**, and **rougher**. Then, add a third object and ask your child to use words that end in **–est** to tell which of the three is softest, smallest, smoothest, etc.
	Understand that adverbs such as **softly** describe verbs.	• Complete Practice Pages 89–91. • Call out actions for your child to demonstrate such as run, skip, sit, talk, or play. As each action is performed, ask your child to tell how it is being done. List adverbs, such as **quickly** and **loudly**, from your child's responses.
	Distinguish between adjectives and adverbs.	• Complete Practice Page 92. • Remind your child that an adjective such as **hot** describes a noun and an adverb such as **happily** describes a verb by telling how, when, or where. Challenge your child to find five examples of each type of word in a favorite book.
Math	Review addition and subtraction with and without regrouping.	• Complete Practice Pages 93–96. • Play "Tic-Tac-Toe" with your child. Before making an **X** or **O**, the player must successfully solve an addition or subtraction problem provided by the other player. • Challenge your child to spend an imaginary $1,000 at an online store. Have him or her round each price to the nearest dollar and use addition and subtraction to make a shopping list.

Adjectives That Compare

Add **er** to most **adjectives** when comparing two nouns. Add **est** to most adjectives when comparing three or more nouns.

Example: The forecaster said this winter is **colder** than last winter.

It is the **coldest** winter on record.

Write the correct form of the adjective in parentheses.

1. The weather map showed that the _____ place of all was Fargo, North Dakota.
(cold)

2. The _____ city of all was Needles, California.
(warm)

3. Does San Diego get _____ than San Francisco?
(hot)

4. The _____ snow of all fell in Buffalo, New York.
(deep)

5. That snowfall was two inches _____ than in Syracuse.
(deep)

6. The _____ place in the country was Wichita, Kansas.
(windy)

7. The _____ winds of all blew there.
(strong)

8. The _____ city in the U.S. was Chicago.
(foggy)

9. Seattle was the _____ of all the cities listed on the map.
(rainy)

10. It is usually _____ in Seattle than in Portland.
(rainy)

Adverbs

Adverbs are words that describe verbs. They tell where, how or when.

Circle the adverb in each of the following sentences.

Example: The doctor worked (carefully.)

1. The skater moved gracefully across the ice.

2. Their call was returned quickly.

3. We easily learned the new words.

4. He did the work perfectly.

5. She lost her purse somewhere.

Complete the sentences below by writing your own adverbs in the blanks.

Example: The bees worked _____ busily _____.

1. The dog barked _____.

2. The baby smiled _____.

3. She wrote her name _____.

4. The horse ran _____.

Adverbs

An **adverb** is a word that can describe a verb. It tells **how**, **when** or **where** an action takes place.

Example:
The snow fell **quietly**. (how)
It snowed **yesterday**. (when)
It fell **everywhere**. (where)

Circle the adverbs in the story. Then, write them under the correct category in the chart.

The snow began early in the day. Huge snowflakes floated gracefully to the ground. Soon, the ground was covered with a blanket of white. Later, the wind began to blow briskly. Outside, the snow drifted into huge mounds. Suddenly, the snow stopped and the children went outdoors. Then, they played in the snow there. They went sledding nearby. Others happily built snow forts. Joyfully, the boys and girls ran around. They certainly enjoyed the snow.

How	When	Where

Adverbs That Compare

Add **er** to an adverb to compare two actions. Add **est** to compare three or more actions.

Example:
This talent show lasted **longer** than last year's did.
It might have lasted **longest** of all the shows.

Circle the correct form of each adverb in parentheses.

1. Cheryl sang (softer, softest) of all the performers.

2. Bill danced (slower, slowest) than Philip.

3. Jill played the drums (louder, loudest) of all the drummers.

4. Carlos sang (longer, longest) than Rita.

5. Jenny tap-danced (faster, fastest) than Paul.

Rule:
If an adverb ends with **ly**, add **more** or **most** to make a comparison.
Use the word **more** before the adverb to compare two actions.
Use **most** to compare three or more actions.

Write **more** or **most** in front of the adverb to make the correct comparison.

1. The audience clapped _____ eagerly this year than last year.

2. Janelle danced _____ daintily of all the ballet dancers.

3. Kristy turned somersaults _____ smoothly than another girl.

4. Charlie played the violin _____ brilliantly of all.

5. Sam read a poem _____ successfully than Ginger.

Adjectives and Adverbs

An **adjective** is used to describe a noun. An **adverb** describes a verb or an action.

Example:
We went into the **busy** pet store. (adjective)
Dad and I walked **quickly** through the mall. (adverb)

Write an adjective or an adverb to describe each **bold** word.

Adjectives	
white	many
adorable	best

Adverbs	
immediately	straight
excitedly	pitifully

1. Dad and I **went** _____ to the back wall.

2. We saw _____ animal **cages**.

3. The _____ **puppies** interested me most.

4. One little beagle **wiggled** _____.

5. I _____ **knew** this was the one I wanted.

6. He was black and brown with _____ **spots**.

7. He **whined** _____.

8. A puppy would be the _____ **present** I could have.

Addition and Subtraction: Regrouping

Addition means "putting together" or adding two or more numbers to find the sum. **Subtraction** means "taking away" or subtracting one number from another to find the difference. To **regroup** is to use 1 ten to form 10 ones, 1 hundred to form 10 tens and so on.

Add or subtract. Regroup when needed.

```
  92        58        63        77
 -47       +26       +18       -38
```

```
  27        31        56        67
 -17       +42       -29       +33
```

```
  72        87        93        54
 +19       -58       -89       +27
```

The soccer team scored 83 goals this year. The soccer team scored 68 goals last year. How many goals did they score in all? _____

How many more goals did they score this year than last year? _____

Addition and Subtraction

Add or subtract using regrouping.

```
   28          82          33          67
   56          49          75          94
 +93         +51        +128        +248
```

```
  683         756         818         956
 -495        +139        -387        +267
```

```
 1,588       4,675       8,732       2,938
 - 989      -2,976      -5,664      +3,459
```

To drive from New York City to Los Angeles is 2,832 miles. To drive from New York City to Miami is 1,327 miles. How much farther is it to drive from New York City to Los Angeles than from New York City to Miami? _____

Addition and Subtraction

Add or subtract, using regrouping when needed.

```
   32          183          456
   68          246          398        643
 + 43        +  89        + 597      - 377
```

```
 1,563        3,586        8,711       9,361
 - 941      + 4,218      - 4,937     - 7,452
```

```
                293
              431          743         849
                                       250
 5,734       +  93        - 529      +  82
+ 6,298
```

```
 1,227
 2,431        9,117
+ 5,792      - 3,828
```

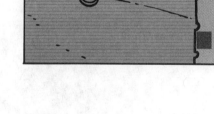

68 + 93 + 146 = _____   73 + 246 + 1,579 = _____

43 + 745 – 29 = _____   128 + 403 + 2,571 = _____

156 + 627 + 541 = _____   97 + 51 + 37 + 79 = _____

Tom walks 389 steps from his house to the video store. It is 149 steps to Elm Street. It is 52 steps from Maple Street to the video store. How many steps is it from Elm Street to Maple Street? _____

Addition and Subtraction

Add or subtract, using regrouping when needed.

38 43 + 21	1,269 2,453 + 8,219	5,792 – 4,814	629 491 + 308	4,697 – 2,988

5,280 – 3,147	68 27 + 42	197 436 + 213	7,321 – 2,789	456 + 974

3,932 + 4,681	492 863 + 57	9,873 + 5,483	4,978 + 2,131	6,235 + 2,986

Sue stocked her pond with 263 bass and 187 trout. 97 fish swam away in a flood. How many fish are left?

_____

Week 9 Skills

Subject	Skill	Multi-Sensory Learning Activities
Reading and Language Arts	Review parts of speech.	• Complete Practice Pages 98–100. • Ask your child to diagram several sentences from a favorite book. Use the sentence diagrams on page 98 as a model. • Encourage your child to write a special type of poem called a **cinquain** using the following format: Line 1: one noun Line 2: two adjectives Line 3: three –**ing** words Line 4: a four-word phrase Line 5: one word
	Write complete sentences, including statements, questions, and commands.	• Complete Practice Pages 101–103. • Look at a famous painting online, such as Salvador Dali's *The Persistence of Memory*. Ask your child to write two statements, two questions, and two commands related to the artwork. Make sure each is punctuated correctly.
Math	Use addition and subtraction to solve word problems.	• Complete Practice Pages 104–106. • Have your child research online to discover numbers related to a favorite amusement park. Numbers might include the height and speed of rides or the average number of guests each day. Ask your child to use the numbers to write five word problems for you to solve. Make story problems for your child to solve, too. • Write addition and subtraction word problems for your child to solve based on characters and scenes from a favorite book or movie.

Parts of Speech

Nouns, pronouns, verbs, adjectives, adverbs and prepositions are all **parts of speech**.

Label the words in each sentence with the correct part of speech.

Example: The   cat   is   fat.
                article   noun   verb   adjective

1. My   cow   walks   in   the   barn.

2. Red   flowers   grow   in   the   garden.

3. The   large   dog   was   excited.

COMPLETE YEAR GRADE 3

Parts of Speech

Ask someone to give you nouns, verbs, adjectives and pronouns where shown. Write them in the blanks. Read the story to your friend when you finish.

The _____ **Adventure**
(adjective)

I went for a _____. I found a really big _____.
(noun)   (noun)

It was so _____ that I _____ all the
(adjective)   (verb)

way home. I put it in my _____. To my amazement, it
(noun)

began to _____. I _____. I took it to my
(verb)   (past-tense verb)

_____. I showed it to all my _____.
(place)   (plural noun)

I decided to _____ it in a box and wrap it up with
(verb)

_____ paper. I gave it to _____ for a
(adjective)   (person)

present. When _____ opened it, _____
(pronoun)   (pronoun)

_____. _____ shouted, "Thank you!
(past-tense verb)   (pronoun)

This is the best _____ I've ever had!"
(noun)

Parts of Speech

Write the part of speech of each underlined word.

NOUN PRONOUN VERB ADJECTIVE ADVERB PREPOSITION

There ① <u>are</u> many ② <u>different</u> kinds of animals. Some animals live in the wild. Some animals live in the ③ <u>zoo</u>. And still others live in homes. The animals that ④ <u>live</u> in homes are called pets.

There are many types of pets. Some pets without fur are fish, turtles, snakes and hermit crabs. Trained birds can fly ⑤ <u>around</u> ⑥ <u>your</u> house. Some ⑦ <u>furry</u> animals are cats, dogs, rabbits, ferrets, gerbils or hamsters. Some animals can ⑧ <u>successfully</u> learn tricks that ⑨ <u>you</u> teach them. Whatever your favorite animal is, animals can be ⑩ <u>special</u> friends!

1._____   4._____

2._____   5._____   7._____   9._____

3._____   6._____   8._____   10._____

Sentence Building

A **sentence** can tell more and more. Read the sentence parts.
Write a word on each line to make each sentence tell more.

1. Mrs. _____ bought a sweater.
      Who?

2. Mrs. _____ bought a sweater and two _____.
      Who?   What?

3. Mrs. _____ bought a sweater and two _____
      Who?   What?

   before leaving the _____ .
                          Where?

4. Mrs. _____ bought a sweater and two _____
      Who?   What?

   before leaving the _____ to pick up _____.
                          Where?   Who?

5. Mrs. _____ bought a sweater and two _____
      Who?   What?

   before leaving the _____ to pick up_____
                          Where?   Who?

   at _____ .
        When?

Kinds of Sentences

Remember: a **statement** tells something, a **question** asks something and a **command** tells someone to do something.

On each line, write a statement, question or command. Use a word from the box in each sentence.

glue	share	decide
enter	add	fold

Example:

Question:

Can he add anything else?

1. Statement: _____

_____

2. Question: _____

_____

3. Command: _____

_____

4. Statement: _____

_____

5. Question: _____

_____

COMPLETE YEAR GRADE 3

Kinds of Sentences

Use the group of words below to write three sentences:
a **statement**, a **question** and a **command**.

| add can these he quickly numbers |

Example:

Statement:

He can add these numbers quickly.

Question:

Can he add these numbers quickly?

Command:

Add these numbers quickly.

| fold here should we it |

1. Statement:

_____

2. Question:

_____

3. Command:

_____

Problem-Solving: Addition, Subtraction

Read and solve each problem. The first one is done for you.

The clown started the day with 200 balloons. He gave away 128 of them. Some broke. At the end of the day he had 18 balloons left. How many of the balloons broke?   54

On Monday, there were 925 tickets sold to adults and 1,412 tickets sold to children. How many more children attended the fair than adults?   _____

At one game booth, prizes were given out for scoring 500 points in three attempts. Sally scored 178 points on her first attempt, 149 points on her second attempt and 233 points on her third attempt. Did Sally win a prize?   _____

The prize-winning steer weighed 2,348 pounds.
The runner-up steer weighed 2,179 pounds.
How much more did the prize steer weigh?   _____

There were 3,418 people at the fair on Tuesday, and 2,294 people on Wednesday. What was the total number of people there for the two days?   _____

Wacky Waldo's Animal Circus

Wacky Waldo has trained a very unusual animal circus. He taught sharks to ride tricycles. He trained mice to scare tigers and snakes to be as cuddly as kittens. He even trained donkeys to fly like sparrows.

1. Wacky Waldo taught 15 sharks to ride tricycles and 34 mice to scare tigers. How many more mice has he taught than sharks?

2. Waldo trained 17 donkeys to fly through the air like little birds. He also taught 18 snakes to cuddle up like little kittens. How many animals were trained altogether?

3. Waldo trained 45 flying donkeys. One night, 26 donkeys flew away. How many donkeys were left?

4. Waldo has 112 flies who have been taught to bite fish and 98 flies who have been taught to chase frogs. What is the total?

5. One evening, 69 sharks rode tricycles. On the same night, 46 whales rode bicycles. How many animals were riding that night?

6. On Sunday, 56 snakes learned to be warm and cuddly. On Monday, 38 more snakes learned how to cuddle up. How many more snakes were trained on Sunday than on Monday?

Lizzy the Lizard

Lizzy the Lizard has a great collection of insects. She is always on the lookout for new and different types of bugs.

1. Lizzy collected 35 ants and 17 beetles in a morning. What was the sum?

2. Lizzy the Lizard caught 43 crickets and 26 grasshoppers in an evening. How many insects did she catch in all?

3. Lizzy found 27 bees and 18 wasps on a tour of her garden. How many insects did she find?

4. Lizzy and her brother Dizzy found 37 stinkbugs and 26 lice on Sunday. How many insects did they find altogether?

5. Lizzy caught 29 mud wasps. Izzy caught 16 waterbugs. Dizzy caught 14 flies. How many bugs did they catch in all?

6. Lizzy found 29 ants in the morning and 9 more ants in the afternoon. How many ants did she find in all?

First Quarter Check-Up

Reading and Language Arts

❏ I know the difference between common and proper nouns.

❏ I can add –**s** or –**es** to make words plural.

❏ I know that pronouns take the place of nouns.

❏ I know that verbs name actions.

❏ I know that helping verbs come before the main verb and that linking verbs join a noun with a describing word.

❏ I can use verbs in the present, past, and future tenses.

❏ I check sentences to make sure subjects and verbs agree.

❏ I know the difference between adjectives and adverbs.

❏ I know which punctuation marks to use at the end of statements, questions, and commands.

Math

❏ I can add multi-digit numbers without regrouping.

❏ I can add multi-digit numbers with regrouping.

❏ I can subtract multi-digit numbers without regrouping.

❏ I can subtract multi-digit numbers with regrouping.

❏ I can solve many addition and subtraction problems mentally.

❏ I can solve addition and subtraction word problems.

Final Project

Make a "Dictionary Quest" for a friend. Write clues that point to pages of a dictionary you own. Examples of clues include "This noun that means 'a tropical bird' is found on page 529," or "This adjective that describes temperature can be found on the page number that equals 385 + 78." Make the last clue point to the page that includes the word **congratulations**. Put a self-sticking note with a smiley face on that page!

Second Quarter Introduction

During the second quarter of the school year, many children are settled into routines at home and at school. Make sure your family's routines include time for playing, eating and talking together, and reading aloud. Supporting your child's learning and development will build his or her confidence in all areas.

Second Quarter Skills

Practice pages in this book for Weeks 10–18 will help your child improve the following skills.

Reading and Language Arts
- Write four kinds of sentences: statements, questions, exclamations, and commands
- Write complete sentences, with subjects and verbs. Avoid fragments and run-ons
- Combine two short sentences into one longer sentence
- Divide words into syllables
- Understand homophones, or words that sound alike but have different spellings and meanings
- Identify word roots and prefixes

Math
- Use addition and subtraction to solve word problems
- Understand the place value of ones, tens, hundreds, and thousands
- Round numbers to the nearest ten, hundred, or thousand
- Count by multiples of 2, 3, 4, 5, and 10
- Understand multiplication
- Practice multiplication
- Find factors

Multi-Sensory Learning Activities

Try these fun activities for enhancing your child's learning and development during the second quarter of the school year. Be sure to choose activities that include speaking, listening, touching, and active movement.

 Reading and Language Arts

Blindfold your child and have him or her touch some unusual objects such as cooked spaghetti coated with oil, sandpaper, a peeled peach, sandpaper, or moss. Touch your child's neck with an ice cube or brush a feather or a stiff brush across his or her arm. Open some spice jars and place them under your child's nose. Keep paper and pen handy so you can write exactly what your child says in response to each sensory experience. Then, remove the blindfold and look at what you wrote. Which sentences are statements that should end with a period? Which are questions that should end with a question mark? Which are exclamations that should end with an exclamation mark? Are any of the sentences commands (such as "Take that away!") that have no subject?

Write a very long run-on sentence on a sheet of paper. It might look like this: *What do you want to do this weekend we could go to the park I know you wanted to watch a movie so we could do that on Saturday maybe we could visit Aunt Heather....* Read the entire sentence to your child quickly, without taking a breath. Explain that it is a run-on sentence that has too many subjects and verbs. Let your child help divide the run-on sentence into several correctly punctuated sentences.

Check your local library for *Dear Deer* by Gene Barretta or *The King Who Rained* by Fred Gwynne. These fun and silly books are all about homophones.

Teach your child the mnemonic phrase **FANBOYS** to help remember the coordinating conjunctions that can be used to join two sentences: **for**, **and**, **nor**, **but**, **or**, **yet**, and **so**. A comma belongs in front of the coordinating conjunction. Ask your child to use different coordinating conjunctions to join these sentences: **I train dancing hippos** and **I fight ninja kangaroos**.

Math

Create a pretend restaurant menu with your child and make up prices together. Then, think of word problems that require adding and subtracting the prices. Solve the problems using play money.

Encourage your child to write word problems about situations that are meaningful to him or her. They could be about items in a collection, friends playing a game, or food needed for a party.

To help with understanding place value, work with real or pretend $1 bills, dimes, and pennies. Explain that $1 equals 100 pennies and one dime equals 10 pennies. Can your child use the money to show 126 cents? 148 cents?

Second Quarter Introduction, cont.

On nine cards or slips of paper, write **1,000–9,000**. On a second set of cards, write **100–900**. On a third set, write **10–90**. On a fourth set, write **1–9**. Put the cards in four stacks. Can your child draw a card from each stack and write the equivalent number?

Make "Multiplication Mysteries" for your child. For example, say, "You can watch TV for the same number of minutes as the product of 5 and 6."

Provide an assortment of buttons, paperclips, pennies, or other small items. Give your child a multiplication problem such as **4 x 4**. Can your child use the objects to represent the problem with four groups of four objects? Can he or she skip-count the objects (example: 4, 8, 12, 16)?

 **Science**

The heart is a strong muscle that pumps oxygen-rich blood to all parts of the body with every beat. Have your child count his or her heart rate for one minute. Then, do some aerobic exercise and count it again. Finally, use multiplication to determine how many times your child's heart beats at resting and elevated rates for 10 minutes, 30 minutes, and 60 minutes.

 **Social Studies**

Read *If You Were At the First Thanksgiving* by Anne Kamma. Ask your child to use what he or she learned from the story to make an acrostic poem from the word **THANKSGIVING**, with each line beginning with one letter of the word.

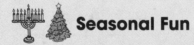 **Seasonal Fun**

Do Christmas trees ever get tired of holding up their branches with all the lights and ornaments? Have your child write a story titled "The Tired Christmas Tree."

Research to find out how Christmas is celebrated in Mexico. Make an ornament-sized "god's eye" or *Ojo Dios* from craft sticks and yarn.

Read *Alexandra's Scroll: The Story of the First Hanukkah* by Miriam Chaikin. Have your child create a new illustration based on the story's characters and setting.

Week 10 Skills

Subject	Skill	Multi-Sensory Learning Activities
Reading and Language Arts	Write statements (telling sentences), questions (asking sentences), and exclamations (sentences that show excitement).	• Complete Practice Pages 112–117. • Have your child choose two favorite books, keeping one and giving one to you. Then, call out either **statement**, **question**, or **exclamation**. Who can find an example of this type of sentence first in his or her book? When found, read the sentence aloud and examine it together. Does it begin with a capital letter? What punctuation mark does it end with? Continue the search with another type of sentence. • Find an interesting photograph in a magazine or on the Internet. Have your child look at it closely and then write five statements, five questions, and five exclamations about it. Make sure each sentence is punctuated correctly.
Math	Use addition and subtraction to solve word problems.	• Complete Practice Pages 118–120. • Choose a number from **1–100**. Can your child write a word problem with an answer that equals that number? Write a problem for a number your child chooses for you, too. • Ask your child to research statistics for a favorite sports team and use some of the numbers to write five word problems about the team. Your child may wish to use the problems to create a worksheet to share with his or her class.

Statements

A **statement** is a sentence that tells something.

Use the words in the box to complete the statements below. Write the words on the lines.

glue	decide	add
share	enter	fold

1. It took ten minutes for Kayla to _____ the numbers.

2. Ben wants to _____ his cookies with me.

3. "I can't _____ which color to choose," said Rocky.

4. _____ can be used to make things stick together.

5. "This is how you _____ your paper in half," said Mrs. Green.

6. The opposite of **leave** is _____.

Write your own statement on the line.

_____

Questions

Questions are asking sentences. They begin with a capital letter and end with a question mark. Many questions begin with the words **who**, **what**, **why**, **when**, **where** and **how**. Write six questions using the question words below. Make sure to end each question with a question mark.

1. Who _____

2. What _____

3. Why _____

4. When _____

5. Where _____

6. How _____

Statements and Questions

Statements are sentences that tell about something. Statements begin with a capital letter and end with a period. **Questions** are sentences that ask about something. Questions begin with a capital letter and end with a question mark.

Rewrite the sentences using capital letters and either a period or a question mark.

Example: walruses live in the Arctic

Walruses live in the Arctic.

1. are walruses large sea mammals or fish

_____

2. they spend most of their time in the water and on ice

_____

3. are floating sheets of ice called ice floes

_____

4. are walruses related to seals

_____

5. their skin is thick, wrinkled and almost hairless

_____

Statements and Questions

Change the statements into questions and the questions into statements.

Example: Jane is happy.   Is Jane happy?
               Were you late?   You were late.

1. The rainbow was brightly colored.

_____

2. Was the sun coming out?

_____

3. The dog is doing tricks.

_____

4. Have you washed the dishes today?

_____

5. Kurt was the circus ringmaster.

_____

6. Were you planning on going to the library?

_____

Word Order in Sentences

You can often make a question out of a statement by changing the word order of the sentence.

Examples:
My family is going on a camping trip. (statement)
Is my family going on a camping trip? (question)

Change the word order to make each statement a question and each question a statement. Write the new sentence on the line.

1. Mom and Dad are going to take turns driving.

_____

2. Ellen is getting the gear together.

_____

3. James is packing the car trunk.

_____

4. Will it be dark when we arrive at the lake?

_____

5. Joey's job is to put up the tent.

_____

6. Will we sit around the fire and tell stories?

_____

Exclamations

Exclamation points are used for sentences that express strong feelings. These sentences can have one or two words or be very long.

Examples: Wait! or **Don't forget to call!**

Add an exclamation point at the end of sentences that express strong feelings.
Add a period at the end of the statements.

1. My parents and I were watching television

2. The snow began falling around noon

3. Wow

4. The snow was really coming down

5. We turned the television off and looked out the window

6. The snow looked like a white blanket

7. How beautiful

8. We decided to put on our coats and go outside

9. Hurry

10. Get your sled

11. All the people on the street came out to see the snow

12. How wonderful

13. The children began making a snowman

14. What a great day

Summer Vacation

Circle the operation needed to solve each problem below.

1. Julie spent 25 afternoons at the beach and 18 afternoons at the neighborhood park. How many more afternoons did Julie spend at the beach than at the park?

   Addition

   Subtraction

2. Melanie needed $6 to go to the skating rink, but she only had $4. How much more money did Melanie need to go skating?

   Addition

   Subtraction

3. At the park, Julie played a game of soccer with her friends. If there were 8 people on Julie's team and 9 on the opposing team, how many people were playing soccer?

   Addition

   Subtraction

4. Cody's summer vacation was 94 days long. If he spent 68 summer days at his aunt's house, how many days were not spent at his aunt's house?

   Addition

   Subtraction

5. The cost to send Julie to summer camp was $350. Her big brother's summer camp cost $450. How much money did Julie's parents spend on summer camp for their two children?

   Addition

   Subtraction

6. Julie and her father went fishing at the lake. Julie caught only 6 fish, while her dad caught 18 fish. How many fish did they catch altogether?

   Addition

   Subtraction

Movie Inventory

Janice helped her mother keep track of movies at the library. Write the answer to each problem on the line.

1. There are 762 movie titles listed in the computer. If Janice entered 287 more names into the computer, how many movie titles would be listed? _____ movie titles

2. One day, 278 movies were checked out. The next day, 192 movies were checked out. How many movies were checked out altogether in those two days? _____ movies

3. Janice liked to count the kids' movies. Janice counted 242 cartoon movies and 179 that were not cartoons. How many movies were in the kids' section? _____ movies

4. In the game section, there are 176 video games for one game system and the same number of games for a different game system. How many video games are there altogether? _____ games

5. Janice counted 195 movies that she had already seen. She found another 178 that she wanted to see. If Janice saw those movies, how many altogether would she have seen? _____ movies

6. The library had 637 patrons last month and 554 patrons this month. How many patrons did the library have altogether in those two months? _____ patrons

Building a House

Read about Jonathan's summer job and write the answer to each problem on the line.

1. Over the summer, Jonathan worked 126 hours. His uncle worked 625 hours. How many more hours did Uncle Jake work than Jonathan?

   _____ more hours

2. It took 630 bricks to build the front wall of the house. The back wall took 725. How many more bricks were needed in the back of the house than in the front of the house?

   _____ more bricks

3. The side walls of the house contained a total of 934 bricks. If the garage took 168 fewer bricks, how many bricks did it take to build the garage?

   _____ bricks

4. They used 245 bricks to build a pillar in the front of the house. If Jonathan laid 150 of those bricks and his uncle did the rest, how many bricks did his uncle lay?

   _____ bricks

5. The bricks in the large pillar cost $282. If the mortar between the bricks cost $218 less, how much did the mortar cost?

   _____ dollars

6. Jonathan earned $360 helping his uncle this summer. Last summer he made $285. How much more did he make this summer than last?

   _____ dollars

Week 11 Skills

Subject	Skill	Multi-Sensory Learning Activities
Reading and Language Arts	Write commands.	• Complete Practice Pages 122 and 123. • Write 10 commands on small sheets of paper. They might include "Jump eight times," "Find a sock," or "Spell your sister's name." Divide the sheets into two stacks, one for you and one for your child. Who can read and perform all the commands in his or her stack the fastest? After the fun, read the commands together, noticing that each sentence has the implied subject **You**.
	Review types of sentences.	• Complete Practice Pages 124–127. • Write these words and punctuation marks on separate index cards: **you, will, climb, the, mountain, ., ?, !**. Ask your child to arrange the cards to make a statement, a question, an exclamation, and a command. Have him or her point to the letter that should be capitalized in each sentence.
Math	Understand place value.	• Complete Practice Pages 128–130. • Help your child understand place value by showing how to write numbers in expanded form. The number **1,246** would be written **one thousand two hundred forty-six**. • Give your child mental math problems such as "What is 200 more than 1,300?" After answering correctly, have your child write the problem, underlining the digit that changed.

Commands

A **command** is a sentence that tells someone to do something.

Use the words in the box to complete the commands below. Write the words on the lines.

glue	decide	add	share	enter	fold

1. _____ a cup of flour to the cake batter.

2. _____ how much paper you will need to write your story.

3. Please _____ the picture of the apple onto the paper.

4. _____ through this door and leave through the other door.

5. Please _____ the letter and put it into an envelope.

6. _____ your toys with your sister.

Write your own command on the lines.

_____

_____

Commands

A **command** is a sentence that tells someone to do something. It ends with a **period**.

The kids at Camp Lagoona have not cleaned their cabin. Their leader is telling them what they have to do. Write eight commands that will tell the campers things they must do to clean the cabin.

1 _____

2 _____

3 _____

4 _____

5 _____

6 _____

7 _____

8 _____

Explaining Sentences

Complete each sentence, explaining why each event might have happened.

She hugged me because _____

_____.

He didn't want to play with us because _____

_____.

We planned to go to the zoo because _____

_____.

I grabbed it away from him because _____

_____.

We clapped loudly because _____

_____.

Review

There are three kinds of sentences.

Statements: Sentences that tell something. Statements end with a period (.).

Questions: Sentences that ask a question. Questions end with a question mark (**?**).

Exclamations: Sentences that express a strong feeling. Exclamations end with an exclamation point (**!**).

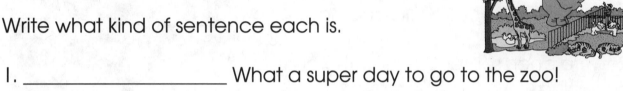

Write what kind of sentence each is.

1. _____ What a super day to go to the zoo!

2. _____ Do you like radishes?

3. _____ I belong to the chess club.

4. _____ It is time to wash the dishes.

5. _____ How much does that cost?

6. _____ Apples grow on trees.

7. _____ Clayton looked out
the window.

8. _____ What a colorful rainbow!

Four Kinds of Sentences

Always begin a sentence with a capital letter. End a statement or a command with a period. End a question with a question mark. End an exclamation with an exclamation point.

Examples:
Grizzly bears are fascinating creatures. (statement)
Do they live in all parts of the world? (question)
Grizzly bears are huge! (exclamation)
Tell me more about bears. (command)

Rewrite each sentence using the correct capitalization and punctuation.

1. grizzly bears live in Wyoming, Montana, Idaho, Alaska and western Canada

2. some grizzlies are eight feet in length

3. did you know that male grizzlies can weigh 800 pounds

4. these bears are huge

5. they can run very quickly

6. that's incredible speed

7. what do grizzly bears eat

8. they eat acorns, roots, berries and leaves

9. they also eat fish, birds, insects and small mammals

Kinds of Sentences

A **statement** is a sentence that tells something.
A **question** is a sentence that asks something.
A **command** is a sentence that tells someone to do something.

Commands begin with a verb or **please**. They usually end with a period. The noun is **you** but does not need to be part of the sentence.

Example: "Come here, please" means "**You** come here, please."

Examples of commands: Stand next to me.
Please give me some paper.

Write **S** in front of the statements, **Q** in front of the questions and **C** in front of the commands. End each sentence with a period or a question mark.

Example:

_____C_____ Stop and look before you cross the street.

_____ 1. Did you do your math homework

_____ 2. I think I lost my math book

_____ 3. Will you help me find it

_____ 4. I looked everywhere

_____ 5. Please open your math books to page three

_____ 6. Did you look under your desk

_____ 7. I looked, but it's not there

_____ 8. Who can add seven and four

_____ 9. Come up and write the answer on the board

_____ 10. Chris, where is your math book

_____ 11. I don't know for sure

_____ 12. Please share a book with a friend

Place Value

The place value of a digit, or numeral, is shown by where it is in the number. For example, in the number **1,234**, **1** has the place value of thousands, **2** is hundreds, **3** is tens and **4** is ones.

Hundred Thousands	Ten Thousands	Thousands	Hundreds	Tens	Ones
9	4	3	8	5	2

Match the numbers in Column A with the words in Column B.

A	B
62,453	two hundred thousands
7,641	three thousands
486,113	four hundred thousands
11,277	eight hundreds
813,463	seven tens
594,483	five ones
254,089	six hundreds
79,841	nine ten thousands
27,115	five tens

Place-Value Puzzle

Complete the puzzle.

ACROSS
A. 3 thousand, 5 hundred 9
C. 100 less than 8,754
E. one hundred sixty-two
G. seven hundred eighty-two
I. 100, 150, 200, ____
J. fifty-one thousand, three hundred twenty-four
L. two
M. 100 less than 9,704
O. three zeros
P. eight
Q. 10,000 more than 56,480
R. one
S. 1 ten, 1 one

DOWN
A. 10 more than 3,769
B. ninety-one
C. 28 backwards
D. 5 hundreds, 8 tens, 5 ones
F. 100 less than 773
H. 5, 10, 15, 20, ____
I. ten less than 24,684
K. 2 tens, 9 ones
L. two thousand, one
N. 1,000; 2,000; 3,000; ____
P. eight hundreds, 6 tens, 1 one

4, 3, 2, 1 Blast Off

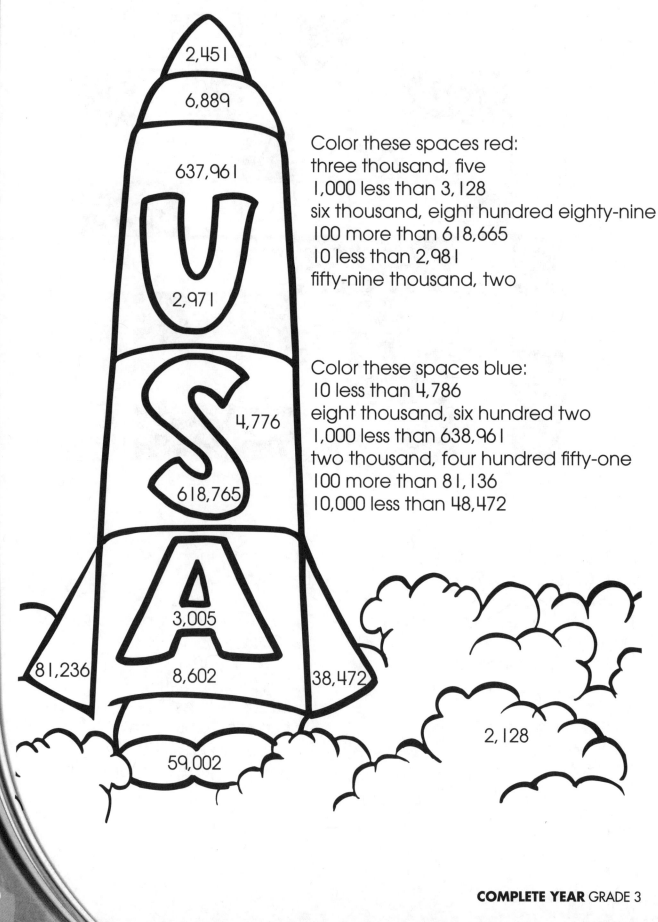

Color these spaces red:
three thousand, five
1,000 less than 3,128
six thousand, eight hundred eighty-nine
100 more than 618,665
10 less than 2,981
fifty-nine thousand, two

Color these spaces blue:
10 less than 4,786
eight thousand, six hundred two
1,000 less than 638,961
two thousand, four hundred fifty-one
100 more than 81,136
10,000 less than 48,472

Numbers on rocket: 2,451 · 6,889 · 637,961 · 2,971 · 4,776 · 618,765 · 3,005 · 81,236 · 8,602 · 38,472 · 59,002 · 2,128

Week 12 Skills

Subject	Skill	Multi-Sensory Learning Activities
Reading and Language Arts	Write complete sentences.	• Complete Practice Pages 132–135. • Have your child proofread a piece of his or her writing, marking the noun in each sentence with a highlighter pen of one color and the verb in each sentence with a highlighter pen of another color. Is every sentence in the piece a complete sentence?
Math	Understand place value.	• Complete Practice Pages 136–139. • Help your child research to find the population of your city or state. Write the number across the top of a large sheet of paper. Can your child write the place value (hundreds, thousands, ten-thousands, etc.) below each digit in the number?
	Round to the nearest ten.	• Complete Practice Page 140. • Have your child roll a pair of dice and write each number rolled as one digit of a two-digit number. Then, ask your child to round the number to the nearest ten. Repeat with more rolls of the dice. • Look for numbers around your home or community. They may include addresses, product weights, or numbers on license plates. Ask your child to round each number found to the nearest ten.

thousands	hundreds	tens	ones
8	6	2	4

Sentences

Remember: every sentence must have a noun that tells who or what is doing something and a verb that tells what the noun is doing.

Parts of each sentence below are missing. Rewrite each sentence, adding a noun or a verb, periods and capital letters.

Example:
read a book every day (needs a noun)

Leon reads a book every day.

1. packed a lunch

_____

2. the crowd at the beach

_____

3. cost too much

_____

4. kangaroos and their babies

_____

5. was too thick to chew

_____

Sentence Identification

A **sentence** is a group of words that tells a whole idea. The mayor's speech has some missing words. Read each group of words. Draw one line under each group of words that makes a sentence. Circle each group of words that does not make a sentence.

I want to thank you for voting for me. I will try to be a good. I plan to work hard for our city. First, I want to build a new children's library. Books are so important to kids. Every child should read at least. Also, I want to improve the city's park and playground. The old picnic tables need. We plan to buy four. These are just a few of. I would like your ideas, too. Please feel free to.

Thank you very.

Choose one of the mayor's mistakes. Add words and write it as a sentence.

_____

_____

_____

_____

A Penny for Your Thoughts

A **phrase** is an **incomplete** thought—it doesn't make sense all by itself. A **sentence** is a **complete** thought.

Circle **phrase** or **sentence** to show whether each group of words below is an incomplete or a complete thought.

1. day of feasting in the village   phrase   sentence

2. it was a string of blue beads   phrase   sentence

3. the chief was pleased   phrase   sentence

4. played drums and danced   phrase   sentence

5. he looked at the ship   phrase   sentence

6. pointed to the north   phrase   sentence

7. rowed toward the ship   phrase   sentence

8. we will tell the chief   phrase   sentence

9. she is sad   phrase   sentence

10. going back to England   phrase   sentence

Add words to the phrases above to make complete thoughts. Don't forget to begin each sentence with a capital letter and end it with a period.

_____

_____

_____

_____

Sentences, Fragments, and Run-Ons

A **complete sentence** tells a complete thought. It contains a subject and a predicate.

A **sentence fragment** does not express a complete thought.

A **run-on sentence** is two or more sentences written together without correct punctuation.

Examples:

Mr. Wilkins went to Alaska last year.
(complete sentence)

First, Mr. Wilkins.
(sentence fragment)

He flew to Seattle he took a plane to Anchorage.
(run-on sentence)

Write **C** for complete, **F** for fragment or **R** for run-on.

_____ 1. Life for children in an Eskimo village is much like life in any town.

_____ 2. The boys and girls.

_____ 3. Children go to school just as you do.

_____ 4. They study reading and English they do math problems and learn to spell and write.

_____ 5. They say the Pledge of Allegiance to the flag before beginning their school work.

_____ 6. Many of the boys and girls wear warm parkas with fur hoods.

_____ 7. They wear warm boots to keep their feet from getting cold.

_____ 8. During festivals, children play games and have contests, they enjoy a game of blanket toss in which the child has to keep his or her balance while being tossed in the air on a blanket of walrus skin.

_____ 9. They also like.

_____ 10. Today, many families have trucks and snowmobiles for transportation rather than dogsleds.

Write That Number

Write the following numbers using digits.

1. six hundred fifty thousand, two hundred twenty-five _____

2. nine hundred ninety-nine thousand, nine hundred ninety-nine _____

3. one hundred six thousand, four hundred thirty-seven _____

4. three hundred fifty-six thousand, two hundred two _____

5. Write the number that is two more than 356,909. _____

6. Write the number that is five less than 448,394. _____

7. Write the number that is ten more than 285,634. _____

8. Write the number that is ten less than 395,025. _____

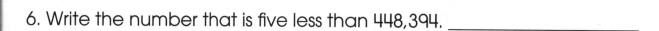

Write the following numbers in word form.

1. 3,208 _____

2. 13,656 _____

Place Value

Place value is the value of a digit, or numeral, shown by where it is in the number. For example, in **1,234**, **1** has the place value of thousands, **2** is hundreds, **3** is tens and **4** is ones.

Write the numbers
in the correct boxes to find
how far the car has traveled.

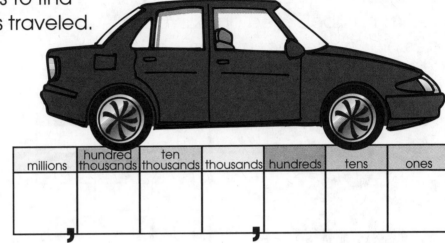

one thousand

six hundreds

eight ones

nine ten thousands

four tens

two millions

five hundred thousands

millions	hundred thousands	ten thousands	thousands	hundreds	tens	ones

How many miles has the car traveled? _____

In the number . . .

2,386	_____	is in the ones place.
4,957	_____	is in the hundreds place.
102,432	_____	is in the ten thousands place.
489,753	_____	is in the thousands place.
1,743,998	_____	is in the millions place.
9,301,671	_____	is in the hundred thousands place.
7,521,834	_____	is in the tens place.

Place Value: Standard Form

For this activity, you will need a number spinner or number cube.

Roll the cube or spin the spinner the same number of times as there are spaces in each place value box. The first number rolled or spun goes in the ones place, the second number in the tens place, and so on.

Example:

thousands	hundreds	tens	ones
4	5	6	7

Standard Form

4,567

	hundreds	tens	ones

_____

thousands	hundreds	tens	ones

_____

ten thousands	thousands	hundreds	tens	ones

_____

hundred thousands	ten thousands	thousands	hundreds	tens	ones

_____

millions	hundred thousands	ten thousands	thousands	hundreds	tens	ones

_____

Write the number words for the numerals above.

_____

_____

_____

_____

_____

Place Value Practice

Use the number cube or spinner to create numbers for the place value boxes below. Then, write the number in expanded notation and standard form.

Example:

thousands	hundreds	tens	ones
8	6	2	4

Standard Form ___8,624___

Expanded Notation ___8,000 + 600 + 20 + 4___

thousands	hundreds	tens	ones

Standard Form _____

Expanded Notation _____

ten thousands	thousands	hundreds	tens	ones

Standard Form _____

Expanded Notation _____

hundred thousands	ten thousands	thousands	hundreds	tens	ones

Standard Form _____

Expanded Notation _____

Write the value of the **4** in each number below.

742,521 _____

456 _____

1,234,567 _____

65,504 _____

937,641 _____

Rounding: The Nearest Ten

If the ones number is 5 or greater, "round up" to the nearest 10. If the ones number is 4 or less, the tens number stays the same and the ones number becomes a zero.

Examples: 15 round up to 20   23 round down to 20   47 round up to 50

7 _____

12 _____

33 _____

27 _____

73 _____

25 _____

39 _____

58 _____

81 _____

94 _____

44 _____

88 _____

66 _____

70 _____

Week 13 Skills

Subject	Skill	Multi-Sensory Learning Activities
Reading and Language Arts	Combine two related sentences into one longer sentence.	• Complete Practice Pages 142–146. • Ask your child to write 10 short sentences describing a character from his or her favorite TV show. Then, help your child combine them into five or fewer sentences using coordinating conjunctions such as **and**, **but**, and **or** and prepositions such as **if**, **when**, and **because**.
Math	Round to the nearest ten, hundred, or thousand.	• Complete Practice Pages 147–150. • Ask your child to choose three places he or she would like to visit: someplace nearby, another state, and another country. Conduct research to find out how many miles away from your home each place is. Then, have your child round the distance to the nearby place to the nearest 10 miles, the distance to the other state to the nearest 100 miles, and the distance to the other country to the nearest 1,000 miles.
Bonus: Social Studies		• Talk with your child about what makes someone a hero. Is it helping others? Getting through a tough situation? Standing up for what you believe in? Help your child choose a hero and write a letter to that person.

Sentence Combining

Combine two sentences to make one sentence. Choose the important word or words from the second sentence. Then, add them to the first sentence where the arrow (↓) is.

Example:

I have a new ↓ skateboard.
It is purple and black.

<u>I have a new purple and black skateboard.</u>

1. I am writing a ↓ letter to my cousin.
   It is a thank you letter.

2. We ate ↓ after the homecoming ball game.
   We ate hot dogs and chili.

3. Every Halloween we watch ↓ movies together.
   We watch scary movies.

4. I must study for my ↓ test.
   My test is in science.

And and But

We can use **and** or **but** to make one longer sentence from two short ones.

Use **and** or **but** to make two short sentences into a longer, more interesting one. Write the new sentence on the line below the two short sentences.

Example:

The skunk has black fur. The skunk has a white stripe.

The skunk has black fur and a white stripe.

1. The skunk has a small head. The skunk has small ears.

_____

2. The skunk has short legs. Skunks can move quickly.

_____

3. Skunks sleep in hollow trees. Skunks sleep underground.

_____

4. Skunks are chased by animals. Skunks do not run away.

_____

5. Skunks sleep during the day. Skunks hunt at night.

_____

Joining Sentences

Joining words are words that make two sentences into one longer sentence. Here are some words that join sentences:

and — if both sentences are about the same noun or verb.
   Example: Tom is in my class at school, **and** he lives near me.

but — if the second sentence says something different from the first sentence.
   Example: Julie walks to school with me, **but** today she is sick.

or — if each sentence names a different thing you could do.
   Example: We could go to my house, **or** we could go to yours.

Join each set of sentences below using the words **and**, **but** or **or**.

1. Those socks usually cost a lot. This pack of ten socks is cheaper.

_____

_____

2. The kangaroo has a pouch. It lives in Australia.

_____

_____

3. The zookeeper can start to work early. She can stay late.

_____

_____

Joining Sentences

If and **when** can be joining words, too.

Read each set of sentences. Then, join the two sentences to make one longer sentence.

Example: The apples will need to be washed.
The apples are dirty.

The apples will need to be washed if they are dirty.

1. The size of the crowd grew. It grew when the game began.

_____

_____

2. Be careful driving in the fog. The fog is thick.

_____

_____

3. Pack your suitcases. Do it when you wake up in the morning.

_____

_____

Joining Sentences

Some words that can join sentences are:

when — **When** we got there, the show had already started.

after — **After** I finished my homework, I watched TV.

because — You can't go by yourself **because** you are too young.

Use the joining words to make the two short sentences into one longer one.

1.  The keeper opened the door. The bear got out.

_____

_____

2.  I didn't buy the tickets. They cost too much.

_____

_____

3. 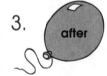 The kangaroo ate lunch. He took a nap.

_____

_____

4. 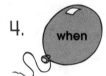 The door opened. The crowd rushed in.

_____

_____

5. 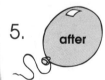 I cut the bread. Everyone had a slice.

_____

_____

Rounding: Tens

Rounding a number means expressing it to the nearest ten, hundred, thousand, and so on. Knowing how to round numbers makes estimating sums, differences and products easier. When rounding to the nearest ten, the key number is in the ones place. If the ones digit is 5 or larger, round up to the next highest ten. If the ones digit is 4 or less, round down to the nearest ten.

Examples:
- Round 81 to the nearest ten.
- 1 is the key digit.
- If it is less than 5, round down.
- Answer: <u>80</u>

- Round 246 to the nearest ten.
- 6 is the key digit.
- If it is more than 5, round up.
- Answer: <u>250</u>

Round these numbers to the nearest ten.

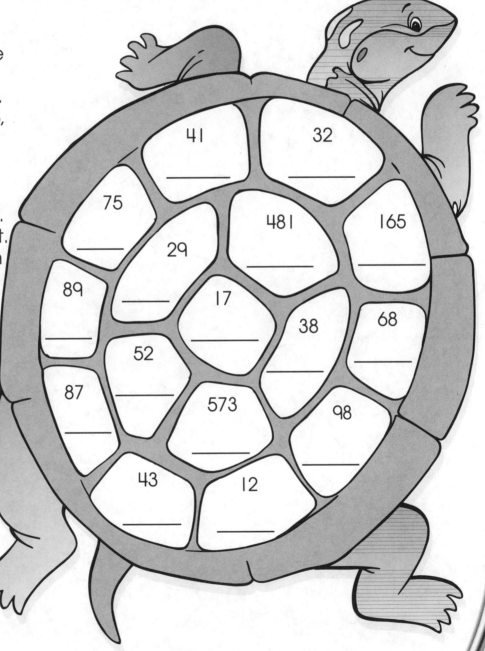

Rounding: The Nearest Hundred

If the tens number is 5 or greater, "round up" to the nearest hundred. If the tens number is 4 or less, the hundreds number remains the same.

Remember: Look at the number directly to the right of the place you are rounding to.

Example:

2<u>3</u>0 round <u>down</u> to 200

4<u>7</u>0 round <u>up</u> to 500

1<u>5</u>0 round <u>up</u> to 200

7<u>3</u>2 round <u>down</u> to 700

456 _____		120 _____	
340 _____		923 _____	
867 _____		550 _____	
686 _____		231 _____	
770 _____		492 _____	

Rounding: Hundreds and Thousands

When rounding to the nearest hundred, the key number is in the tens place. If the tens digit is 5 or larger, round up to nearest hundred. If the tens digit is 4 or less, round down to the nearest hundred.

Examples:

Round 871 to the nearest hundred.
7 is the key digit.
If it is more than 5, round up.
Answer: <u>900</u>

Round 421 to the nearest hundred.
2 is the key digit.
If it is less than 4, round down.
Answer: <u>400</u>

Round these numbers to the nearest hundred.

255 _____   368 _____   443 _____   578 _____

562 _____   698 _____   99 _____   775 _____

812 _____   592 _____   124 _____   10,235 _____

When rounding to the nearest thousand, the key number is in the hundreds place. If the hundreds digit is 5 or larger, round up to the nearest thousand. If the hundreds digit is 4 or less, round down to the nearest thousand.

Examples:

Round 7,932 to the nearest thousand.
9 is the key digit.
If it is more than 5, round up.
Answer: <u>8,000</u>

Round 1,368 to the nearest thousand.
3 is the key digit.
If it is less than 4, round down.
Answer: <u>1,000</u>

Round these numbers to the nearest thousand.

8,631 _____   1,248 _____   798 _____

999 _____   6,229 _____   8,461 _____

9,654 _____   4,963 _____   99,923 _____

Rounding

Round these numbers to the nearest ten.

18 _____   33 _____   82 _____   56 _____

24 _____   49 _____   91 _____   67 _____

Round these numbers to the nearest hundred.

243 _____   689 _____   263 _____   162 _____

389 _____   720 _____   351 _____   490 _____

463 _____   846 _____   928 _____   733 _____

Round these numbers to the nearest thousand.

2,638 _____   3,940 _____   8,653 _____

6,238 _____   1,429 _____   5,061 _____

7,289 _____   2,742 _____   9,460 _____

3,109 _____   4,697 _____   8,302 _____

Round these numbers to the nearest ten thousand.

11,368 _____   38,421 _____

75,302 _____   67,932 _____

14,569 _____   49,926 _____

93,694 _____   81,648 _____

26,784 _____   87,065 _____

57,843 _____   29,399 _____

Week 14 Skills

Subject	Skill	Multi-Sensory Learning Activities
Reading and Language Arts	Identify the subject of a sentence.	• Complete Practice Pages 152–154. • Cut long strips of construction paper. Fold over several inches at the left edge of each strip to form a flap. Open the flap and write a sentence about an animal on each strip. Use this format: **The bird gathered twigs for its nest**. When folded, the flap should cover the subject of each sentence (example: **The bird**). Show the strips to your child with the flaps folded in. Ask him or her to read each predicate, try to guess the subject of each sentence, and unfold the flap to check the guess.
	Identify the predicate of a sentence.	• Complete Practice Pages 155 and 156. • Use the sentence strips from the previous activity. Ask your child to underline the verb in each predicate. Can your child think of a different subject to match each predicate?
Math	Count by multiples of 2, 3, 4, 5, and 10.	• Complete Practice Pages 157–160. • Ask your child to jump rope, dance to music, or do another rhythmic activity while counting by 2s, 3s, 4s, 5s, and 10s. • Gather a collection of small items such as pennies, checkers, or beads. Ask your child to arrange them in rows and columns to make them easy to count. Then, help your child skip-count each row to find the total number of items.

Subjects of Sentences

The **subject** of a sentence tells who or what the sentence is about.

Example:

<u>**The buffalo**</u> provided the Plains Native Americans with many things.

↑
(subject)

Underline the subject of each sentence.

1. The Plains Native Americans used almost every part of the buffalo.

2. Their tepees were made of buffalo hides.

3. Clothing was made from the hides of buffalo and deer.

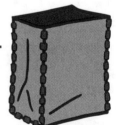

4. They ate the meat of the buffalo

5. Buffalo stomachs were used as pots for cooking.

6. Bones were used for tools and utensils.

7. The tail was used as a flyswatter.

8. Horns were used as scrapers and cups.

9. Buffalo manure was dried and used for fuel.

10. A kind of glue could be made from the hooves.

Simple Subjects

A **simple subject** is the main noun or pronoun in the complete subject.

Draw a line between the subject and the predicate. Circle the simple subject.

Example: The black (bear) | lives in the zoo.

1. Penguins look like they wear tuxedos.

2. The seal enjoys raw fish.

3. The monkeys like to swing on bars.

4. The beautiful peacock has colorful feathers.

5. Bats like dark places.

6. Some snakes eat small rodents.

7. The orange and brown giraffes have long necks.

8. The baby zebra is close to his mother.

Compound Subjects

Compound subjects are two or more nouns that have the same predicate.

Combine the subjects to create one sentence with a compound subject.

Example: Jill can swing.
Whitney can swing.
Luke can swing.
Jill, Whitney and Luke can swing.

1. Roses grow in the garden. Tulips grow in the garden.

_____

2. Apples are fruit. Oranges are fruit. Bananas are fruit.

_____

3. Bears live in the zoo. Monkeys live in the zoo.

_____

4. Jackets keep us warm. Sweaters keep us warm.

_____

Predicates of Sentences

The **predicate** of a sentence tells what the subject is or does.

Juan is interested in collecting rocks.

↑   ↑

(subject)   (predicate)

Underline the predicate part of each sentence.

1. Juan looks for rocks everywhere he goes.

2. He has found many interesting rocks in his own backyard.

3. Juan showed me a piece of limestone with fossils in it.

4. Limestone is a kind of sedimentary rock.

5. It is formed underwater from the shells of animals.

6. Juan told me that some rocks come from deep inside the Earth.

7. Molten rock comes out of a volcano.

8. The lava cools to form igneous rock.

9. Heat and pressure inside the Earth cause igneous and sedimentary rock to change form.

10. This changed rock is called metamorphic rock.

11. Metamorphic rock is often used in building.

12. I want to become a "rock hound," too!

Compound Predicates

A **compound predicate** has two or more verbs joined with the word **and**.

Dad **picks up** Sam. Dad **drives** Sam to the dentist.

Dad **picks up and drives** Sam to the dentist.

If the sentence has a compound predicate, write **CP** on the line. If it does not have a compound predicate, write **NO**.

_____ 1. Dad and Sam park the car and go inside.

_____ 2. Sam reads and watches TV while waiting for the dentist.

_____ 3. Dad visits with another patient.

_____ 4. The hygienist comes into the room and gets Sam.

_____ 5. The hygienist cleans, polishes and x-rays Sam's teeth.

_____ 6. The dentist examines Sam's teeth and checks the x-rays.

_____ 7. The dentist gives Sam a toothbrush to take home.

_____ 8. Sam thanks the dentist.

Combine the predicate parts of the two sentences below to make a compound predicate. Write the new sentence on the line.

1. Sam wiggles his loose tooth. Sam pulls his loose tooth.

_____

2. Sam smiles. Sam shows Dad the empty space in his mouth.

_____

Skipping Through the Tens

Skip-count by tens. Begin with the number on the first line. Write each number that follows.

0, _____ , _____ , _____ , _____ , _____ , _____ , _____ , _____ , 100

3, _____ , _____ , _____ , 53 , _____ , _____ , _____ , 103

1, _____ , _____ , _____ , _____ , _____ , _____ , 81 , _____ , _____

8, _____ , _____ , _____ , _____ , 68 , _____ , _____ , _____ , _____

6, _____ , _____ , _____ , _____ , _____ , _____ , _____ , _____ , _____

4, _____ , _____ , _____ , _____ , _____ , _____ , _____ , _____ , 104

2, _____ , _____ , _____ , _____ , _____ , _____ , _____ , 92 , _____

5, _____ , _____ , 45 , _____ , _____ , _____ , _____ , _____ , _____

What is ten more than ...

26 _____   29 _____

44 _____   77 _____

53 _____   91 _____

24 _____   49 _____

Counting to 100

Count by twos:

		6	8			16		22					
30						44							56
			66						78				
						100							

Count by threes:

3	6					21						39	
				57							75		
	90				102								

Count by fours:

4	8								40				
60								88		100			

Skip-Counting

Skip-counting is a quick way to count by skipping numbers. For example, when you skip-count by 2s, you count 2, 4, 6, 8, and so on. You can skip-count by many different numbers such as 2s, 4s, 5s, 10s and 100s.

The illustration below shows skip-counting by 2s to 14.

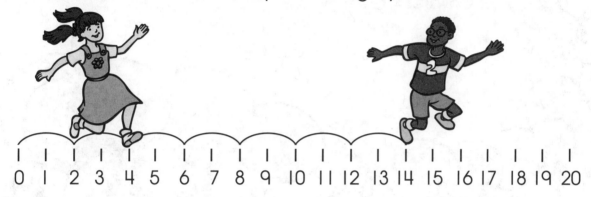

Use the number line to help you skip-count by 2s from 0 to 20.

0, _____ , _____ , _____ , 8, _____ , _____ , 14, _____ , _____ , _____ .

Skip-count by 3s by filling in the rocks across the pond.

Multiples

A **multiple** is the product of a specific number and any other number. For example, the multiples of 2 are 2 (2 x 1), 4 (2 x 2), 6, 8, 10, 12, and so on.

Write the missing multiples.

Example: Count by 5s.
5, 10, 15, 20, 25, 30, 35.
These are multiples of 5.

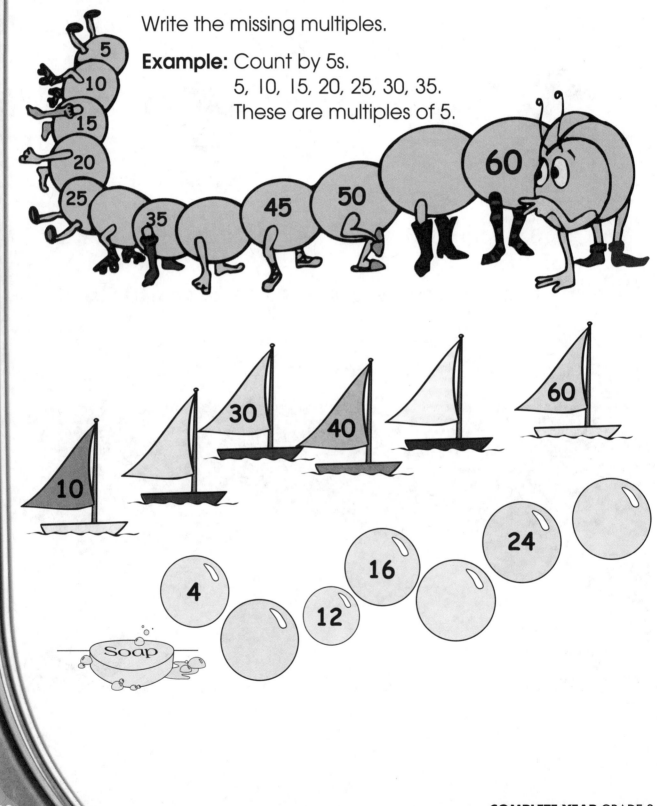

Week 15 Skills

Subject	Skill	Multi-Sensory Learning Activities
Reading and Language Arts	Divide words into syllables.	• Complete Practice Pages 162–166. • Have your child examine a printed or online dictionary to see how words are divided into syllables. Ask him or her to notice that each syllable in a word contains at least one vowel sound and letter. Then, ask your child to spell a long word such as **helicopter**. How does breaking the word into syllables help to spell it correctly?
Math	Understand multiplication.	• Complete Practice Pages 167–170. • Help your child understand that multiplication is repeated addition. For example, say, "If there are four people eating dinner, and each one wants two rolls, we can find out how many rolls we need by adding $2 + 2 + 2 + 2 = 8$. Or, there is an easier way. We can think that four groups of two equals eight. Four times two is eight." Whenever possible, let your child arrange objects in groups and count the groups to help visualize multiplication problems.
Bonus: Science		• Talk about the six types of simple machines: levers, pulleys, wedges, wheels, screws, and inclined planes. Search for photos on the Internet that show examples of each type of machine. Then, look for real-life examples around your home or community.

Syllables

All words can be divided into syllables. **Syllables** are word parts which have one vowel sound in each part.

Draw a line between the syllables and write the word on the correct line below. The first one is done for you.

lit|tle	bumblebee	pillow
truck	dazzle	dog
pencil	flag	angelic
rejoicing	ant	telephone

I SYLLABLE	**2 SYLLABLES**	**3 SYLLABLES**
	little	

Syllables

When the letters **le** come at the end of a word, they sometimes have the sound of **ul**, as in **raffle**.

Draw a line to match the syllables so they make words. The first one is done for you.

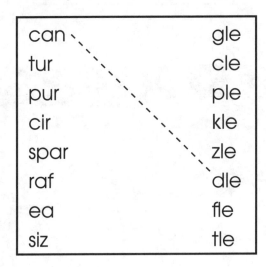

Use the words you made to complete the sentences. One is done for you.

1. Will you buy a ticket for our school <u>raffle</u>?

2. The _____ pulled his head into his shell.

3. We could hear the bacon _____ in the pan.

4. The baby had one _____ on her birthday cake.

5. My favorite color is _____.

6. Look at that diamond _____!

7. The bald _____ is our national bird.

8. Draw a _____ around the correct answer.

Quilting Bee

Follow the code to color the quilt squares.

> 1-syllable words = blue   3-syllable words = green
> 2-syllable words = red   4-syllable words = yellow

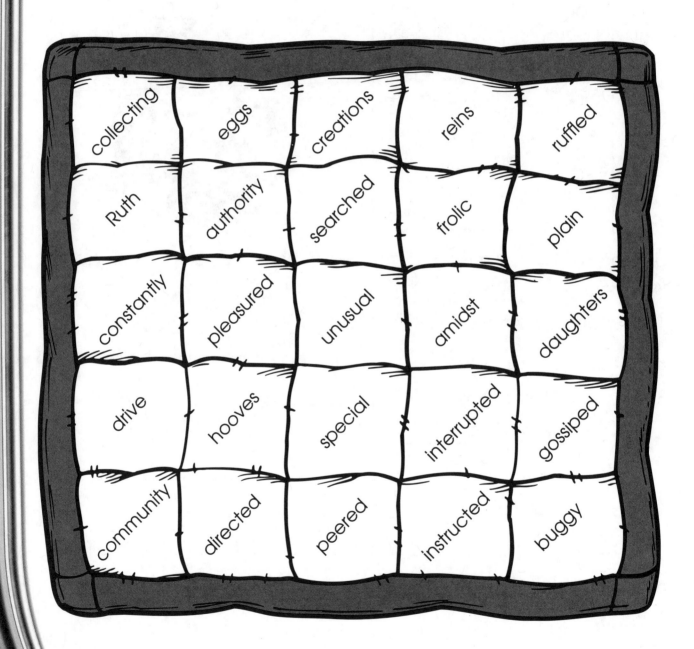

Syllables

A **syllable** is a word—or part of a word—with only one vowel sound. Some words have just one syllable, such as **cat, dog** and **house**. Some words have two syllables, such as **in-sist** and **be-fore**. Some words have three syllables, such as **re-mem-ber**; four syllables, such as **un-der-stand-ing**; or more. Often, words are easier to spell if you know how many syllables they have.

Syl-la-bles

Write the number of syllables in each word below.

Word	Syllables	Word	Syllables
1. amphibian	_____	11. want	_____
2. liter	_____	12. communication	_____
3. guild	_____	13. pedestrian	_____
4. chili	_____	14. kilo	_____
5. vegetarian	_____	15. autumn	_____
6. comedian	_____	16. dinosaur	_____
7. warm	_____	17. grammar	_____
8. piano	_____	18. dry	_____
9. barbarian	_____	19. solar	_____
10. chef	_____	20. wild	_____

Next to each number, write words with the same number of syllables.

1 _____ _____ _____ _____

2 _____ _____ _____ _____

3 _____ _____ _____ _____

4 _____ _____ _____ _____

5 _____ _____ _____ _____

Syllables

Write each word from the box next to the number that shows how many syllables it has.

fuss	paragraph	phone	friendship	freedom
defend	flood	alphabet	rough	laughter

One: _____ _____ _____ _____

Two: _____ _____ _____ _____

Three: _____ _____

How many syllables are there in the word **friendship**?

Circle the two words in each row that have the same number of syllables as the first word.

Example: fact	(clay)	happy	(phone)	command
rough	freckle	pump	accuse	ghost
jacket	flood	laughter	defend	paragraph
accident	paragraph	carpenter	stomach	castle
comfort	agree	friend	friendship	health
fuss	collect	blend	freedom	hatch
alphabet	thankful	Christmas	enemy	unhappy
glowing	midnight	defending	grading	telephone

Multiplication

Multiplication is a short way to find the sum of adding the same number a certain amount of times. For example, **4 x 7 = 28** instead of **7 + 7 + 7 + 7 = 28**.

Study the example. Solve the problems.

Example:

3 + 3 + 3 = 9
3 threes = 9
3 x 3 = 9

7 + 7 = 14
2 sevens = 14
2 x 7 = 14

4 + 4 + 4 + 4 = ____
4 fours = ____
4 x ____ = ____

5 + 5 = ____
2 fives = ____
2 x ____ = ____

2 + 2 + 2 + 2 = ____
4 twos = ____
4 x ____ = ____

6 + 6 = ____
2 sixes = ____
2 x ____ = ____

Multiplication

Multiplication is repeated addition.
Draw a picture for each problem.
Then, write the missing numbers.
Example:
Draw 2 groups of three apples.

$$3 + 3 = 6$$
or $$2 \times 3 = 6$$

Draw 3 groups of four hearts.	Draw 2 groups of five boxes.
 $4 + 4 + 4 =$ ___ or $3 \times$ ___ $=$ ___	$5 +$ ___ $=$ ___ or $2 \times$ ___ $=$ ___

Draw 6 groups of two circles.

$2 +$ ___ $+$ ___ $+$ ___ $+$ ___ $+$ ___ $=$ ___
or $6 \times$ ___ $=$ ___

Draw 7 groups of three triangles.

$3 +$ ___ $+$ ___ $+$ ___ $+$ ___ $+$ ___ $+$ ___ $=$ ___
or   ___ $\times$ ___ $=$ ___

Multiplication

Study the example. Draw the groups and write the total.

Example:

2×3

$2 + 2 + 2$ $= \rightarrow 6$

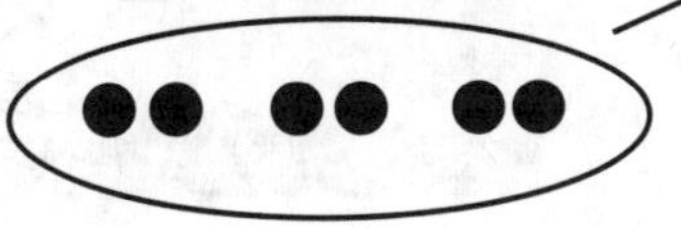

3×4

___ + ___ + ___ = _____

2×5

___ + ___ = _____

5×3

___ + ___ + ___ + ___ + ___ = _____

Multiplication

Solve the problems.

$9 + 9 = \underline{18}$

2 nines = _____

$2 \times 9 = $ _____

$7 + 7 = $ _____

2 sevens = _____

$2 \times \underline{7} = $ _____

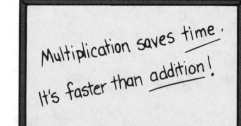

Multiplication saves time.
It's faster than addition!

$4 + 4 + 4 + 4 = $ _____

$\underline{4}$ fours = _____

_____ $\times 4 = $ _____

$8 + 8 + 8 + 8 + 8 = $ _____

_____ eights = _____

_____ $\times 8 = $ _____

$5 + 5 + 5 = $ _____

_____ fives = _____

_____ $\times 5 = $ _____

$9 + 9 = $ _____

_____ nines = _____

_____ $\times 9 = $ _____

$6 + 6 + 6 = $ _____

_____ sixes = _____

_____ $\times 6 = $ _____

$3 + 3 = $ _____

_____ threes = _____

_____ $\times 3 = $ _____

$7 + 7 + 7 + 7 = $ _____

_____ sevens = _____

_____ $\times 7 = $ _____

$2 + 2 = $ _____

_____ twos = _____

_____ $\times 2 = $ _____

Week 16 Skills

Subject	Skill	Multi-Sensory Learning Activities
Reading and Language Arts	Understand homophones, or words that sound alike but have different spellings and meanings.	• Complete Practice Pages 172–175. • The homophones **its** (The dog lost its collar) and **it's** (It's raining) are frequently confused. Have your child create a worksheet or word puzzle that provides practice for using each word correctly. Another practice page might help with these frequently confused homophones: **to**, **too**, and **two**. • Invite your child to draw funny illustrations for these homophone phrases: **a bare bear**, **a hare's hair**, **a towed toad**, **Aunt ant**.
Math	Practice multiplication.	• Complete Practice Pages 177–180. • Help your child make flash cards for basic multiplication facts. Show how to draw group of dots on the front of each card to illustrate the problem. For example, the 3 x 7 card would show three groups of seven dots. • Using the flash cards described in the activity above, practice multiplication facts with your child for three minutes each day. How many problems can your child answer correctly in three minutes? Can he or she beat that total the next day?

Homophones

Homophones are words that sound the same but are spelled differently and have different meanings.

Use the homophones in the box to answer the riddles below.

main	meat	peace	dear	to
mane	meet	piece	deer	too

1. Which word has the word **pie** in it? _____

2. Which word rhymes with **ear** and is an animal? _____

3. Which word rhymes with **shoe** and means **also**? _____

4. Which word has the word **eat** in it and is something you might eat? _____

5. Which word has the same letters as the word **read** but in a different order? _____

6. Which word rhymes with **train** and is something on a pony? _____

7. Which word, if it began with a capital letter, might be the name of an important street? _____

8. Which word sounds like a number but has only two letters? _____

9. Which word rhymes with and is a synonym for **greet**? _____

10. Which word rhymes with the last syllable in **police** and can mean quiet? _____

Homophones: Sentences

Write a word from the box to complete each sentence.

main	meat	dear	two
mane	meet	deer	too

1. The horse had a long, beautiful _____.

   The _____ idea of the paragraph was boats.

2. Let's _____ at my house to do our homework.

   The lion was fed _____ at mealtime.

3. We had _____ kittens.

   Mike has a red bike. Tom does, _____.

4. The _____ ran in front of the car.

   I begin my letters with " _____ Mom."

Homophones: Spelling

Circle the word in each sentence which is not spelled correctly. Then, write the word correctly.

1. Please meat me at the park. _____

2. I would like a peace of pie. _____

3. There were too cookies left. _____

4. The horse's main needed to be brushed._____

5. We saw a dear in the forest. _____

Homophones

Cut out each honeybee at the bottom of the page and glue it on the flower with its homophone.

cut ✂ -

Multiplication

Multiplication is a short way to find the sum of adding the same number a certain amount of times. For example, we write $7 \times 4 = 28$ instead of $7 + 7 + 7 + 7 = 28$.

Study the example. Multiply.

Example:
There are two groups of seashells.
There are 3 seashells in each group. $2 \times 3 = 6$
How many seashells are there in all?

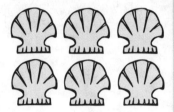

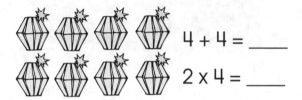

$4 + 4 = \underline{\hspace{1cm}}$

$2 \times 4 = \underline{\hspace{1cm}}$

$3 + 3 + 3 = \underline{\hspace{1cm}}$

$3 \times 3 = \underline{\hspace{1cm}}$

2 x3	3 x5	4 x3	6 x2	7 x3
5 x2	6 x3	4 x2	7 x2	8 x3
5 x5	9 x4	8 x5	6 x6	9 x3

Multiplication

Multiply.

3 x5	4 x6	3 x8

5 x5	4 x8	5 x4

6 x7	3 x9	2 x8	7 x6	9 x4

6 x8	5 x6	7 x7	5 x3	8 x9

A riverboat makes 3 trips a day every day.
How many trips does it make in a week? _____

Multiplication

Factors are the numbers multiplied together in a multiplication problem. The answer is called the **product**. If you change the order of the factors, the product stays the same.

Example:

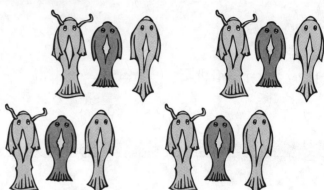

There are 4 groups of fish.
There are 3 fish in each group.
How many fish are there in all?

$$4 \times 3 = 12$$

factor x factor = product

Draw 3 groups of 4 fish.

$$3 \times 4 = 12$$

Compare your drawing and answer with the example. What did you notice?

Fill in the missing numbers. Multiply.

$5 \times 4 =$ _____ $3 \times 6 =$ _____ $4 \times 2 =$ _____

$4 \times 5 =$ _____ $6 \times 3 =$ _____ $2 \times 4 =$ _____

3 x7	7 x3	2 x9	9 x2	8 x4	4 x8
5 x2	2 x5	6 x3	3 x6	5 x6	6 x5

Multiplication: Zero and One

Any number multiplied by zero equals zero. One multiplied by any number equals that number. Study the example. Multiply.

Example:

How many full sails are there in all?

2 boats x **1** sail on each boat = **2** sails

How many full sails are there now?

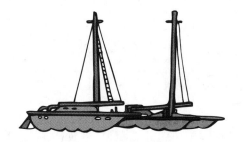

2 boats x **0** sails = **0** sails

Multiply.

1 x5	2 x1	3 x0	4 x1	0 x6	7 x0

9 x1	8 x0	3 x1	4 x0	7 x1	6 x1

Week 17 Skills

Subject	Skill	Multi-Sensory Learning Activities
Reading and Language Arts	Understand homophones, or words that sound alike but have different spellings and meanings.	• Complete Practice Pages 182–187. • Write homophone pairs such as **sale/sail**, **be/bee**, and **eight/ate** on a sheet of paper. Then, give a clue to one of the words. Challenge your child to answer your riddle by pointing to the correctly spelled word.
Math	Practice multiplication.	• Complete Practice Pages 188–190. • Discuss with your child the commutative property of multiplication. This rule states that if 3 x 2 = 6, then 2 x 3 must equal 6 as well. Practice multiplication facts with your child while driving in the car. If he or she gives the correct answer to a problem such as 6 x 4, switch the order to practice the commutative property by asking, "What is 4 x 6?"
Bonus: Social Studies		• Provide a globe, atlas, world map, or interactive online map for your child to explore. Point out the seven continents (Asia, Africa, North America, South America, Europe, Australia, and Antarctica) and the four oceans (Atlantic, Pacific, Indian, and Arctic). Then, draw or print out a blank world map. Can your child write in the names of the continents and oceans?

Homophones: Rhymes

Use homophones to create two-lined rhymes.

Example: I found it a **pain**
To comb the horse's **mane**!

1. _____

_____

2. _____

_____

3. _____

_____

Homophones

Homophones are words that sound the same but are spelled differently and have different meanings.

Example:

sew

sow

so

Read the sentences and write the correct word in the blanks.

Example:

blue	**blew**	She has **blue** eyes.
		The wind **blew** the barn down.

eye   I   He hurt his left _____ playing ball.

_____ like to learn new things.

see   sea   Can you _____ the winning runner from here?

He goes diving for pearls under the _____.

eight ate   The baby _____ the banana.

Jane was _____ years old last year.

one   won   Jill _____ first prize at the science fair.

I am the only _____ in my family with red hair.

be   bee   Jenny cried when a _____ stung her.

I have to _____ in bed every night at eight o'clock.

two to too   My father likes _____ play tennis.

I like to play, _____.

It takes at least _____ people to play.

Homophones

Circle the correct word to complete each sentence. Then, write the word on the line.

1. I am going to _____ a letter to my grandmother.
   right, write

2. Draw a circle around the _____ answer.
   right, write

3. Wait an _____ before going swimming.
   our, hour

4. This is _____ house.
   our, hour

5. He got a _____ from his garden.
   beat, beet

6. Our football team _____ that team.
   beat, beet

7. Go to the store and _____ a loaf of bread.
   by, buy

8. We will drive _____ our house.
   by, buy

9. It will be trouble if the dog _____ the cat.
   seas, sees

10. They sailed the seven _____.
    seas, sees

11. We have _____ cars in the garage.
    to, too, two

12. I am going _____ the zoo today.
    to, too, two

13. My little brother is going, _____.
    to, too, two

Homophones

Homophones are words that sound the same but have different spellings and meanings.

Complete each sentence using a word from the box.

blew	night	blue	knight	hour	in	ant	inn
our	aunt	meet	too	two	to	meat	

1. A red _____ crawled up the wall.

2. It will be one _____ before we can go back home.

3. Will you _____ us later?

4. We plan to stay at an _____ during our trip.

5. The king had a _____ who fought bravely.

6. The wind _____ so hard that I almost lost my hat.

7. His jacket was _____.

8. My_____ plans to visit us this week.

9. I will come _____ when it gets too cold outside.

10. It was late at _____ when we finally got there.

11. _____ of us will go with you.

12. I will mail a note _____ someone at the bank.

13. Do you eat red _____?

14. We would like to join you, _____.

15. Come over to see _____ new cat.

Homophones

Circle the words that are not used correctly. Write the correct word above the circled word. Use the words in the box to help you. The first one has been done for you.

road	see	one	be	so	I	brakes	piece	there
wait	not	some	hour	would	no	deer	you	heard

Jake and his family were getting close to Grandpa's. It had taken

them nearly an ~~our~~ *hour* to get their, but Jake knew it was worth it. In his

mind, he could already sea the pond and could almost feel the cool

water. It had been sew hot this summer in the apartment.

"Wood ewe like a peace of my apple, Jake?" asked his big sister

Clare. "Eye can't eat any more."

"Know, thank you," Jake replied. "I still have sum of my fruit left."

Suddenly, Dad slammed on the breaks. "Did you see that dear on

the rode? I always herd that if you see won, there might bee more."

"Good thinking, Dad. I'm glad you are a safe driver. We're knot very

far from Grandpa's now. I can't weight!"

Hairs on Hares?

Words that sound alike but are spelled differently and have different meanings are called **homophones**. On the line before each homophone, write the letter of the phrase that best defines the word.

_____ 1. hare   A. any creature hunted for food

_____ 2. hair   B. a mass of unbaked bread

_____ 3. peer   C. a body part used to smell

_____ 4. pier   D. something that is owed

_____ 5. doe   E. the end of an animal's body

_____ 6. dough   F. an animal related to the rabbit

_____ 7. bare   G. a large furry animal with a short tail

_____ 8. bear   H. to look closely; to gaze

_____ 9. dew   I. to beg for or ask for by prayer

_____ 10. due   J. a female deer, hare or rabbit

_____ 11. nose   K. a platform built out over water

_____ 12. knows   L. a story

_____ 13. prey   M. naked; without any covering

_____ 14. pray   N. growth that covers the scalp of a person or the body of a mammal

_____ 15. tail   O. understands; to be certain of something

_____ 16. tale   P. water droplets

Multiplication

Time yourself as you multiply. How quickly can you complete this page?

3 x2	8 x7	1 x0	1 x6	3 x4	0 x4
4 x1	4 x4	2 x5	9 x3	9 x9	5 x3
0 x8	2 x6	9 x6	8 x5	7 x3	4 x2
3 x5	2 x0	4 x6	1 x3	0 x0	3 x3

Multiplication Table

Complete the multiplication table. Use it to practice your multiplication facts. Do you notice any patterns?

X	0	1	2	3	4	5	6	7	8	9	10
0	0										
1		1									
2			4								
3				9							
4					16						
5						25					
6							36				
7								49			
8									64		
9										81	
10											100

Multiplying

When multiplying, the first factor tells how many groups there are.

$\underline{5} \times 3 =$ ___   There are 5 groups.

The second factor tells how many there are in each group.

$5 \times \underline{3} =$ ___   There are 3 in each group.

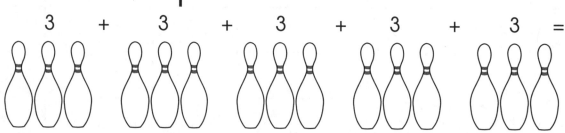

3   +   3   +   3   +   3   +   3   =   ___

5 groups of 3 equal **15**.

Mark, David and Bill met at the park to launch rockets. They each launched their rocket 4 times! How many rocket launches were there altogether?

$3 \times 4 =$ ____

Multiply.

$$\begin{array}{cc} 5 \\ \times\,2 \\ \hline \end{array} \qquad \begin{array}{cc} 3 \\ \times\,6 \\ \hline \end{array} \qquad \begin{array}{cc} 2 \\ \times\,7 \\ \hline \end{array} \qquad \begin{array}{cc} 3 \\ \times\,9 \\ \hline \end{array} \qquad \begin{array}{cc} 8 \\ \times\,2 \\ \hline \end{array} \qquad \begin{array}{cc} 4 \\ \times\,5 \\ \hline \end{array}$$

$4 \times 9 =$ ___ $4 \times 8 =$ ___ $5 \times 7 =$ ___

$6 \times 2 =$ ___ $5 \times 3 =$ ___ $5 \times 5 =$ ___

Week 18 Skills

Subject	Skill	Multi-Sensory Learning Activities
Reading and Language Arts	Identify root words.	• Complete Practice Page 192. • Have your child draw a large tree and write a root word such as **sleep** among its roots. Then, show your child how to write related words such as **sleepy**, **asleep**, **sleeps**, and **sleeping** on the branches and leaves of the tree.
	Identify prefixes.	• Complete Practice Pages 193–196. • Choose a common prefix such as **bi** ("two"), **non** ("not"), **sub** ("under"), **re** ("again"), **pre** ("before"), **dis** ("not"), or **mis** ("wrong"). Take turns with your child brainstorming words that include the prefix. The first one to run out of ideas chooses the next prefix. Talk about how the addition of each prefix changes the meaning of the word.
Math	Practice multiplication.	• Complete Practice Pages 197–199. • Give your child situations such as "There are six children playing. Each child has three toys." Challenge your child to provide and solve the related multiplication problem (6 x 3 = 18).
	Find factors.	• Complete Practice Page 200. • Use a deck of multiplication flash cards. Call out a number such as **10**, **12**, **18**, or **24**. How many flash cards can your child find whose problems have that product?

The Root of the Problem

Underline the root of each word in the list. Then, circle the root words in the word search. Words may go up, down, across, backwards and diagonally.

1. planting
2. mending
3. fishing
4. golden
5. swimming
6. certainly
7. suddenly
8. arrows
9. foolish
10. sounds
11. sighing
12. rushing
13. safely
14. asleep
15. longer
16. arms
17. stones
18. bandits

A	P	L	A	N	T	H	S	I	F
R	O	C	E	R	T	A	I	N	O
M	E	N	D	D	N	U	O	S	O
I	A	E	L	P	R	E	K	I	L
W	R	D	O	G	N	O	L	G	E
S	R	D	G	O	R	U	S	H	F
N	O	U	T	S	L	E	E	P	A
V	W	S	T	I	D	N	A	B	S

Prefixes

Prefixes are word parts added to the beginning of a root word. Prefixes add to or change the meaning of the word.

Example: remake — to make something again

re — again   un — not   dis — not or reverse   in — in or not

Read the meanings on each treasure chest lid. Then, glue the correct word onto each treasure chest.

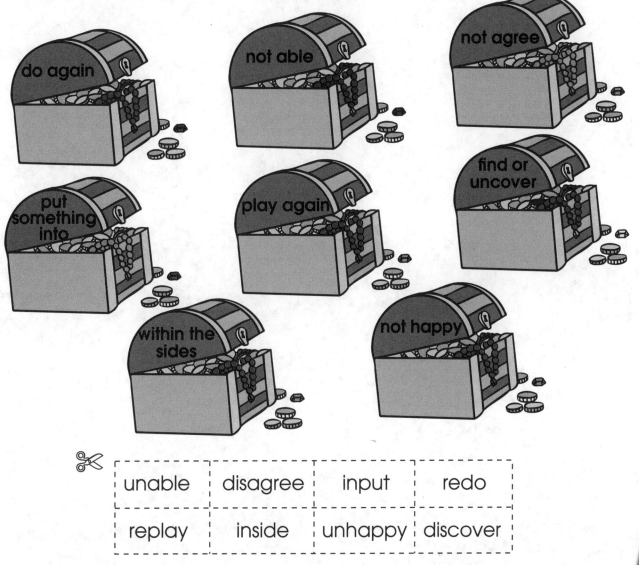

- do again
- not able
- not agree
- put something into
- play again
- find or uncover
- within the sides
- not happy

| unable | disagree | input | redo |
| replay | inside | unhappy | discover |

Prefixes: Sentences

Match each sentence with the word that completes it.
Then, write the word on the line.

1. The farmer was _____ because it •   • input
   didn't rain.

2. The scientist tried to _____ the •   • redo
   secret formula.

3. The child _____ his report •   • unhappy
   into the computer.

4. We were _____ to do the •   • disagree
   work without help.

5. My brother and I _____ about •   • replay
   which show to watch.

6. The umpire called for a _____ of •   • discover
   the game.

7. We had to stay _____ when •   • inside
   it got cold.

8. I spilled my milk on my paper and had to •   • unable
   _____ my homework.

What a Recipe!

Write the words that mean the same. Circle your answers in the puzzle.

Hint: All words start with the prefix **un**, **dis** or **re**.

u	n	a	r	e	b	u	i	l	d	i	s	l	i	k	e
u	n	f	a	i	r	n	n	o	i	n	o	r	e	d	o
n	o	e	r	l	u	n	u	n	s	a	f	e	r	f	u
s	d	i	s	a	g	r	e	e	o	b	z	f	e	o	n
e	u	n	t	i	e	d	r	r	b	a	u	i	d	x	f
e	n	r	o	u	t	r	y	s	e	b	n	l	o	m	r
n	e	e	u	n	h	a	p	p	y	d	i	l	s	u	i
r	e	u	s	t	e	d	r	e	w	r	i	t	e	s	e
u	n	h	u	r	t	s	o	r	e	w	a	s	h	l	n
v	e	s	u	u	s	d	i	s	a	p	p	e	a	r	d
p	i	c	r	e	w	r	a	p	i	o	n	s	i	k	l
r	e	o	p	e	n	a	u	n	f	o	l	d	e	d	y

Clues:

1. Not happy _____
2. Not true _____
3. To not obey _____
4. Not hurt _____
5. To not like _____
6. Not safe _____
7. To fill again _____
8. Not fair _____
9. To wrap again _____
10. Not seen _____

11. To not appear _____
12. To write again _____
13. Wash again _____
14. Not tied _____
15. Not folded _____
16. To not agree _____
17. To do again _____
18. To open again_____
19. Not friendly_____
20. To build again _____

Racing to the Finish

Solve the multiplication problems below.

5 x 3	2 x 8	4 x 6	9 x 3

7 x 5	3 x 9	4 x 2	6 x 2	4 x 4	0 x 6

3 x 2	7 x 2	6 x 5	3 x 4	8 x 3	4 x 5

5 x 2	7 x 4	6 x 3	4 x 8	2 x 2	8 x 5

3 x 7	5 x 5	5 x 9	9 x 2	4 x 6	9 x 4

Out of Sight!

Solve the multiplication problems below.

$$
\begin{array}{r}
11 \\
\times\ 4 \\
\hline
\end{array}
\qquad
\begin{array}{r}
92 \\
\times\ 1 \\
\hline
\end{array}
$$

$$
\begin{array}{r}
23 \\
\times\ 3 \\
\hline
\end{array}
\qquad
\begin{array}{r}
43 \\
\times\ 2 \\
\hline
\end{array}
\qquad
\begin{array}{r}
58 \\
\times\ 1 \\
\hline
\end{array}
$$

$$
\begin{array}{r}
22 \\
\times\ 4 \\
\hline
\end{array}
\quad
\begin{array}{r}
89 \\
\times\ 1 \\
\hline
\end{array}
\quad
\begin{array}{r}
21 \\
\times\ 4 \\
\hline
\end{array}
\quad
\begin{array}{r}
10 \\
\times\ 5 \\
\hline
\end{array}
\quad
\begin{array}{r}
44 \\
\times\ 2 \\
\hline
\end{array}
\quad
\begin{array}{r}
11 \\
\times\ 6 \\
\hline
\end{array}
$$

$$
\begin{array}{r}
11 \\
\times\ 5 \\
\hline
\end{array}
\quad
\begin{array}{r}
10 \\
\times\ 4 \\
\hline
\end{array}
\quad
\begin{array}{r}
11 \\
\times\ 8 \\
\hline
\end{array}
\quad
\begin{array}{r}
32 \\
\times\ 3 \\
\hline
\end{array}
\quad
\begin{array}{r}
42 \\
\times\ 2 \\
\hline
\end{array}
\quad
\begin{array}{r}
57 \\
\times\ 1 \\
\hline
\end{array}
\quad
\begin{array}{r}
11 \\
\times\ 3 \\
\hline
\end{array}
$$

$$
\begin{array}{r}
64 \\
\times\ 1 \\
\hline
\end{array}
\quad
\begin{array}{r}
10 \\
\times\ 7 \\
\hline
\end{array}
\quad
\begin{array}{r}
23 \\
\times\ 2 \\
\hline
\end{array}
\quad
\begin{array}{r}
33 \\
\times\ 2 \\
\hline
\end{array}
\quad
\begin{array}{r}
22 \\
\times\ 4 \\
\hline
\end{array}
\quad
\begin{array}{r}
10 \\
\times\ 9 \\
\hline
\end{array}
$$

$$
\begin{array}{r}
21 \\
\times\ 3 \\
\hline
\end{array}
\quad
\begin{array}{r}
22 \\
\times\ 3 \\
\hline
\end{array}
\quad
\begin{array}{r}
24 \\
\times\ 2 \\
\hline
\end{array}
\quad
\begin{array}{r}
41 \\
\times\ 2 \\
\hline
\end{array}
\quad
\begin{array}{r}
49 \\
\times\ 1 \\
\hline
\end{array}
$$

$$
\begin{array}{r}
12 \\
\times\ 4 \\
\hline
\end{array}
\qquad
\begin{array}{r}
87 \\
\times\ 1 \\
\hline
\end{array}
$$

The Caped Cow

Multiply.

| 12 x 9 | 22 x 8 | 32 x 5 | 19 x 9 | 22 x 7 | 33 x 4 | 27 x 2 |

| 14 x 6 | 38 x 2 | 25 x 3 | 15 x 4 | 16 x 5 | 28 x 3 | 18 x 5 |

| 14 x 7 | 13 x 5 | 24 x 4 | 13 x 6 | 29 x 2 | 17 x 4 | 36 x 2 |

| 29 x 3 | 14 x 5 | 18 x 4 | 19 x 3 | 28 x 2 | 17 x 5 | 19 x 4 |

Factor Trees

Factors are the smaller numbers multiplied together to make a larger number. Factor trees are one way to find all the factors of a number.

Example:

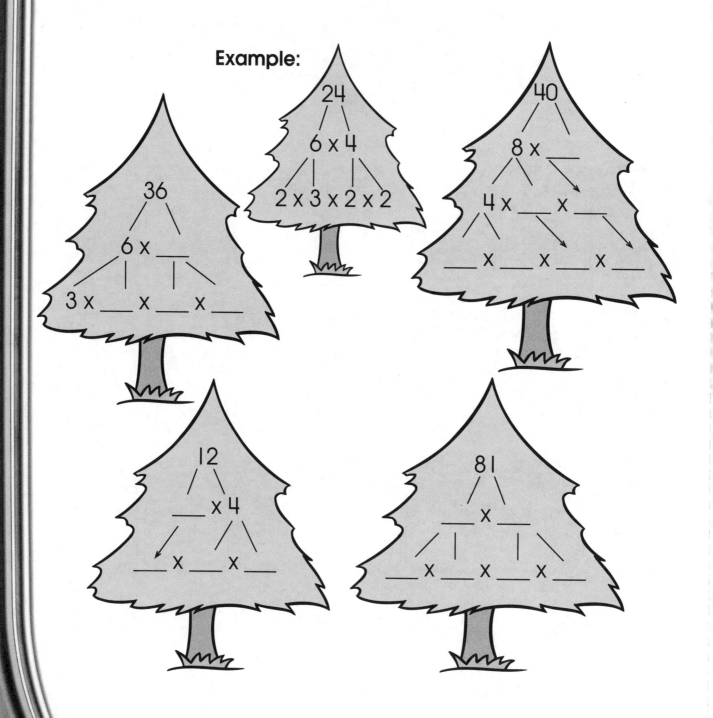

COMPLETE YEAR GRADE 3

Second Quarter Check-Up

Reading and Language Arts

❑ I can write statements, questions, exclamations, and commands.

❑ I can write complete sentences that include a subject and a verb.

❑ I avoid fragments and run-on sentences.

❑ I can join two shorter sentences into one longer sentence.

❑ I can count the number of syllables in a word.

❑ I can spell homophones correctly in sentences.

❑ I can identify roots and prefixes in words.

Math

❑ I can use addition and subtraction to solve word problems.

❑ I can tell how many ones, tens, hundreds, and thousands are in a given number.

❑ I can round numbers to the nearest ten, hundred, or thousand.

❑ I can count by multiples of 2, 3, 4, 5, and 10.

❑ I understand that multiplication takes the place of repeated addition.

❑ I can solve multiplication problems.

❑ I can find the factors of a number.

Final Project

Read *One Grain of Rice: A Mathematical Folktale* by Demi. Think about how multiplication is used in the story to double the amount of rice each day. Ask your parent to give you one penny today, two pennies the next day, four pennies the following day, and so on, for seven days. How much money will you have by the end? When the week is over, write the story of the doubling pennies in a little illustrated book.

Third Quarter Introduction

In the weeks after the winter or mid-year break, students are often ready to tackle new learning challenges. In many classrooms, brand-new concepts and skills are introduced during third quarter that may be difficult for your child. You can help at home by encouraging your child and providing positive learning support using resources found in *Complete Year*.

Third Quarter Skills

Practice pages in this book for Weeks 19–27 will help your child improve the following skills.

Reading and Language Arts
- Understand that a suffix can be added to the end of a root word
- Use quotation marks correctly
- Understand possessive pronouns and words that show ownership by adding an apostrophe and **s**
- Capitalize names of days, months, cities, states, etc.
- Proofread for spelling errors
- Identify causes and effects
- Use context clues to understand and use new vocabulary words
- Understand figurative language

Math
- Understand division
- Solve division problems, including those that have remainders
- Use multiplication and division to solve word problems
- Follow the order of operations when solving problems
- Understand symmetry
- Understand fractions
- Compare fractions, identify equivalent fractions, and convert fractions to decimals
- Use fractions and decimals to solve word problems
- Tell time using analog and digital clocks

Multi-Sensory Learning Activities

Try these fun activities for enhancing your child's learning and development during the third quarter of the school year. Be sure to choose activities that include speaking, listening, touching, and active movement.

Reading and Language Arts

Review the suffixes below with your child. Ask him or her to choose several to include in a poster or digital presentation about roots and suffixes.

er, or: one who (examples: **painter**, **governor**)
ment, ness: state or quality of (examples: **treatment**, **shyness**)
able, ible: capable of (examples: **comfortable**, **visible**)
ful: full of (examples: **handful**, **forceful**)
ish, y: like; pertaining to (examples: **reddish**, **weedy**)
less: without (examples: **wingless**, **careless**)
ly: like; in the nature of (examples: **friendly**, **nicely**)

Make a copy of the unpunctuated story below. Ask your child to read it with expression. When your child becomes frustrated, talk about the importance of punctuation. Read the story aloud. Help your child fill in the punctuation marks and missing capital letters, commas, periods, apostrophes, and quotation marks.

George and Maria sat next to each other in the lunch room last Tuesday that day George had forgotten his lunch at home what am i going to do i am so hungry cried george don't worry responded Maria my dad gave me a huge lunch I ate all my snack earlier and I'm really not that hungry do you like cheese sandwiches yes thank you so much maria that is very kind you're a good friend sniffled George.

Have your child make up a silly word, such as **grwarble**, and write a sentence that uses the word and includes context clues to its meaning. Read the sentence and guess the meaning of the word.

2 8 4 9 6 Math

Teach your child to use multiplication to check the answers to division problems. If 15 ÷ 3 = 5, then 3 x 5 = 15. When your child practices a division problem, ask him or her to think of a related multiplication problem.

Ask your child to write multiplication and division word problems based on the number of students in his or her class at school. For example, if there are 28 students in a class and each student needs 12 paperclips for a project,

Third Quarter Introduction, cont.

how many paperclips are needed in all? If there are 28 students in a class and the teacher asks them to get into groups of 4, how many groups will there be?

Draw circles on index cards, partitioning each into 2, 4, 6, 8, 10, or 12 equal wedges. Color in one or more wedges on each card. Then, prepare a second set of cards that name the fractions, such as $\frac{1}{2}$ or $\frac{3}{8}$, that are illustrated by the circles. Mix up the cards, place them facedown in an array on a tabletop, and use them to play "Memory" with your child.

Science

To make a sundial, find a sunny location and draw a circle in the dirt. Place a stick in the center of the circle pointing straight up. Use a compass to find north and draw a line in the circle pointing north. This line will be 12:00 on a clock face. Draw lines for the other hours. Observe where the shadow of the stick falls. The shadow should match the hour. (Note: The time may be off because of daylight savings time or because you live on the edge of a time zone.)

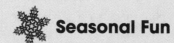

Social Studies

Have your child choose a country and research its recipes and customs. Then, invite your child to plan a special meal to celebrate the country. Your child should choose recipes, help with shopping and food preparation, and share interesting facts.

❄ Seasonal Fun

Make indoor "snow" by pouring a box of baking soda into a bowl. Mix in a little glitter and peppermint extract (optional). Then, add water a tablespoon at a time and stir until the mixture has a good consistency for modeling. Use the "snow" to make a mini snowman!

Have your child use a free Web site to make a crossword puzzle or word search with words related to winter.

Week 19 Skills

Subject	Skill	Multi-Sensory Learning Activities
Reading and Language Arts	Add suffixes to root words to make new words.	• Complete Practice Pages 206–209. • Roll a die and choose one of the suffixes listed on page 218. Can a partner write that many words that include the suffix? If yes, it is the partner's turn to roll and choose. If not, roll and choose again. • Challenge your child to find 10 words with suffixes in a favorite chapter book and write them on a sheet of paper. Ask your child to underline the root word for each. What other suffixes could be added to those roots to make new words?
Math	Understand that division is finding out how many times one number is contained in another number.	• Complete Practice Pages 211–214. • Play with 24 coins, checkers, interlocking blocks, or other counters. Ask your child to divide them into equal groups of 2, 4, 6, 8, and 12. In each case, ask how many equal groups were created. Then, write the related division problem (example: $24 \div 8 = 3$) to help your child understand division. • Help your child understand the relationship between multiplication and division. Provide 15 small pieces of candy and ask your child to use them to show $3 \times 5 = 15$. Then, ask your child to divide the 15 candies into three equal groups and count the candies in each group to show $15 \div 3 = 5$.

Suffixes

A **suffix** is a word part added to the end of a word. Suffixes add to or change the meaning of the word.

Example: sad + ly = sadly

Below are some suffixes and their meanings.

ment	state of being, quality of, act of
ly	like or in a certain way
ness	state of being
ful	full of
less	without

The words in the box have suffixes. Use the suffix meanings above to match each word with its meaning below. Write the words on the lines.

friendly	cheerful	safely	sleeveless	speechless
kindness	amazement	sickness	peaceful	excitement

1. in a safe way __ __ __ __ __ __
                      6

2. full of cheer __ __ __ __ __ __ __ __
                              2

3. full of peace __ __ __ __ __ __ __
                      4

4. state of being amazed __ __ __ __ __ __ __ __ __
                                          5

5. state of being excited __ __ __ __ __ __ __ __ __
                                      1

6. without speech __ __ __ __ __ __ __ __ __
                                      3

Use the numbered letters to find the missing word below.
You are now on your way to becoming a

__ __ __ __ __ __ of suffixes!
5 6 3 1 4 2

Suffixes: Adverbs

Adverbs are words that describe verbs. Adverbs tell where, when or how. Most adverbs end in the suffix **ly**.

Complete each sentence with the correct part of speech.

Example:

Hank	wrote	here.
who? (noun)	what? (verb)	where? (adverb)

1.

	was lost	
who? (noun)	what? (verb)	where? (adverb)

2.

		quickly.
who? (noun)	what? (verb)	how? (adverb)

3.

	felt	
who? (noun)	what? (verb)	how? (adverb)

4. My brother

who? (noun)	what? (verb)	when? (adverb)

5.

	woke up	
who? (noun)	what? (verb)	when? (adverb)

6.

		gladly.
who? (noun)	what? (verb)	how? (adverb)

Suffixes: Sentences

Use a word from the box to complete each sentence.

cheerful	softness	encouragement
kindness	safely	friendly

1. The _____ dog licked me and wagged his tail.

2. Jeff is happy and _____.

3. To ride your bike _____ , you should wear a helmet.

4. My aunt is known for her thoughtfulness and _____.

5. I love the _____ of my cat's fur.

6. The teacher gave her class a lot of _____.

Suffixes: Root Words

A **root word** is a word before a suffix is added.

Example: In the word **hope**ful, the root word is **hope**.

DON'T BE CLUELESS!

Each egg contains a root word. Cut out each egg and match it with a basket so that it forms a new word. Write the new word on the lines on the basket.

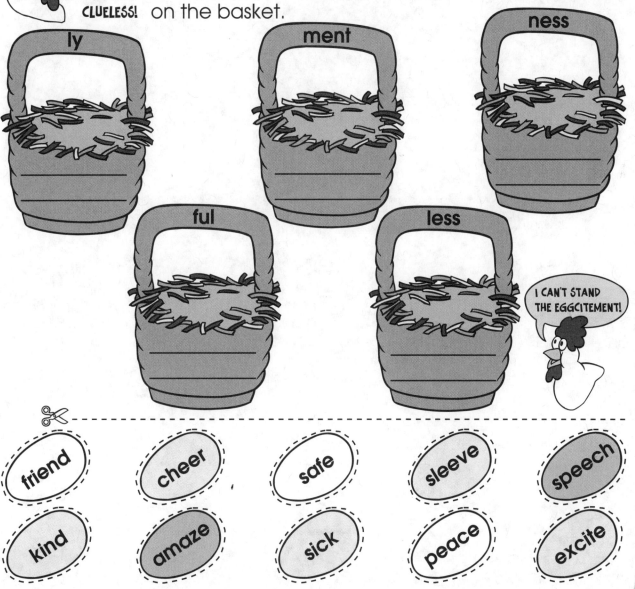

Dividing by 0 to 2

Follow the steps below to divide by 0, 1, or 2.

$$\frac{8}{2\overline{\smash{\big)}16}}$$ quotient = 8   divisor = 2   dividend = 16

When **zero** is divided by a number, the quotient is always **0**!

$0 \div 6 = 0$ 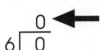 $0 \div 3 = 0$ $0 \div 25 =$

$\dfrac{0}{6\overline{\smash{\big)}0}}$ 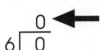 $\dfrac{0}{3\overline{\smash{\big)}0}}$ $25\overline{\smash{\big)}0}$

When you divide by **one**, the quotient is always the number you are dividing.

$7 \div 1 = 7$ $16 \div 1 = 16$ $12 \div 1 =$
same

$1\overline{\smash{\big)}7}^{\,7}$ same $1\overline{\smash{\big)}16}^{\,16}$ $1\overline{\smash{\big)}12}$

When you divide by **two**, the quotient is always $\frac{1}{2}$ of the number you are dividing.

$6 \div 2 = 3$ 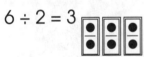 $10 \div 2 = 5$ $14 \div 2 = 7$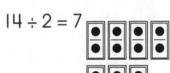

$2\overline{\smash{\big)}6}^{\,3}$ $\underline{3}$ groups of 2 $2\overline{\smash{\big)}10}^{\,5}$ $\underline{5}$ groups of 2 $2\overline{\smash{\big)}14}$ $\underline{}$ groups of 2

$6\overline{\smash{\big)}0}^{\,0}$ $2\overline{\smash{\big)}8}$ $1\overline{\smash{\big)}4}$ $16\overline{\smash{\big)}0}$ $24\overline{\smash{\big)}0}$ $2\overline{\smash{\big)}18}$

$0 \div 7 =$ _____ $14 \div 1 =$ _____ $6 \div 2 =$ _____ $12 \div 2 =$ _____ $4 \div 1 =$ _____

Dividing by 2 to 5

1. | Determine how many there are altogether (the dividend).

12 notes in all

2. | Decide how many will go into each group (the divisor).

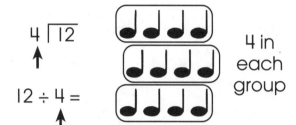

4 in each group

3. | How many groups were made (the quotient)?

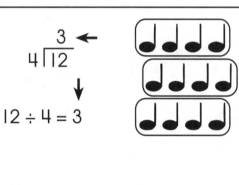

3 groups in all

Division is fun.

Divide.

$$\overset{4}{4\overline{)16}} \qquad 2\overline{)6} \qquad 5\overline{)25} \qquad 3\overline{)18} \qquad 3\overline{)24}$$

$$15 \div 5 = \underline{} \qquad 12 \div 4 = \underline{} \qquad 36 \div 4 = \underline{} \qquad 10 \div 2 = \underline{} \qquad 21 \div 3 = \underline{}$$

Dividing by 6 to 9

Three ways to find the quotient of $6\overline{)18}$ or $18 \div 6$ are:

1.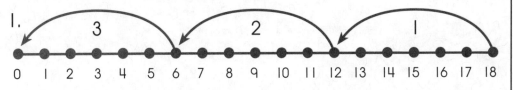

Start at 18 (dividend). Leap at intervals of 6 (divisor) to get to 0.

$$\frac{3}{6\overline{)18}}$$ ← How many times did you leap? 3 (the quotient)

2.

Start with 18 fish.	Put them in 6 groups.	How many will there be in each group?

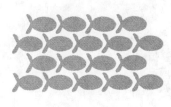

$\overline{)18}$

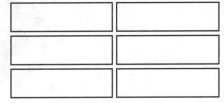

$\overline{)18}$

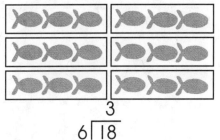

$\frac{3}{6\overline{)18}}$

3.

Start with 18 bees.	Put them into groups of 6.	How many groups do you have?

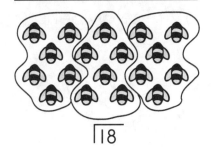

$\overline{)18}$

$\overline{)18}$

Notice that the answers are the same!

$\frac{3}{6\overline{)18}}$

Divide.

$\dfrac{4}{6\overline{)24}}$ $8\overline{)56}$ $6\overline{)36}$ $21 \div 7 = \underline{\quad}$ $64 \div 8 = \underline{\quad}$ $12 \div 6 = \underline{\quad}$

Dividing by 2 to 9

Do you know why the quotient is always one when the divisor and dividend are the same?

Here's Why!

If there are a total of 8 kittens,

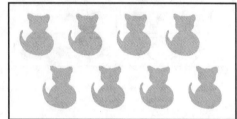

and 8 in each group,

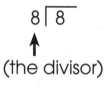

then there will be one group.
There is 1 group of 8 kittens.

(the dividend)

8⟌8
↑
(the divisor)

8⟌8 ←
(the quotient)

Always check division problems by multiplying. The quotient (1) times the divisor (8) is equal to the dividend (8).

8⟌8   8 x 1 = 8   6⟌12   6 x 2 = 12

Divide.

8⟌8   9⟌45   6⟌42   7⟌7   8⟌32   3⟌9

21 ÷ 3 = ___   18 ÷ 6 = ___   48 ÷ 8 = ___   63 ÷ 9 = ___   30 ÷ 6 = ___

Week 20 Skills

Subject	Skill	Multi-Sensory Learning Activities
Reading and Language Arts	Add **ed**, **ing** and other suffixes to root words.	• Complete Practice Pages 216–218. • Ask your child to select a passage from a chapter book and look at its verbs. Do most verbs end in **ed** (indicating past tense), or with **ing** or **s** (indicating present tense)? Have your child rewrite the passage to change the tense from past to present or from present to past, changing the ending of each verb accordingly.
	Review prefixes, suffixes, and root words.	• Complete Practice Page 219. • Have two partners write lists of words. Award one point for a root word (such as **fortune**), two points for a root word with a prefix or suffix (such as **fortunately**), and three points for a root word with a prefix and a suffix (such as **unfortunately**). Who can reach 20 points first?
Math	Practice division.	• Complete Practice Pages 220–223. • Help your child make flash cards for basic division facts. Show how to draw groups of dots on the front of each card to illustrate the problem. For example, the 12 ÷ 4 card would show three groups of four dots. Use the cards to practice for three minutes each day.
	Solve division problems with remainders.	• Complete Practice Page 224. • Ask your child to use 13 coins, checkers, or other counters to show the problem 13 ÷ 3. Emphasize that 13 does not divide equally into three groups. The answer is four with a remainder of one.

Word Endings

Follow the rules to color each balloon.

> **Rule 1:** Add **ed** to most verbs to show the past tense. Color these words **blue**.
>
> **Rule 2:** If the verb ends in **e**, drop the **e** and add **ed**. Color these words **green**.
>
> **Rule 3:** If the verb has a short vowel followed by a single consonant, double the final consonant and add **ed**. Color these words **red**.
>
> **Rule 4:** If the verb ends in **y**, change the **y** to **i** and add **ed**. Color these words **yellow**.

Hop-Hopped-Hopping!

Help bouncy Bing hop home. If you can add an **ed** or **ing** to a word, color that lily pad **green**. Do not color the other lily pads.

Bing is certainly a frog of action. All the words he hopped on are…

_____.

Suffixes

A **suffix** is a word part added to the end of a root (base) word. It changes or adds to the meaning.

Read each suffix and its meaning. Write two words that use that suffix.

Suffix	Meaning	Examples
er	someone who	painter,_____
ful	full of	_____
less	without	_____
ed	happened in the past	_____
ly	like	_____
s	more than one	_____
able	able to do	_____
ness	being like	_____
ment	act or quality of	_____
en	made of	_____

A Little More

Attach the suffixes and prefixes to as many words as possible from the list below to make new words. Many combinations are possible. Some root word endings will have to be changed slightly.

broke	grace	comfort	thought	timid	water
merry	luck	travel	thank	heart	oil
few	farm	convenient	scare	fortunate	chop
beauty	happy	correct	wood	like	most

Division

Division is a way to find out how many times one number is contained in another number. For example, $28 \div 4 = 7$ means that there are seven groups of four in 28.

Study the example. Divide.

Example:

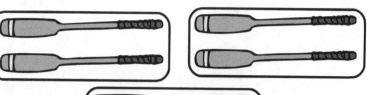

There are 6 oars.
Each canoe needs 2 oars.
How many canoes can be used?

Circle groups of 2.
There are 3 groups of 2.

$$
\begin{array}{ccccc}
6 & \div & 2 & = & 3 \\
\text{oars} & & \text{number} & & \text{canoes} \\
& & \text{of oars} \\
& & \text{needed} \\
& & \text{per canoe}
\end{array}
$$

$9 \div 3 =$ _____ 　　　$8 \div 2 =$ _____ 　　　$16 \div 4 =$ _____

$15 \div 5 =$ _____ 　　　$18 \div 2 =$ _____ 　　　$20 \div 4 =$ _____

$21 \div 7 =$ _____ 　　　$24 \div 6 =$ _____ 　　　$12 \div 2 =$ _____

Division

Divide. Draw a line from the boat to the sail with the correct answer.

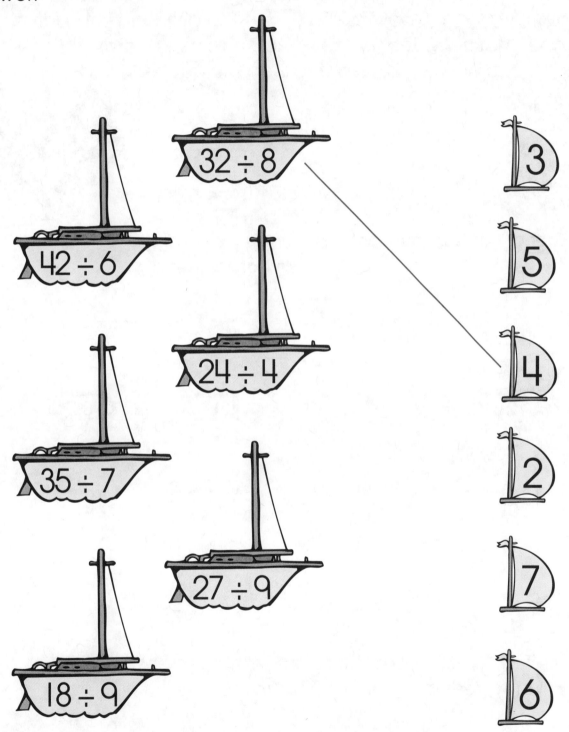

Division

Division is a way to find out how many times one number is contained in another number. The ÷ sign means "divided by." Another way to divide is to use ⌐‾. The **dividend** is the larger number that is divided by the smaller number, or **divisor**. The answer of a division problem is called the **quotient**.

Study the example. Divide.

Example:

$$20 \div 4 = 5$$

dividend   divisor   quotient

quotient
↕
$$4 \overline{\smash{)}20}$$
↕   ↕
divisor dividend

$35 \div 7 =$ ____ $7 \overline{\smash{)}35}$ $42 \div 6 =$ ____ $6 \overline{\smash{)}42}$

$2 \overline{\smash{)}12}$ $3 \overline{\smash{)}18}$ $4 \overline{\smash{)}36}$ $5 \overline{\smash{)}50}$

$6 \overline{\smash{)}24}$ $7 \overline{\smash{)}21}$ $8 \overline{\smash{)}32}$ $9 \overline{\smash{)}27}$

$36 \div 6 =$ ____ $28 \div 4 =$ ____ $15 \div 5 =$ ____ $12 \div 2 =$ ___

A tree farm has 36 trees. There are 4 rows of trees.
How many trees are there in each row?   _____

Division: Zero and One

Study the rules of division and the examples. Divide, then write the number of the rule you used to solve each problem.

Examples:

Rule 1: $1\overline{)5}$ Any number divided by 1 is that number.

Rule 2: $5\overline{)5}$ Any number except 0 divided by itself is 1.

Rule 3: $7\overline{)0}$ Zero divided by any number is zero.

Rule 4: $0\overline{)7}$ You cannot divide by zero.

$1\overline{)6}$ Rule ____ $4 \div 1 =$ ____   Rule ____

$7\overline{)7}$ Rule ____ $9 \div 9 =$ ____   Rule ____

$9\overline{)0}$ Rule ____ $7 \div 1 =$ ____   Rule ____

$1\overline{)4}$ Rule ____ $6 \div 0 =$ ____   Rule ____

Mr. R Means Business

Solve the division problems below. Write the remainders.

Use me when a problem doesn't come out even.

$$\begin{array}{r} 6 \\ 4\overline{)24} \end{array}$$ **NO REMAINDER**

$$\begin{array}{r} 5\,R\,2 \\ 4\overline{)22} \\ -20 \\ \hline \end{array}$$ **2 REMAINDER**

$$5\overline{)28}\;\;^{5\,R}$$ $$4\overline{)19}\;\;^{4\,R}$$ $$8\overline{)26}\;\;^{3\,R}$$ $$7\overline{)45}\;\;^{6\,R}$$

$$3\overline{)26}\;\;^{R}$$ $$2\overline{)19}\;\;^{R}$$ $$6\overline{)51}\;\;^{R}$$ $$9\overline{)65}\;\;^{R}$$

$$8\overline{)43}\;\;^{R}$$ $$9\overline{)59}\;\;^{R}$$ $$7\overline{)33}\;\;^{R}$$ $$4\overline{)27}\;\;^{R}$$

Week 21 Skills

Subject	Skill	Multi-Sensory Learning Activities
Reading and Language Arts	Use quotation marks correctly for writing dialogue.	• Complete Practice Pages 226–229. • Have your child choose a funny or memorable scene from a recorded movie, video, or TV show. Ask your child to write each line from the scene, pausing as needed to catch all the words. Remind your child to use quotation marks correctly.
Math	Solve division problems with remainders.	• Complete Practice Pages 230–234. • Use the board from any board game you own. Alternately, create a game board that shows a simple path. Also use the division problems from page 233 or other division problems with remainders. On each turn, the player solves a division problem and moves ahead the same number of spaces as the remainder. If the answer is correct, the player goes again. If the answer is not correct, the player must go back the same number of spaces as the correct remainder. The first player to reach the end of the path wins.
Bonus: Science		• Discuss the importance of reducing the amount of trash your family produces. Have your child help weigh the bag(s) of trash your family throws out this week. Can you reduce that weight next week? Your child may wish to record trash weights for several weeks and show them on a simple graph.

Quotation Marks

Quotation marks are punctuation marks that tell what is said by a person. Quotation marks go before the first word and after the punctuation of a direct quote. The first word of a direct quote begins with a capital letter.

Example: Katie said, "Never go in the water without a friend."

Put quotation marks around the correct words in the sentences below.

Example: "Wait for me, please," said Laura.

1. John, would you like to visit a jungle? asked his uncle.

2. The police officer said, Don't worry, we'll help you.

3. James shouted, Hit a home run!

4. My friend Carol said, I really don't like cheeseburgers.

_____

Write your own quotations by answering the questions below. Be sure to put quotation marks around your words.

1. What would you say if you saw a dinosaur?

_____

_____

2. What would your best friend say if your hair turned purple?

_____

_____

Quotation Marks

Put quotation marks around the correct words in the sentences below. Then, write the sentences.

1. Can we go for a bike ride? asked Katrina.

_____

2. Yes, said Mom.

_____

3. Let's go to the park, said Mike.

_____

4. Great idea! said Mom.

_____

5. How long until we get there? asked Katrina.

_____

6. Soon, said Mike.

_____

7. Here we are! exclaimed Mom.

_____

Talking Bits

Quotation marks are a signal that someone is saying something. Put quotation marks around the words that someone is saying in these sentences based on Beverly Cleary's character Ramona Quimby.

Example: "What if you have to back up?" asked Ramona.

1. Ramona could hear her father say, Now, don't worry.

2. Hurry up, Ramona, Mrs. Quimby was calling.

3. There's something wrong with the car, Ramona told Beezus.

4. Yard Ape yelled, Hi, Egghead!

5. Marsha was whispering, It's okay. It's okay.

6. She could hear her mother's words, Let's go home now.

7. How are you feeling? her father asked.

8. You'll feel better later, Ramona's mother said gently.

9. Ramona almost dreamed about Yard Ape yelling, Hey, Egghead!

10. Mrs. Whaley would surely say, What a super nuisance she is!

Rabbit Remark

For each of the quotes below, add a set of quotation marks around exactly what was said.

Examples: "That's a good sign," said Rahm.
He called, "You can come out now."

1. I think it is time for us to build the nursery, Silla said.

2. When do you think it will happen? asked Rahm.

3. Silla said, When the moon is round again.

4. How many children do you think we'll have? asked Rahm.

Rewrite these quotes, adding a set of quotation marks, a capital letter at the beginning and a period or question mark at the end.

1. there is no way of telling, she answered

_____

_____

2. let's just wait and see, said Silla

_____

_____

Division: Remainders

Division is a way to find out how many times one number is contained in another number. For example, $28 \div 4 = 7$ means that there are seven groups of four in 28. The **dividend** is the larger number that is divided by the smaller number, or **divisor**. The **quotient** is the answer in a division problem. The **remainder** is the amount left over. The remainder is always less than the divisor.

Study the example. Find each quotient and remainder.

Example:
There are 11 dog biscuits.
Put them in groups of 3.
There are 2 left over.

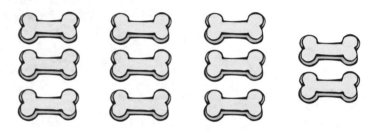

Remember: The remainder must be less than the **divisor!**

$3 \overline{)13}$ $4 \overline{)17}$ $6 \overline{)32}$ $5 \overline{)26}$

$9 \div 4 =$ ____ $12 \div 5 =$ ____ $26 \div 4 =$ ____ $49 \div 9 =$ ____

The pet store has 7 cats.
Two cats go in each
cage. How many cats
are left over?

_____

Divisibility Rules

A number is divisible... by 2 if the last digit is 0 or even (2, 4, 6, 8).
by 3 if the sum of all digits is divisible by 3.
by 4 if the last two digits are divisible by 4.
by 5 if the last digit is a 0 or 5.
by 10 if the last digit is 0.

Example: 250 is divisible by <u>2, 5, 10</u>

Tell what numbers each of these numbers is divisible by.

3,732 _____   439 _____

50 _____   444 _____

7,960 _____   8,212 _____

104,924 _____   2,345 _____

Division

Division is a way to find out how many times one number is contained in another number. For example, $28 \div 7 = 4$ means that there are 4 groups of 7 in 28.

Division problems can be written two ways: $36 \div 6 = 6$ or $6\overline{)36}$

These are the parts of a division problem:

dividend ➔ $36 \div 6 = 6$ ← quotient

divisor ↗

Divide.

$$\text{divisor} \rightarrow 6\overline{)36} \begin{array}{c} 6 \leftarrow \text{quotient} \\ \leftarrow \text{dividend} \end{array}$$

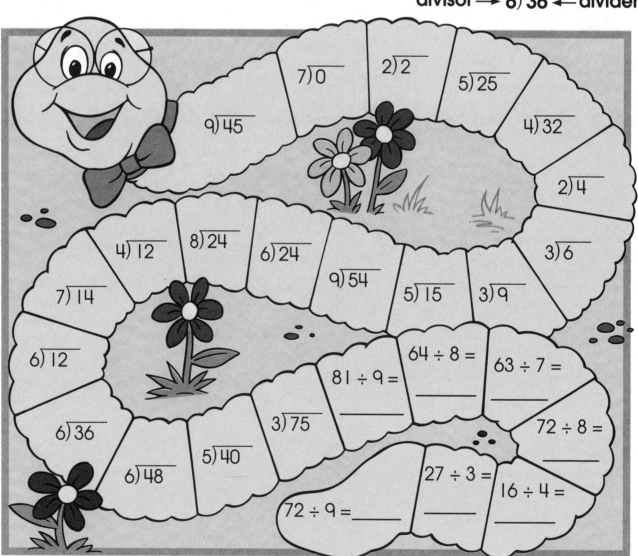

$9\overline{)45}$ $7\overline{)0}$ $2\overline{)2}$ $5\overline{)25}$ $4\overline{)32}$ $2\overline{)4}$

$7\overline{)14}$ $4\overline{)12}$ $8\overline{)24}$ $6\overline{)24}$ $9\overline{)54}$ $5\overline{)15}$ $3\overline{)9}$ $3\overline{)6}$

$6\overline{)12}$

$6\overline{)36}$ $6\overline{)48}$ $5\overline{)40}$ $3\overline{)75}$ $81 \div 9 =$ ____ $64 \div 8 =$ ____ $63 \div 7 =$ ____

$72 \div 8 =$ ____

$72 \div 9 =$ ____ $27 \div 3 =$ ____ $16 \div 4 =$ ____

Division With Remainders

Sometimes, groups of objects or numbers cannot be divided into equal groups. The **remainder** is the number left over in the quotient of a division problem. The remainder must be smaller than the divisor.

Example:

Divide 18 butterflies into groups of 5. You have 3 equal groups, with 3 butterflies left over.

$18 \div 5 = 3 \text{ R}3$

or

$$\begin{array}{r} 3 \text{ R}3 \\ 5\overline{)18} \\ -15 \\ \hline 3 \end{array}$$

Divide. Some problems may have remainders.

 $9\overline{)84}$ $7\overline{)65}$ $8\overline{)25}$ $5\overline{)35}$ $5\overline{)34}$

$4\overline{)25}$ $6\overline{)56}$ $4\overline{)7}$ $7\overline{)16}$ $8\overline{)37}$

 $7\overline{)27}$ $2\overline{)5}$ $2\overline{)4}$ $8\overline{)73}$ $4\overline{)9}$

 $9\overline{)46}$ $5\overline{)17}$ $2\overline{)3}$ $4\overline{)13}$ $5\overline{)25}$

Division: Larger Numbers

Follow the steps for dividing larger numbers.

Example: **Step 1:** Divide the tens first. **Step 2:** Divide the ones next.

$$3\overline{)66}$$

$$\begin{array}{r} 2 \\ 3\overline{)66} \\ -6 \\ \hline 06 \end{array}$$

$$\begin{array}{r} 22 \\ 3\overline{)66} \\ -6 \\ \hline 06 \\ -6 \\ \hline 0 \end{array}$$

Divide.

$$4\overline{)84} \qquad 2\overline{)90} \qquad 2\overline{)64} \qquad 2\overline{)50} \qquad 3\overline{)45}$$

$$3\overline{)75} \qquad 3\overline{)36} \qquad 4\overline{)92} \qquad 2\overline{)76} \qquad 5\overline{)65}$$

In some larger numbers, the divisor goes into the first two digits of the dividend.

Example:

$$9\overline{)729}$$

$$\begin{array}{r} 8 \\ 9\overline{)729} \\ -72 \\ \hline 09 \end{array}$$

$$\begin{array}{r} 81 \\ 9\overline{)729} \\ -72 \\ \hline 09 \\ -9 \\ \hline 0 \end{array}$$

Divide.

$$7\overline{)630} \qquad 5\overline{)125} \qquad 6\overline{)486} \qquad 5\overline{)100} \qquad 6\overline{)540}$$

Week 22 Skills

Subject	Skill	Multi-Sensory Learning Activities
Reading and Language Arts	Use possessive pronouns to show ownership.	• Complete Practice Page 236. • Print a short fable or folktale from the Internet. Ask your child to read it and circle possessive pronouns such as **my**, **our**, **your**, **his**, **her**, **its**, and **theirs**. Then, ask your child to draw an arrow back from each possessive pronoun to the noun that tells who the owner is.
	Add **'s** to nouns to show ownership.	• Complete Practice Pages 237–240. • Provide self-sticking notes for your child to stick on objects around the house that belong to different family members. On each, have him or her write possessive nouns such as **Dad's shoes** or **Keisha's bed**.
Math	Practice division with and without remainders.	• Complete Practice Page 241. • Remind your child to align numbers carefully according to their place values when solving long division problems. Suggest that he or she use a colored pencil to draw vertical lines between columns of digits written to solve division problems.
	Use multiplication and division to solve problems, including word problems.	• Complete Practice Pages 242–244. • Make up word problems related to an interesting place or event. For example, during a trip to the zoo, ask how many pounds of food the lions need if each lion eats four pounds, or how many monkey toys are needed if one toy is provided for every three monkeys.

Possessive Pronouns

Possessive pronouns show ownership.

Example: his hat, **her** shoes, **our** dog

We can use these pronouns before a noun:
my, our, your, his, her, its, their

Example: That is **my** bike.

We can use these pronouns on their own:
mine, yours, ours, his, hers, theirs, its

Example: That is **mine**.

Write each sentence again, using a pronoun instead of the words in bold letters. Be sure to use capitals and periods.

Example:

My **dog's** bowl is brown.　　　　**Its** bowl is brown.

1. That is **Lisa's** book. _____

2. This is **my pencil**. _____

3. This hat is **your hat**. _____

4. Fifi is **Kevin's** cat. _____

5. That beautiful house is **our home**.

_____

6. **The gerbil's** cage is too small.

_____

Apostrophes

Apostrophes are used to show ownership by placing an **'s** at the end of a single person, place or thing.

Example: Mary**'s** cat

Add an **apostrophe** and an **s** to the words to show ownership of a person, place or thing.

1. That is Holly   flower garden.

2. Mark   new skates are black and green.

3. Mom threw away Dad   old shoes.

4. Buster   food dish was lost in the snowstorm.

Apostrophes can also be used in place of the missing letters in a contraction.

Example: do n**o**t = don**'**t

Write the apostrophes in the contractions below.

1. We didn t think that the ice cream would melt so fast.

2. They re never around when we re ready to go.

3. Didn t you need to make a phone call?

4. Who s going to help you paint the bicycle red?

Possessive Nouns

A **possessive noun** shows ownership or possession.

Add an **apostrophe** and **s** to a singular noun.
   Example: the dog**'s** bone, Chris**'s** puppy

Add an **apostrophe** and an **s** (**'s**) to a plural noun that does not end in **s**.
   Example: the children**'s** turtle

Add an **apostrophe** (**'**) to a plural noun that ends in **s**.
   Example: the two pet**s'** cages.

Circle the answers.

1. Our class's pet show was last Friday.
   How many classes had a pet show?   one   more than one

2. The students' pets were interesting.
   How many students had pets?   one   more than one

3. The girl's hamster got out of the cage.
   How many girls had hamsters?   one   more than one

4. The snake's meal was a mouse.
   How many snakes were there?   one   more than one

5. The mice's cage was next to the snakes.
   How many mice were there?   one   more than one

6. The puppies' barking was disturbing.
   How many puppies were there?   one   more than one

7. The chicken's clucking was noisy.
   How many chickens were there?   one   more than one

8. The box turtle's shell protected it well.
   How many box turtles were there?   one   more than one

Ownership

We add **'s** to nouns (people, places or things) to tell who or what owns something.

Read the sentences. Fill in the blanks to show ownership.

Example: The doll belongs to **Sara**.
It is **Sara's** doll.

1. Sparky has a red collar.

_____ collar is red.

2. Jimmy has a blue coat.

_____ coat is blue.

3. The tail of the cat is short.

The _____ tail is short.

4. The name of my mother is Karen.

My _____ name is Karen.

Ownership

Read the sentences. Choose the correct word and write it in the sentences below.

1. The _____ lunchbox is broken.   boys   boy's

2. The _____ played in the cage.   gerbil's   gerbils

3. _____ hair is brown.   Anns   Ann's

4. The _____ ran in the field.   horse's   horses

5. My _____ coat is torn.   sister's   sisters

6. The _____ fur is brown.   cats   cat's

7. Three _____ flew past our window.   birds   bird's

8. The _____ paws are muddy.   dogs   dog's

9. The _____ neck is long.   giraffes   giraffe's

10. The _____ are big and powerful.   lion's   lions

Division

Divide.

$7\overline{)860}$ $\quad$ $6\overline{)611}$ $\quad$ $8\overline{)279}$ $\quad$ $4\overline{)338}$ $\quad$ $6\overline{)979}$

$3\overline{)792}$ $\quad$ $5\overline{)463}$ $\quad$ $6\overline{)940}$ $\quad$ $4\overline{)647}$ $\quad$ $3\overline{)814}$

$7\overline{)758}$ $\quad$ $5\overline{)356}$ $\quad$ $4\overline{)276}$ $\quad$ $8\overline{)328}$ $\quad$ $9\overline{)306}$

$4\overline{)579}$ $\quad$ $8\overline{)932}$ $\quad$ $3\overline{)102}$ $\quad$ $2\overline{)821}$ $\quad$ $6\overline{)489}$

The video store has 491 DVDs.
The store sells 8 DVDs a day.
How many days will it take
to sell all of the DVDs? _____

Multiplication and Division Review

Multiply or divide. Fill in the blanks with the missing numbers or **x** or ÷ signs. The first one is done for you.

5 x 4 = 20   6 x 8 = ____   7 x ____ = 14

3 _ 6 = 18   7 x 2 = ____   ____ x 3 = 24

6 _ 2 = 3   24 ÷ 6 = ____   6 x 5 = ____

25 _ 5 = 5   49 ÷ 7 = ____   8 x ____ = 32

3 _ 8 = 24   18 ÷ 3 = ____   9 x 5 = ____

12 _ 3 = 4   9 x 8 = ____   6 x ____ = 36

COMPLETE YEAR GRADE 3

Problem-Solving: Multiplication, Division

Read and solve each problem.

Jeff and Terry are planting a garden. They plant 3 rows of green beans with 8 plants in each row. How many green bean plants are there in the garden? _____

There are 45 tomato plants in the garden. There are 5 rows of them. How many tomato plants are in each row? _____

The children have 12 plants each of lettuce, broccoli and spinach. How many plants are there in all? _____

Jeff planted 3 times as many cucumber plants as Terry. He planted 15 of them. How many did Terry plant? _____

Terry planted 12 pepper plants. He planted twice as many green pepper plants as red pepper plants. How many green pepper plants are there? _____

How many red pepper plants? _____

Raising a Family

Omar and his family live a very simple life. Omar's father raises coffee plants on their one-acre farm. Omar's mother and father work very hard to earn the money to send Omar and his brother and two sisters to school. It costs $75 a year for primary school for each child. To earn more money, Omar's father works as a stonemason for $5 a day. Omar's mother works at a large farm for $2 a day.

1. How many days will Omar's father have to work as a stonemason to pay for 1 year of Omar's primary school? (**Hint:** Count by 5s.) _____

2. How many days will Omar's father have to work to pay for the other three children's primary school each year? (**Hint:** Add your answer from #1 three times.) _____

3. One pair of children's shoes costs $10. How many days will Omar's mother have to work to buy him a pair of shoes? _____

4. How many days will Omar's mother have to work to buy the other three children new pairs of shoes? _____

5. How much will it cost to buy shoes for all four children? (**Hint:** Count by 10s.) _____

Week 23 Skills

Subject	Skill	Multi-Sensory Learning Activities
Reading and Language Arts	Capitalize names of people and pets, places, days of the week, months of the year, and holidays.	• Complete Practice Page 246. • Print 12 free blank monthly calendar pages from the Internet. Have your child write in names of months, days, and holidays. Add birthdates of family members and friends. Remind your child to begin each proper noun with a capital letter.
	Capitalize the names of cities and states and use a comma between them.	• Complete Practice Page 247. • Ask your child to plan a road trip to three different U.S. states. Have him or her write an itinerary, using a comma between each capitalized city and state name.
	Proofread for spelling.	• Complete Practice Pages 248–251. • Send your child short text or e-mail messages that have spelling errors. Ask your child to correct the errors and send the messages back to you.
Math	Use the order of operations to solve math problems.	• Complete Practice Pages 252 and 253. • Teach your child the phrase **pardon my dear aunt sally** to help remember the order of operations: **p**arentheses, **m**ultiplication, **d**ivision, **a**ddition, **s**ubtraction.
	Understand symmetry.	• Complete Practice Page 254. • Have your child cut shapes from construction paper and fold them in half. Are they symmetrical?
Bonus: Science		• Most creatures have two identical or nearly identical sides. Are there any animals whose bodies are not symmetrical? Research to find out.

Capitalization

The names of **people**, **places** and **pets**, the **days of the week**, the **months of the year** and **holidays** begin with a capital letter.

Read the words in the box. Write the words in the correct column with capital letters at the beginning of each word.

ron polsky	tuesday	march	april
presidents' day	saturday	woofy	october
blackie	portland, oregon	corning, new york	molly yoder
valentine's day	fluffy	harold edwards	arbor day
bozeman, montana	sunday		

People

_____

_____

_____

Places

_____

_____

_____

Pets

_____

_____

_____

Days

_____

_____

_____

Months

_____

_____

_____

Holidays

_____

_____

_____

Capitalization and Commas

We capitalize the names of cities and states. We use a comma to separate the name of a city and a state.

Use capital letters and commas to write the names of the cities and states correctly.

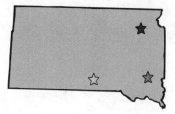

Example:

sioux falls south dakota   _Sioux Falls, South Dakota_

1. plymouth massachusetts   _____

2. boston massachusetts   _____

3. philadelphia pennsylvania   _____

4. white plains new york   _____

5. newport rhode island   _____

6. yorktown virginia   _____

7. nashville tennessee   _____

8. portland oregon   _____

9. mansfield ohio   _____

Spelling

Circle the word in each sentence that is not spelled correctly. Then, write the word correctly.

1. John isn't shelfish at all. _____

2. He sharred his lunch with me today. _____

3. I was careles and forgot to bring mine. _____

4. My father says if I planed better,
   that wouldn't happen all the time. _____

5. John is kind of quiet, and I used
   to think he was shie. _____

6. Now, I know he is really thotful. _____

7. He's also very polyte and always
   asks before he borrows anything. _____

8. He would never just reach over
   and grabb something he wanted. _____

9. I'm glad John desided to be my friend. _____

Spelling

Circle the word in each sentence that is not spelled correctly. Then, write the word correctly.

1. Be sure to stopp at the red light. _____

2. The train goes down the trak. _____

3. Please put the bred in the toaster. _____

4. I need another blok to finish. _____

5. The beasst player won a trophy. _____

6. Blow out the candles and make a wiish. _____

7. The truk blew its horn. _____

Review

Circle the words that are not spelled correctly in the story. Then, write each word correctly on the lines below.

One day, Peter and I were sitting on a bench at the park. A polise woman came and sat in the empty spase beside us. "Have you seen a little dog with thik black fur?" she asked. She was very poolite. "Remember that dog?" I asked Peter. "He was just here!" Peter nodded. He was too shie to say anything.

"Give us his adress," I said. "We'll find him and take him home." She got out a pensil and wrote the addres in the senter of a piece of paper. Peter and I desided to walk down the street the way the dog had gone. There was a krowd of people at a cherch we passed, but no dog.

Then it started getting late. "We'd better go home," Peter said. "I can't see in this drakness, anyway."

As we turned around to go back, there was the little dog! He had been following us! We took him to the adress. The girl who came to the door grabed him and hugged him tight. "I'm sorry I let you wander away," she told the dog. "I'll never be so carless again." I thought she was going to kis us, too. We left just in time!

_____   _____   _____

_____   _____   _____

_____   _____   _____

_____   _____   _____

_____   _____   _____

_____   _____   _____

Review

Circle the two words in each sentence that are not spelled correctly. Then, write the words correctly.

1. Arn't you going to shere your cookie with me?

_____   _____

2. We planed a long time, but we still wern't ready.

_____   _____

3. My pensil hassn't broken yet today.

_____   _____

4. We arn't going because we don't have the correct adress.

_____   _____

5. Youve stired the soup too much.

_____   _____

6. Weave tried to be as neet as possible.

_____   _____

7. She hasnt seen us in this darknes.

_____   _____

Order of Operations

When you solve a problem that involves more than one operation, this is the order to follow:

Parentheses first, then do multiplication and division in order from left to right. Finally, do all addition and subtraction steps, in order from left to right. These rules are called **Order of Operations**.

Example:

$$2 + (3 \times 5) - 2 = 15$$
$$2 + 15 - 2 = 15$$
$$17 - 2 = 15$$

Solve the problems using the correct order of operations.

$(5 - 3) + 4 \times 7 = \underline{\hspace{1cm}}$ $1 + 2 \times 3 + 4 = \underline{\hspace{1cm}}$

$6 \times 3 - 1 = \underline{\hspace{1cm}}$ $(8 \div 2) \times 4 = \underline{\hspace{1cm}}$

$9 \div 3 \times 3 + 0 = \underline{\hspace{1cm}}$ $5 - 2 \times 1 + 2 = \underline{\hspace{1cm}}$

Order of Operations

Use +, −, x and ÷ to complete the problems so the number sentence is true.

Example: 4 __+__ 2 __−__ 1 = 5

(8 ____ 2) ____ 4 = 8

(1 ____ 2) ____ 3 = 1

9 ____ 3 ____ 9 = 3

(7 ____ 5) ____ 1 = 2

8 ____ 5 ____ 4 = 10

5 ____ 4 ____ 1 = 1

Perfect Symmetry

A figure that can be separated into two matching parts is **symmetric**.

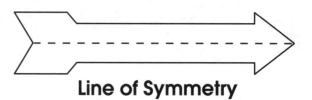

Line of Symmetry

Is the dotted line a line of symmetry?

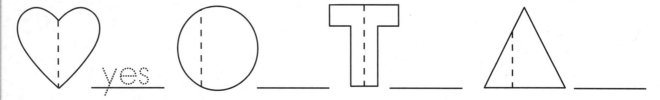

yes

Draw the matching part.

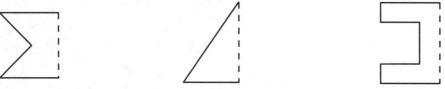

Use letters to make symmetric words.

Make your own symmetric words.

_ _ _ _ _ _ _ _ _ _

Week 24 Skills

Subject	Skill	Multi-Sensory Learning Activities
Reading and Language Arts	Review common spelling patterns.	• Complete Practice Pages 256–260. • Use a variety of strategies for practicing words that are difficult to spell. Have your child try spelling words while clapping, tapping his or her foot, or jumping rope.
Math	Understand fractions.	• Complete Practice Pages 261 and 262. • Cut a snack such as an apple or a slice of cheese into thirds, fourths, or fifths. As your child eats, ask him or her to name a fraction to describe how much is left. • Draw large shapes on blank paper. Then, give directions to your child such as "color half of the circle green" or "make two-thirds of the rectangle polka-dotted."
	Compare fractions and choose equivalent fractions.	• Complete Practice Pages 263 and 264. • Ask your child to use construction paper and markers to create an equivalent fraction collage. See how many different ways there are to show equivalent fractions for $\frac{1}{2}$. Display the completed artwork on the refrigerator or wall.
Bonus: Social Studies		• Ask your child to research Martin Luther King Day, Presidents' Day, or another national holiday and design a postage stamp to honor it. Have your child explain how the stamp's design reflects the meaning of the holiday.

C, K, CK Words: Spelling

Write the words from the box that answer the questions.

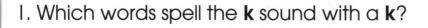

| crowd | keeper | cost | pack | kangaroo | thick |

1. Which words spell the **k** sound with a **k**?

_____

2. Which words spell the **k** sound with a **c**?

_____

3. Which words spell the **k** sound with **ck**?

_____

4. Circle the letters that spell the **k** sound in these words:

cook   black   cool   kite

cake   pocket   poke

5. Which words from the box rhyme with each of these?

tossed _____   deeper _____

proud _____   all in blue _____

C, K, CK Words: Spelling

The **k** sound can be spelled with a **c**, **k** or **ck** after a short vowel sound.

Use the words from the box to complete the sentences. Use each word only once.

crowd	keeper
cost	pack
kangaroo	thick

1. On sunny days, there is always a _____ of people at the zoo.

2. It doesn't _____ much to get into the zoo.

3. We always get hungry, so we _____ a picnic lunch.

4. We like to watch the _____.

5. Its _____ tail helps it jump and walk.

6. The _____ always makes sure the cages are clean.

S Words: Spelling

The **s** sound can be spelled with an **s**, **ss**, **c** or **ce**.

Use the words from the box to complete the sentences below. Write each word only once.

center	pencil	space
address	police	darkness

1. I drew a circle in the _____ of the page.

2. I'll write to you if you tell me your _____.

3. She pushed too hard and broke the point on her _____.

4. If you hear a noise at night, call the _____.

5. It was night, and I couldn't see him in the _____.

6. There's not enough _____ for me to sit next to you.

S Words: Spelling

Write the words from the box that answer the questions.

| center | pencil | space | address | police | darkness |

1. Which words spell the **s** sound with **ss**?

_____

2. Which words spell **s** with a **c**?

_____

_____

3. Which words spell **s** with **ce**?

_____

4. Write two other words you know that spell **s** with an **s**.

_____

5. Circle the letters that spell the **s** sound in these words.

decide   kiss   careless   ice

cost   fierce   sentence

6. Put these letters in order to make words from the box.

sdsdera _____   sdserakn _____

clipoe _____   clipne _____

capse _____   retnce _____

C Words: Spelling

The letter **c** can make the **k** sound or the **s** sound.

Example: **c**ount, **c**ity

Write **k** or **s** to show how the **c** in each word sounds.

cave	_____	copy	_____	force	_____
become	_____	dance	_____	city	_____
certain	_____	contest	_____	cool	_____

Use the words from the box to answer these questions.

center	pencil	space	address	police	darkness

1. Which word begins with the same sound as **simple** and ends with the same sound as **fur**? _____

2. Which word begins with the same sound as **average** and ends with the same sound as **circus**? _____

3. Which word begins with the same sound as **popcorn** and ends with the same sound as **glass**? _____

4. Which word begins and ends with the same sounds as **pool**?

   _____

5. Which word begins with the same sound as **city** and ends with the same sound as **kiss**? _____

6. Which word begins and ends with the same sounds as **delicious**?

   _____

Fractions

A **fraction** is a number that names part of a whole, such as $\frac{1}{2}$ or $\frac{1}{3}$.

Write the fraction that tells what parrt of each figure is colored. The first one is done for you.

Example:

    2 parts shaded
    5 parts in the whole figure

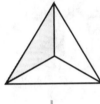

$\frac{1}{3}$

_____

_____

_____

_____

_____

_____

_____

_____

_____

Fractions: Division

A **fraction** is a number that names part of an object. It can also name part of a group.

Study the example. Divide by the bottom number of the fraction to find the answers.

Example:

There are 6 cheerleaders.
$\frac{1}{2}$ of the cheerleaders are boys.
How many cheerleaders are boys?

6 cheerleaders ÷ 2 groups = 3 boys

$\frac{1}{2}$ of 6 = 3 $\frac{1}{2}$ of 8 = __4__

$\frac{1}{2}$ of 10 = ____ $\frac{1}{3}$ of 9 = ____ $\frac{1}{5}$ of 10 = ____

$\frac{1}{4}$ of 12 = ____ $\frac{1}{8}$ of 32 = ____ $\frac{1}{3}$ of 27 = ____

$\frac{1}{5}$ of 30 = ____ $\frac{1}{2}$ of 14 = ____ $\frac{1}{9}$ of 18 = ____

$\frac{1}{6}$ of 24 = ____ $\frac{1}{3}$ of 18 = ____ $\frac{1}{10}$ of 50 = ____

Fractions: Equivalent

Fractions that name the same part of a whole are equivalent fractions.

Example:

$$\frac{1}{2} = \frac{2}{4}$$

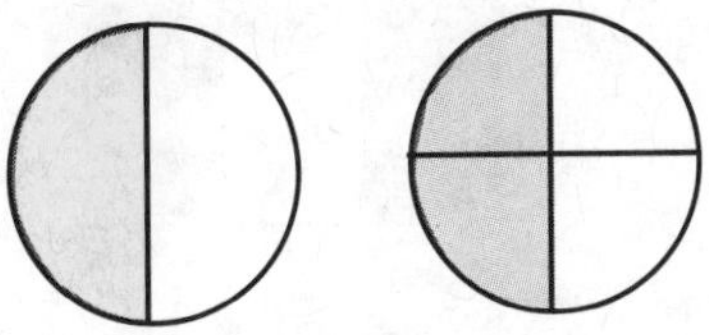

Fill in the numbers to complete the equivalent fractions.

$$\frac{1}{4} = \frac{\boxed{}}{8}$$

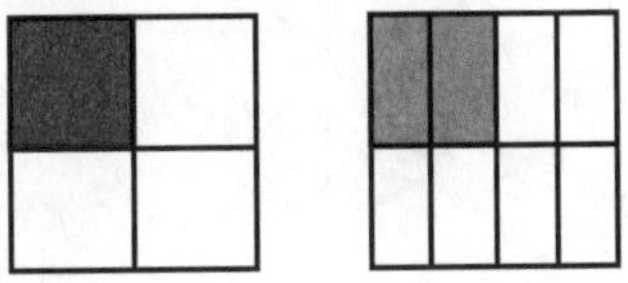

$$\frac{2}{3} = \frac{\boxed{}}{6}$$

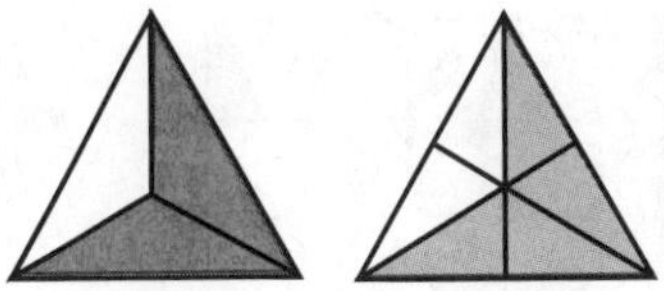

$$\frac{1}{6} = \frac{\boxed{}}{12}$$

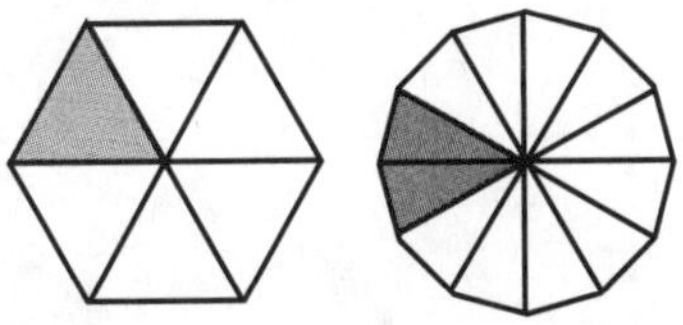

$$\frac{2}{3} = \frac{\boxed{}}{6}$$

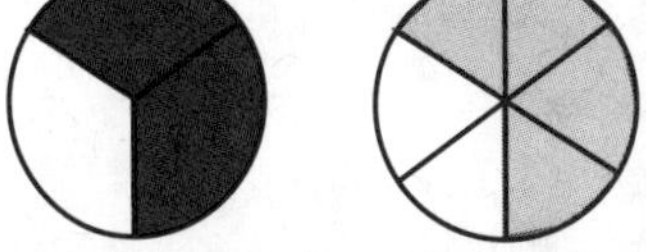

$$\frac{1}{3} = \frac{\boxed{}}{12}$$

$$\frac{1}{5} = \frac{\boxed{}}{15}$$

$$\frac{1}{4} = \frac{\boxed{}}{8}$$

$$\frac{1}{2} = \frac{\boxed{}}{6}$$

$$\frac{2}{3} = \frac{\boxed{}}{9}$$

$$\frac{2}{6} = \frac{\boxed{}}{18}$$

Fractions: Comparing

Circle the fraction in each pair that is larger.

Example:

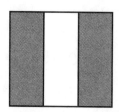

$$\left(\frac{2}{3}\right)$$

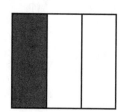

$$\frac{1}{3}$$

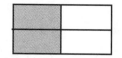

$$\frac{2}{4}$$

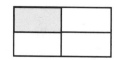

$$\frac{1}{4}$$

$$\frac{1}{8}$$

$$\frac{2}{8}$$

$$\frac{1}{2}$$

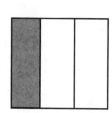

$$\frac{1}{3}$$

$$\frac{2}{3}$$

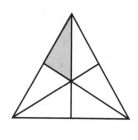

$$\frac{1}{6}$$

$\frac{1}{4}$ or $\frac{1}{6}$ $\frac{1}{5}$ or $\frac{1}{7}$ $\frac{1}{8}$ or $\frac{1}{4}$

Week 25 Skills

Subject	Skill	Multi-Sensory Learning Activities
Reading and Language Arts	Understand cause and effect.	• Complete Practice Pages 266–270. • Read *Camp Ghost-Away* by Judy Delton. Challenge your child to describe five examples of cause and effect in the story. • Have your child write safety guidelines for something he or she likes to do, such as swimming or riding a scooter. Ask what might happen if the guidelines are not followed.
Math	Convert fractions to decimals.	• Complete Practice Pages 271–273. • Provide 10 dimes and explain that each coin equals one-tenth of a dollar, or 0.1. Challenge your child to choose different numbers of dimes and write the equivalent fractions and decimal numbers.
	Add and subtract decimals.	• Complete Practice Page 274. • Ask your child to use a grocery store ad to find the prices of ingredients needed for a meal or snack. Can he or she write the price for each item in a column, aligning the decimal points, and add them to find the total price?
Bonus: Social Studies		• Search for photographs of national symbols such as the Liberty Bell, the Statue of Liberty, the American flag, or the bald eagle. Ask your child to choose one and write a paragraph explaining why it is a good symbol for the country. The paragraph should contain at least three supporting reasons.

Boo...

Each sentence tells something that happened. Find a sentence in the box below that tells why it might have happened and write it on the line.

1. Roger and Sonny dressed up like ghosts. _____

_____

2. Molly couldn't float. _____

_____

3. One of the boat oars fell into the lake. _____

_____

4. Molly's arms itched. _____

_____

5. Roger and Sonny had to clean the kitchen. _____

_____

6. Molly was angry with Roger and Sonny. _____

_____

- Their joke caused the mess.
- They wanted to play a joke and scare the girls.
- Molly touched a poison ivy plant.
- Molly didn't think it was funny to scare people.
- The oar was too heavy for Molly to hold.
- She needed to relax all of her muscles.

If...Then

Underline the **cause** with red and the **effect** with blue.

1. Dorothy lay down to take a nap, for the long walk had made her tired.

2. The ladder they had made was so heavy, they couldn't pull it over the wall.

3. The group realized they should be careful in this dainty country because the people could be hurt easily.

4. The Joker had many cracks over his body because he always tried to stand on his head.

5. The dolls have stiff joints when they are on a store shelf, because they have been waiting so long for someone to take them home.

6. The Lion attacked the great spider, because it had been eating the animals of the forest.

7. The forest animals bowed to the Lion as their king, because he had killed their enemy.

8. The animals asked the Lion to save them, because he was thought of as King of the Beasts.

9. Traveling through the forest was difficult, because the forest floor was covered with thick grass and muddy holes.

10. Dorothy loved the princess doll and wanted to take her home, because she was beautiful.

Cause and Effect

A **cause** is the reason for an event. An **effect** is what happens as a result of a cause.

Circle the cause and underline the effect in each sentence. They may be in any order. The first one has been done for you.

1. (The truck hit an icy patch) and <u>skidded off the road.</u>

2. When the door slammed shut, the baby woke up crying.

3. Our soccer game was cancelled when it began to storm.

4. Dad and Mom are adding a room onto the house since our family is growing.

5. Our car ran out of gas on the way to town, so we had to walk.

6. The home run in the ninth inning helped our team win the game.

7. We had to climb the stairs because the elevator was broken.

8. We were late to school because the bus had a flat tire.

Cause and Effect

Cause and effect sentences often use clue words to show the relationship between two events. Common clue words are **because**, **so**, **when**, and **since**.

Read the sentences on pages 269 and 270. Circle each clue word. The first one has been done for you.

1. I'll help you clean your room, (so) we can go out to play sooner.

2. Because of the heavy snowfall, school was closed today.

3. She was not smiling, so her mother wanted her school pictures taken again.

4. Mrs. Wilderman came to school with crutches today, because she had a skating accident.

5. When the team began making too many mistakes at practice, the coach told them to take a break.

Cause and Effect

6. Our telephone was not working, so I called the doctor from next door.

7. The police officer began to direct traffic, since the traffic signal was not working.

8. The class will go out to recess when the room is cleaned up.

9. "I can't see you because the room is too dark," said Jordan.

10. He has to wash the dishes alone because his sister is sick.

11. Since the bus had engine trouble, several children were late to school.

12. Monday was a holiday, so Mom and Dad took us to the park.

Decimals

A **decimal** is a number with one or more numbers to the right of a decimal point. A **decimal point** is a dot placed between the ones place and the tens place of a number, such as 2.5.

Example:

$\frac{3}{10}$ can be written as .3   They are both read as **three-tenths**.

Write the answer as a decimal for the shaded parts.

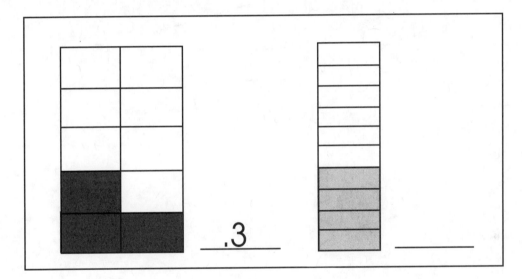

Color parts of each object to match the decimals given.

.7   .6   .5

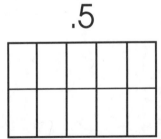

Decimals

A **decimal** is a number with one or more numbers to the right of a decimal point, such as 6.5 or 2.25. **Equivalent** means numbers that are equal.

Draw a line between the equivalent numbers.

.8	$\frac{5}{10}$
five-tenths	$\frac{8}{10}$
.7	$\frac{6}{10}$
.4	.3
six-tenths	$\frac{2}{10}$
three-tenths	$\frac{7}{10}$
.2	$\frac{9}{10}$
nine-tenths	$\frac{4}{10}$

Decimals: Greater Than 1

Write the decimal for the part that is shaded.

Example: $2\frac{4}{10}$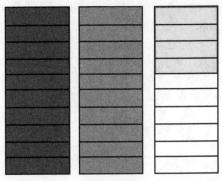

Write: 2.4   Read: two and four-tenths

$1\frac{2}{10}$ = ____

$3\frac{6}{10}$ = ____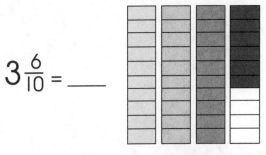

$2\frac{3}{10}$ = ____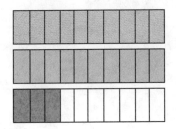

$2\frac{7}{10}$ = ____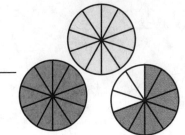

Write each number as a decimal.

four and two-tenths = ____   seven and one-tenth = ____

$3\frac{4}{10}$ = ____ $6\frac{9}{10}$ = ____ $8\frac{3}{10}$ = ____ $7\frac{5}{10}$ = ____

Decimals: Addition and Subtraction

Decimals are added and subtracted in the same way as other numbers. Simply carry down the decimal point to your answer.

Add or subtract.

Examples:

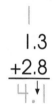

```
  1.3              4.5
+2.8             -2.2
 4.1              2.3
```

```
  1.3        4.6           5.1           6.7
+2.2       -3.4         +8.8          -4.3
```

```
  7.9        6.4          11.4           0.5
-3.7       +8.7          - 9.5          +3.6
```

9.3 + 1.2 = ____   2.5 - 0.7 = ____   1.2 + 5.0 = ____

Bob jogs around the school every day. The distance for one time around is .7 of a mile. If he jogs around the school two times, how many miles does he jog every day?

_____

Week 26 Skills

Subject	Skill	Multi-Sensory Learning Activities
Reading and Language Arts	Use context clues to help define new vocabulary words.	• Complete Practice Pages 276–280. • Have your child read aloud an interesting article from a newspaper or magazine. When your child comes to an unfamiliar word, help him or her look for context clues to guess its meaning. Then, look up the word in the dictionary to confirm the definition. • Let your child decorate a craft stick with question marks and a pair of eyes. When reading together, let your child point the stick at unknown words. Then, search the surrounding words for clues to the new word's meaning.
Math	Review multiplication, division, and fractions.	• Complete Practice Page 281. • Make a math "Tic-Tac-Toe" board. In each square, write one or more multiplication, division, or fractions problems. Then, play the game with your child. A player who solves the problems correctly can write **X** or **O** in the box.
	Use fractions to solve word problems.	• Complete Practice Pages 282–284. • Write word problems for your child such as "A class has 24 students. If $\frac{1}{8}$ of them play a musical instrument, how many play a musical instrument?" Challenge your child to draw a visual model to help solve each problem.

Vocabulary

Write a word from the box to complete each sentence. Use each word only once.

| glue | enter | share | add | decide | fold |

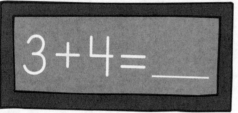

1. I know how to _____ 3 and 4.

2. Which book did you _____ to read?

3. Go in the door that says "_____ ."

4. I will _____ a yellow circle for the sun onto my picture.

5. I help _____ the clothes after they are washed.

6. She will_____ her banana with me.

Vocabulary

Find the picture that matches each sentence below. Then, complete each sentence with the word under the picture.

list

spill

search

pound

toast

load

1. I will _____ until I find it.

2. Be careful you don't _____ the paint.

3. Is that _____ too heavy for you?

4. They made _____ for breakfast.

5. Please go to the store and buy a _____ of butter.

6. Is my name on the _____?

Vocabulary

Find the picture that matches each sentence below. Then, complete the sentence with the word under the picture.

hug

plan

clap

stir

drag

grab

1. She will _____ where to go on her trip.

2. _____ that big box over here, please.

3. My little brother always tries to _____ my toys.

4. May I help you _____ the soup?

5. I like to _____ my dog because he is so soft.

6. After she played, everyone started to _____.

Sentences

Use the words in the box to complete each sentence.

fast	wish	truck	bread	sun
best	stop	track	lunch	block

 Race cars can go very _____.

 Carol packs a _____ for Ted before school.

 Throw a penny in the well and make a _____.

 The _____ had a flat tire.

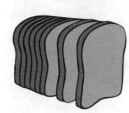 My favorite kind of _____ is whole wheat.

Sentences

Use the words in the box to complete each sentence.

lame	goal	pain	few	bike
street	fright	nose	gray	fuse

1. Look both ways before crossing the _____.

2. My _____ had a flat tire.

3. Our walk through the haunted house
   gave us such a _____.

4. I kicked the soccer ball and scored a _____.

5. The _____ clouds mean rain is coming.

6. Cover your _____ when you sneeze.

7. We blew a _____ at my house last night.

Review

Solve.

$$\begin{array}{r} 3 \\ \times\,6 \\ \hline \end{array} \qquad \begin{array}{r} 3 \\ \times\,8 \\ \hline \end{array} \qquad \begin{array}{r} 9 \\ \times\,8 \\ \hline \end{array} \qquad \begin{array}{r} 9 \\ \times\,5 \\ \hline \end{array} \qquad \begin{array}{r} 7 \\ \times\,2 \\ \hline \end{array}$$

$$5\overline{)25} \qquad 2\overline{)6} \qquad 3\overline{)18} \qquad 8\overline{)24} \qquad 7\overline{)49}$$

$\dfrac{1}{3}$ of 12 = _____ $\dfrac{1}{7}$ of 28 = _____ $\dfrac{1}{9}$ of 45 = _____

Color parts to match the fractions given.

$\dfrac{1}{3}$ 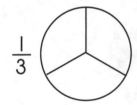 $\dfrac{2}{4}$ $\dfrac{2}{6}$

The Mystery of the Missing Sweets

Some mysterious person is sneaking away with pieces of desserts from Sam Sillicook's diner. Help him figure out how much is missing.

1. What fraction of Sam's Super Sweet Chocolate Cream Cake is missing?

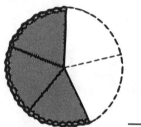

_____

2. What fraction of Sam's Heavenly Tasting Cherry Cream Tart is missing?

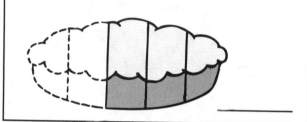

_____

3. What fraction of Sam's Tastee Toffee Coffee Cake is missing?

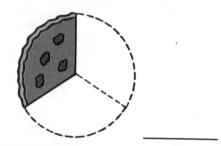

_____

4. What fraction of Sam's Luscious Licorice Candy Cake is missing?

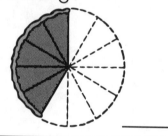

_____

5. What fraction of Sam's Tasty Tidbits of Chocolate Ice Cream is missing?

_____

6. Sam's Upside-Down Ice-Cream Cake is very famous. What fraction has vanished?

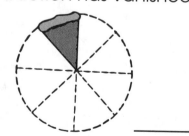

_____

The Mouse Family

The Mouse family found a feast of pies. Color the pies to illustrate the problem and answer the question on the line.
Write the fraction addition problem in the space.

Example:
If Mindy Mouse ate one-third of a pie and her sister Martha ate
another one-third of the pie, how much total pie did they eat? $\dfrac{2}{3}$

    $\dfrac{1}{3} + \dfrac{1}{3} = \dfrac{2}{3}$

1. Max Mouse found a whole pie and ate one-fifth of it. When he was hungry later, he ate another two-fifths. How much of the pie did he eat? _____

2. If Mindy gave three-eighths of a pie to her uncle and two-eighths to her cousin, how much did she give away? _____

3. Mr. Mouse demanded, "No more pie before bedtime!" Mindy handed her father one-fifth of a pie and Max handed his father another one-fifth. What part of a whole pie was Mr. Mouse holding? _____

4. If Max ate three-fifths of a pie and Mindy ate two-fifths of a pie, who ate more pie? _____

Ellie's Candy Bars

Ellie loves candy bars. Sometimes, she eats too many and gets a stomachache. Color the candy bars to illustrate the problem. Then, answer the questions. Use different colors, if necessary. Show the subtraction problem with numbers in the space.

Example:

Although Ellie is not supposed to eat candy before lunch, she secretly ate two-fifths of a candy bar. How much of the candy bar is left?

$\dfrac{3}{5}$

 $\qquad \dfrac{5}{5} - \dfrac{2}{5} = \dfrac{3}{5}$

1. At school, Ellie gave one friend four-sixths of a candy bar and another friend two-sixths. How much more did the first friend get than the second friend? _____

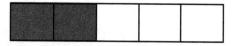

2. If Ellie broke off one-seventh of a candy bar, how much would be left? _____

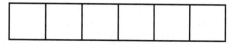

3. Ellie started with six-sevenths of a candy bar. She ate four-sevenths. How much of the candy bar is left? _____

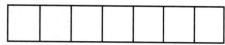

4. Ellie's mom bought a candy bar and ate four-fifths of it. How much of the candy bar did she save to eat later? _____

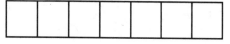

5. Ellie's sister divided a candy bar into 4 equal pieces. She gave Ellie 1 piece. How much of the candy bar was left? _____

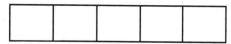

Week 27 Skills

Subject	Skill	Multi-Sensory Learning Activities
Reading and Language Arts	Use picture clues and context clues to find information and use new words in writing.	• Complete Practice Pages 286–289. • Provide a notebook where your child can keep lists of words and definitions related to school subject areas or topics of interest. For example, if your child is interested in ocean animals, he or she might list **marine**, **mollusk**, **plankton**, or **reef**. • Encourage your child to read a nonfiction book about a topic of interest. After reading, ask your child to make a short glossary that defines 10 key words from the book. Slip the glossary in the back of the book for other readers to use.
	Understand idioms and figurative language.	• Complete Practice Page 290. • Read *There's a Frog in My Throat* by Loreen Leedy. This book is about how funny idioms can be, especially when they are taken literally.
Math	Tell time using analog clocks and digital clocks.	• Complete Practice Pages 291–294. • When you are out with your child at stores, restaurants, and other public places, be on the lookout for analog clocks. Help your child read the positions of the hands and determine the time. Compare to times shown digitally on your phone or another device.

Completing a Story

Use **c**, **k**, or **ck** words to complete this story. Some of the verbs are past tense and need to end with **ed**. Use the word box on page 256 if you need help.

One day, Kevin and I _____ a lunch and went to the

zoo. There was a big _____ of people. Kevin wanted

to see the _____. When we got to the

_____ cage, we met the _____

whose name was Carla. "How much does it _____ $ to

keep a _____?" Kevin asked the _____.

"Our grass at home is really _____ NOT THIN , and that's

what  _____ eat, right?"

"You must have a big cage and clean it every day," Carla the

_____ told Kevin. Kevin got quiet very quickly.

"I'll just keep coming here to see _____ in

the cage you clean," he said.

Making Sentences

Sentences can tell what people are saying. What could each person be saying in the scene below? Write a sentence in each speech bubble.

Levers

simple
easier
fulcrum
force
load
distance
A
B

Use the words from the box to complete the sentences.

Mandy wants to try to lift her dad off the ground. Where should Mandy stand on the board? By standing on point ___, Mandy can lift her dad.

The board resting on the log is an example of a _____ machine called a **lever**. A lever has three parts—the **force**, the **fulcrum** and the **load**. Mandy is the force. The point on which the lever turns is called the _____. And Mandy's dad, the object to be lifted, is called the _____. The greater the _____ between the _____ and the fulcrum, the _____ it is to lift the load. The closer the distance between the **force** and the **fulcrum**, the harder it is to lift the load.

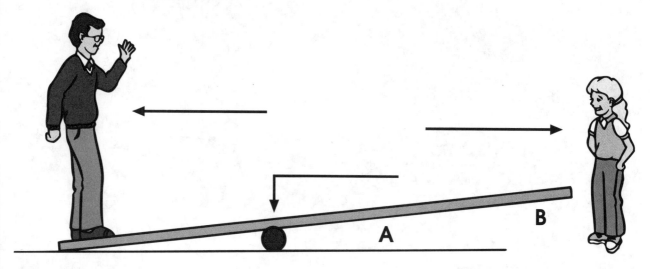

Label the picture of Mandy and her father with these words: **load**, **force** and **fulcrum**.

Six-Legged Friends

The largest group of animals belongs
to the group called **invertebrates**,
or animals without backbones.
This large group is the **insect** group.

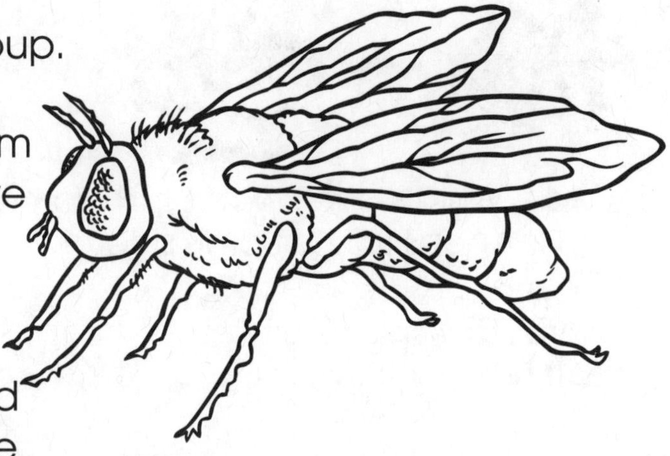

Insects are easy to tell apart from
other animals. Adult insects have
three body parts and six legs.
The first body part is the **head**.
On the head are the mouth,
eyes and antennae. The second
body part is the **thorax**. On it are
the legs and wings. The third part
is the **abdomen**. On it are small
openings for breathing.

Color the body parts of the insect above.
head — red, thorax — yellow, abdomen — blue

Draw an insect below. Make your insect a one-of-a-kind. Be sure it
has the correct number of body parts, legs, wings and antennae.
Fill in the information below.

Insect's name: _____   Warning:_____

Length: _____   _____

Where found: _____   _____

Food: _____   _____

Cool Heads

Circle the sentence that means the same as the numbered sentence.

1. Eddie Whitestone always had something up his sleeve.
   a. He keeps things up his sleeve.   b. He liked to plan surprises.

2. His room was a pigsty.
   a. It is very messy.   b. He lives with pigs.

3. She would be late if she didn't step on it.
   a. She needs to hurry.   b. She needs to step on something.

4. Sometimes David can be hardheaded.
   a. His head is very hard.   b. He can be stubborn.

5. Roger always tries to keep a cool head.
   a. He tries to be calm.   b. He keeps ice on his head.

6. Horseplay is not allowed in the hall.
   a. No horses are allowed in the hall.   b. No playing is allowed in the hall.

7. Ali Baba wraps up another mystery.
   a. He solves the mystery.   b. He wraps the mystery in paper.

8. Ali Baba keeps an eye on Eddie Whitestone.
   a. He draws an eye on Eddie's shirt.   b. He watches him.

9. His neighbors skip town.
   a. They skip all over town.   b. They leave town.

10. The criminal is in hot water.
    a. He is standing in hot water.   b. He is in trouble.

Time

Write the time shown on each clock.

Example:

7:15

7:00

_____

_____

_____

_____

_____

_____

_____

_____

_____

Time: a.m. and p.m.

In telling time, the hours between 12:00 midnight and 12:00 noon are a.m. hours. The hours between 12:00 noon and 12:00 midnight are p.m. hours.

Draw a line between the times that are the same.

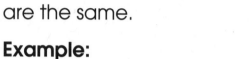

Example:

7:30 in the morning   7:30 a.m.

half-past seven a.m.

seven thirty in the morning

9:00 in the evening   9:00 p.m.

nine o'clock at night

six o'clock in the evening   8:00 a.m.

3:30 a.m.   six o'clock in the morning

4:15 p.m.   6:00 p.m.

eight o'clock in the morning   eleven o'clock at night

quarter past five in the evening   three thirty in the morning

11:00 p.m.   four fifteen in the evening

6:00 a.m.   5:15 p.m.

Time: Minutes

A minute is a measurement of time. There are sixty seconds in a minute and sixty minutes in an hour.

Write the time shown on each clock.

Example:

Each mark is one minute.
The hand is at mark number 6.

Write: 5:06

Read: six minutes after five.

_____

_____

_____

_____

_____

_____

_____

_____

_____

_____

_____

_____

Time: Addition

Add the hours and minutes together.
(Remember, 1 hour equals 60 minutes.)

Example:

    2 hours 10 minutes
+ 1 hour 50 minutes
3 hours 60 minutes
       (1 hour)
4 hours

    4 hours 20 minutes
+ 2 hours 10 minutes
6 hours 30 minutes

  9 hours
+ 2 hours

  1 hour
+ 5 hours

  6 hours
+ 3 hours

  6 hours 15 minutes
+ 1 hour 15 minutes

10 hours 30 minutes
+ 1 hour   10 minutes

3 hours 40 minutes
+ 8 hours 20 minutes

11 hours 15 minutes
+ 1 hour 30 minutes

4 hours 15 minutes
+ 5 hours 45 minutes

7 hours 10 minutes
+ 1 hour   30 minutes

Third Quarter Check-Up

Reading and Language Arts

❑ I know how to add suffixes to root words.

❑ I can use quotation marks to show what someone said.

❑ I can show ownership by using a possessive pronoun or by adding **'s**.

❑ I capitalize days, months, cities, states, and other proper nouns.

❑ I check my writing for spelling errors.

❑ When reading, I think about what caused an event to happen.

❑ I can use context clues to help define a new word.

❑ I understand idioms such as "hit the road."

Math

❑ I can solve division problems with and without remainders.

❑ I can use multiplication and division to solve word problems.

❑ I know the order of operations.

❑ I can tell whether or not a shape is symmetrical.

❑ I can identify equivalent fractions and change a fraction into a decimal.

❑ I can use fractions and decimals to solve word problems.

❑ I can tell time using digital and analog clocks.

Final Project

Examine the labels on several packaged snack foods. Focus on the calorie information. Think about how much of the food you would likely eat at one time (which may or may not be similar to the serving size stated on the package). Then, use multiplication and division to find out how many actual servings are in the package and how many calories are in each serving. Create a graph to show the information.

Fourth Quarter Introduction

As the school year nears its end, many students are feeling confident about the new skills they have learned as third graders. This may be evident in more fluent reading of longer stories and books, increased vocabulary, and a greater understanding of fractions and other more abstract math concepts. As the days get warmer and children play outside in the evenings, don't forget to maintain school day routines and continue to support your child's academic growth at home.

Fourth Quarter Skills

Practice pages in this book for Weeks 28–36 will help your child improve the following skills.

Reading and Language Arts
- Sequence story events in a logical order
- Learn the parts of a paragraph
- Find the main idea
- Choose appropriate research materials to answer questions
- Understand fiction and nonfiction texts
- Read, write, and follow directions
- Read maps, graphs, and other visual aids

Math
- Tell time from digital and analog clocks
- Solve problems with money amounts
- Measure length with standard and metric units
- Explore weight and volume
- Find the perimeter of a shape
- Find the area of a shape
- Make and interpret graphs
- Understand scale drawings (maps)

Multi-Sensory Learning Activities

Try these fun activities for enhancing your child's learning and development during the fourth quarter of the school year. Be sure to choose activities that include speaking, listening, touching, and active movement.

 Reading and Language Arts

Have your child write a story that gives directions for finding something in your neighborhood. Include a simple map. Then, take a walk together.

Encourage your child to read a short newspaper, magazine, or online article about a topic that he or she finds interesting. Ask your child to share three details from the article. Then ask, "What main idea do those details support?"

Encourage your child to wonder about how something works. It could be a mobile phone, the human eye, or a procedure used at school. Ask your child to read and research to answer his or her questions and then write a short explanation that includes a visual aid such as a diagram, chart, or time line.

Build stories with your child while riding in the car. You may wish to make up a funny character and create stories about his or her ongoing adventures. Start a story at the beginning, middle, or end. Take turns filling in the gaps.

2 8 4 9 6 Math

Ask your child to estimate how long it takes him or her to get ready for school in the morning. Include eating breakfast, brushing teeth, etc. Have your child draw analog clocks on a poster to show what time he or she should begin each step. Display the poster in your child's bedroom or in the bathroom.

Ask your child to imagine receiving $100 to spend in any way he or she likes. How many items would he or she buy? What is the price of each item? How much money would be left after purchasing each item? Have your child write a long subtraction problem to show the amounts.

Point to an item in the room and ask your child to guess its length in inches, feet, centimeters, or meters. Then, have your child use a ruler to check the guess. How close was it?

Ask your child to measure each wall of a room in your home and find the room's perimeter in feet, yards, and inches. Is it necessary for your child to measure all four walls? Why or why not?

Using the measurements from the previous activity, ask your child to find the area of one room of your home in square feet. Then, have your child research the cost of carpet or other flooring per square foot. How much would it cost to have new flooring installed in the room?

Help your child design a survey to collect data from family members and friends about favorite foods, TV shows, school subject areas, or other topics. After conducting the survey, encourage your child to use software or graph paper to create a graph that shows the results.

Fourth Quarter Introduction, cont.

 **Science**

Rainwater, rivers, and oceans move sand, silt, clay, rock, and soil. These materials settle into layers that can be observed around water and in rocks and mountains. Visit a river or streambed with your child, looking for examples of sediment and layering. Back at home, try this experiment. In a quart jar, mix $\frac{1}{3}$ cup sand, silt, and soil with two teaspoons baking soda and a few pebbles. Add one cup of water, screw on the cover, and shake. Observe the contents of the jar. Draw one picture to show the materials right away and another picture in 15 minutes. Compare the two drawings.

 Social Studies

Invite your child to choose one of these early explorers of the Americas: Christopher Columbus, Amerigo Vespucci, Ponce De Leon, Henry Hudson, Samuel de Champlain, or Hernando De Soto. Help your child research the person's life and discoveries. Then, provide a blank map and encourage your child to use it to show the route of the explorer's journey.

 Seasonal Fun

Gather white flowers such as carnations, mums, or daisies and divide them among several glass jars or vases. Fill each vase with water and add a few drops of food coloring. Watch as the colored water travels up the flower stems and into the flower petals.

Make a fish kite. Glue crepe paper to cover a toilet paper roll. Add crepe paper fins on the body and several long tails to flow from the back. Use a marker to add eyes, or glue on wiggle eyes. Punch two holes on either side toward the front of the roll and thread a piece of string through the holes. Tie the string to a short twig or dowel rod. Have fun running and playing with your kite on a windy day.

Week 28 Skills

Subject	Skill	Multi-Sensory Learning Activities
Reading and Language Arts	Put events in a logical sequence.	• Complete Practice Pages 300–304. • Read *Just Plain Fancy* by Patricia Polacco. Then, have your child write eight events from the story on eight strips of paper. Can he or she put the strips in order and use them to retell the story? • Encourage your child to wonder about how a bee makes honey, how a seed sprouts, how rainwater enters the water cycle, or how something else happens. Help your child research the process and draw or write at least five steps involved.
Math	Tell time using analog clocks; subtract time.	• Complete Practice Pages 305 and 306. • Remind your child that there are 24 hours in one day. Can he or she begin with 24 hours and subtract time spent sleeping, attending school, eating, and doing chores each day? How many hours of free time does your child have in a typical day?
	Count coins and $1, $5, and $10 bills.	• Complete Practice Pages 307 and 308. • Read *Alexander, Who Used to Be Rich Last Sunday* by Judith Viorst. Then, have your child use real or pretend money to model each amount of money that Alex spends.

Sequencing

Read each story. Circle the phrase that tells what happened before.

1. Beth is very happy now that she has someone to play with. She hopes that her new sister will grow up quickly!

   A few days ago . . .
   Beth was sick.
   Beth's mother had a baby.
   Beth got a new puppy.

2. Sara tried to mend the tear. She used a needle and thread to sew up the hole.

   While playing, Sara had . . .
   broken her bicycle.
   lost her watch.
   torn her shirt.

3. The movers took John's bike off the truck and put it in the garage. Next, they moved his bed into his new bedroom.

   John's family . . .
   bought a new house.
   went on vacation.
   bought a new truck.

4. Katie picked out a book about dinosaurs. Jim, who likes sports, chose two books about baseball.

   Katie and Jim . . .
   went to the library.
   went to the playground.
   went to the grocery.

Sequencing

Read each story. Circle the sentence that tells what might happen next.

1. Sam and Judy picked up their books and left the house. They walked to the bus stop. They got on a big yellow bus.

   What will Sam and Judy do next?
   They will go to school.
   They will visit their grandmother.
   They will go to the store.

2. Maggie and Matt were playing in the snow. They made a snowman with a black hat and scarf. Then, the sun came out.

   What might happen next?
   It will snow again.
   They will play in the sandbox.
   The snowman will melt.

3. Megan put on a big floppy hat and funny clothes. She put green make-up on her face.

   What will Megan do next?
   She will go to school.
   She will go to a costume party.
   She will go to bed.

4. Mike was eating a hot dog. Suddenly, he smelled smoke. He turned and saw a fire on the stove.

   What will Mike do next?
   He will watch the fire.
   He will call for help.
   He will finish his hot dog.

Sequencing

Number these sentences from 1 to 5 to show the correct order of the story.

Building a Treehouse

_____ They had a beautiful treehouse!

_____ They got wood and nails.

___1___ Jay and Lisa planned to build a treehouse.

_____ Now, they like to eat lunch in their treehouse.

_____ Lisa and Jay worked in the backyard for three days building the treehouse.

A School Play

_____ Everyone clapped when the curtain closed.

_____ The girl who played Snow White came onto the stage.

_____ All the other school children went to the gym to see the play.

_____ The stage curtain opened.

___1___ The third grade was going to put on a play about Snow White.

Sequencing

Number these sentences from 1 to 8 to show the correct order of the story.

_____ Jack's father called the family doctor.

_____ Jack felt much better as his parents drove him home.

_____ Jack woke up in the middle of the night with a terrible pain in his stomach.

_____ The doctor told Jack's father to take Jack to the hospital.

_____ Jack called his parents to come help him.

_____ At the hospital, the doctors examined Jack. They said the problem was not serious. They told Jack's parents that he could go home.

_____ Jack's mother took his temperature. He had a fever of 103 degrees.

_____ On the way to the hospital, Jack rested in the backseat. He was worried.

Just Swallow It!

Using the diagram, number the sentences in the correct order to show what happens when you swallow a bite of food.

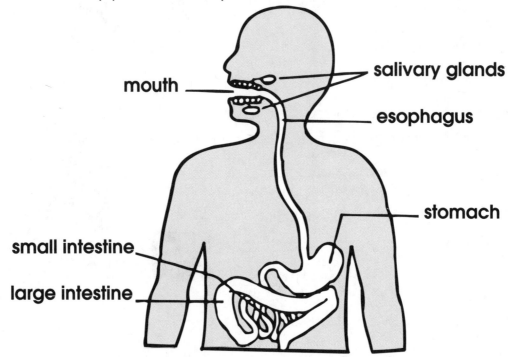

_____ While your teeth are breaking the food into tiny pieces, saliva is making the food softer.

_____ Whatever the body cannot use goes into the large intestine.

_____ While the food is in your stomach, more juices help to dissolve it.

_____ When the food in your mouth is soft enough, you swallow it.

_____ When the food has dissolved in your stomach, it goes to your small intestine.

_____ As you swallow your food, it moves down the esophagus to your stomach.

_____ Use your teeth to take a bite of the sandwich.

_____ While the food is in your small intestine, the body absorbs whatever it needs.

Time: Subtraction

Subtract the hours and minutes.
(Remember, 1 hour equals 60 minutes.)
"Borrow" from the "hours" if you need to.

Example:

$$
\begin{array}{r}
5 \qquad 70 \\
\cancel{6}\text{ hours } \cancel{10}\text{ minutes} \\
-\ 2\text{ hours } 30\text{ minutes} \\
\hline
3\text{ hours } 40\text{ minutes}
\end{array}
$$

12 hours	5 hours	2 hours
- 2 hours	- 3 hours	- 1 hour

5 hours 30 minutes	9 hours 45 minutes	11 hours 50 minutes
- 2 hours 15 minutes	- 3 hours 15 minutes	- 4 hours 35 minutes

12 hours 00 minutes	7 hours 15 minutes	8 hours 10 minutes
- 6 hours 30 minutes	- 5 hours 30 minutes	- 4 hours 40 minutes

Solar Scholars

Write the time.

8:20

_____

_____

_____

_____

_____

_____

_____

_____

_____

_____

_____

Money: Coins and Dollars

dollar = 100¢ or $1.00

 penny =
1¢ or $.01

 nickel =
5¢ or $.05

 dime =
10¢ or $.10

 quarter =
25¢ or $.25

 half-dollar =
50¢ or $.50

Write the amount for each group of money shown. Use a dollar sign and decimal point. The first one is done for you.

 $.07

 _____

 _____

 _____

 _____

 _____

Money: Five-Dollar Bill and Ten-Dollar Bill

Write the amount for each group of money shown. Use a dollar sign and decimal point. The first one is done for you.

Five-dollar bill =
5 one-dollar bills

Ten-dollar bill =
2 five-dollar bills or
10 one-dollar bills

$15.00

_____

_____

_____

7 one-dollar bills, 2 quarters _____

2 five-dollar bills, 3 one-dollar bills, half-dollar _____

3 ten-dollar bills, 1 five-dollar bill, 3 quarters _____

COMPLETE YEAR GRADE 3

Week 29 Skills

Subject	Skill	Multi-Sensory Learning Activities
Reading and Language Arts	Put story events in a logical order.	• Complete Practice Pages 310–314. • After your child watches an episode from a favorite TV show, ask him or her to recall events from the story in order. Invite your child to think about how the outcome of the story might have been different if one of the events changed. Finally, suggest that your child write a summary of a new episode for the TV series that includes a logical series of events.
Math	Add, subtract, and compare money amounts.	• Complete Practice Pages 315–318. • When your child helps you with grocery shopping, challenge him or her to save your family at least $5 by using coupons, switching brands to those on sale, or deciding that some items are not really needed. As you shop, suggest that your child use mental math, scrap paper and pencil, or a calculator to add the cost savings.
Bonus: Social Studies		• Ask your child to create a time line showing the history of the town or city closest to your home. When did Native American tribes live there? When was the town first settled? When was its population counted most recently? Encourage your child to include all these milestones on the time line.

Sequencing: A Story

This is a story from *The McGuffey Second Reader*. This is a very old book your great-great-grandparents may have used to learn to read.

Read the story on pages 310 and 311, then answer the questions on page 312.

The Crow and the Robin

One morning in the early spring, a crow was sitting on the branch of an old oak tree. He felt very ugly and cross and could only say, "Croak! Croak!" Soon, a little robin, who was looking for a place to build her nest, came with a merry song into the same tree. "Good morning to you," she said to the crow.

But the crow made no answer; he only looked at the clouds and croaked something about the cold wind. "I said, 'Good morning to you,'" said the robin, jumping from branch to branch.

"I wonder how you can be so merry this morning," croaked the crow.

"Why shouldn't I be merry?" asked the robin. "Spring has come and everyone ought to be happy."

"I am not happy," said the crow. "Don't you see those black clouds above us? It is going to snow."

"Very well," said the robin, "I shall keep on singing until the snow comes. A merry song will not make it any colder."

"Caw, caw, caw," croaked the crow. "I think you are very foolish."

Sequencing: A Story

The Crow and the Robin

The robin flew to another tree and kept on singing, but the crow sat still and made himself very unhappy. "The wind is so cold," he said. "It always blows the wrong way for me."

Very soon the sun came out, warm and bright, and the clouds went away, but the crow was as cross as ever.

The grass began to spring up in the meadows. Green leaves and flowers were seen in the woods. Birds and bees flew here and there in the glad sunshine. The crow sat and croaked on the branch of the old oak tree.

"It is always too warm or too cold," said he. "To be sure, it is a little pleasant just now, but I know that the sun will soon shine warm enough to burn me up. Then before night, it will be colder than ever. I do not see how anyone can sing at such a time as this."

Just then the robin came back to the tree with a straw in her mouth for her nest. "Well, my friend," asked she, "where is your snow?"

"Don't talk about that," croaked the crow. "It will snow all the harder for this sunshine."

"And snow or shine," said the robin, "you will keep on croaking. For my part, I shall always look on the bright side of things and have a song for every day in the year."

Which will you be like—the crow or the robin?_____

Sequencing: The Story

These sentences retell the story of "The Crow and the Robin" but are out of order.

Write the numbers **1** through **10** on the lines to show the correct sequence. The first one has been done for you.

___ Although the sun came out and the clouds went away, the crow was still as cross as ever.

___ "I shall always . . . have a song for every day in the year," said the robin.

1 The crow sat on the branch of an old oak tree and could only say, "Croak, Croak!"

___ "This wind is so cold. It always blows the wrong way," the crow said.

___ The crow said, "It is going to snow."

___ The robin said good morning to the crow.

___ The crow told the robin that he thought she was very foolish.

___ The grass began to spring up in the meadows.

___ The robin was jumping from branch to branch as she talked to the crow.

___ The robin came back with straw in her mouth for her nest.

Order in the Story!

Wilbur wants to make sure that you never forget how Charlotte spins the TERRIFIC web. Number the boxes in the order Charlotte might spin the letters.

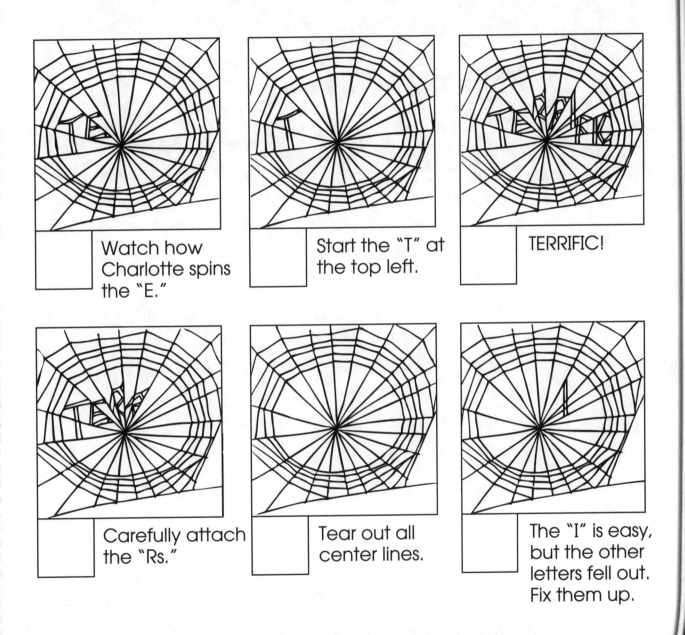

Watch how Charlotte spins the "E."

Start the "T" at the top left.

TERRIFIC!

Carefully attach the "Rs."

Tear out all center lines.

The "I" is easy, but the other letters fell out. Fix them up.

Create your own web! First, design a web using a pencil and paper. Use your own name or any fun word. Dribble white glue lines, one at a time, over the pencil design. Quickly lay pieces of yarn on the glue lines.

Waterworks

Use the diagram to help you number the sentences in the order that tells how water is purified.

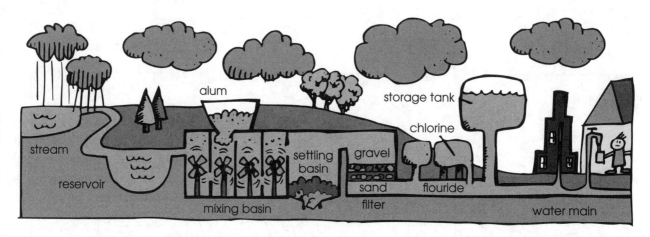

____ Smaller pipes carry the water to the faucets in our homes.

____ As the water flows to the filter, the alum and dirt sink to the bottom of the settling basin.

____ The water in the reservoir goes through a large pipe into a mixing basin.

____ Now that the water is as clean as possible, it is stored in a huge storage tank.

____ First, raindrops fall into streams, lakes and rivers.

____ Water leaves the storage tank through water mains.

____ A chemical called alum is added to take the dirt out of the water.

____ Turn the faucet handle and you have water.

____ The clear, filtered water passes through a pipe where fluoride and chlorine are added.

____ Then, the streams and rivers flow into a reservoir.

____ Smaller pipes carry the water from the water main to our homes.

Money: Counting Change

Subtract the money using decimals to show how much change a person would receive in each of the following.

Example:
Bill had 3 dollars.
He bought a baseball for $2.83.
How much change did he receive?

$3.00
-$2.83
$0.17

Paid 2 dollars.

_____

Paid 1 dollar.

_____

Paid 5 dollars.

_____

Paid 10 dollars.

_____

Paid 4 dollars.

_____

Paid 7 dollars.

_____

Money: Comparing

Compare the amount of money in the left column with the price of the object in the right column. Is the amount of money in the left column enough to purchase the object in the right column? Circle yes or no.

Example:

Alice has 2 dollars. She wants to buy a jump rope for $1.75. Does she have enough money?

(Yes) No

       Yes No

      Yes No

       Yes No

Review

Complete each clock to show the time written below it.

7:15

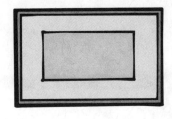
3:07

6:25

Write the time using a.m. or p.m.

seven twenty-two in the evening _____

three fifteen in the morning _____

eight thirty at night _____

Write the correct amount of money.

_____

_____

 Joey paid $4.67 for a model car. He gave the clerk a five-dollar bill. How much change should he receive? _____

Your Answer's Safe With Me

Find the right "combination" to open each safe. Draw the bills and coins needed to make each amount.

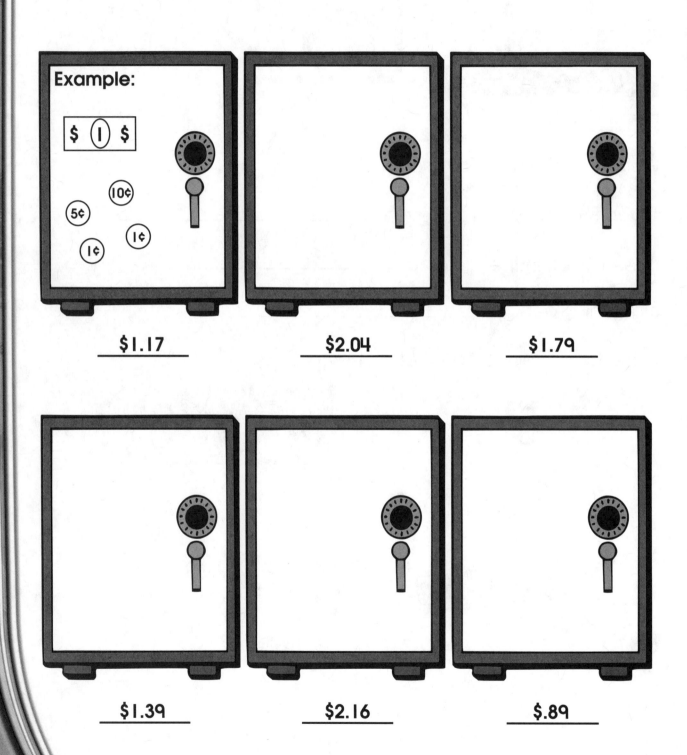

Example:

$1.17

$2.04

$1.79

$1.39

$2.16

$.89

Week 30 Skills

Subject	Skill	Multi-Sensory Learning Activities
Reading and Language Arts	Understand the parts of a paragraph.	• Complete Practice Pages 320–325. • Photocopy a paragraph from a science or social studies textbook, a newspaper or magazine article, or a nonfiction book. After reading the paragraph, can your child underline the topic sentence, number each supporting detail, and underline the concluding sentence? • When your child expresses an opinion about what he or she wants to do, eat, watch on TV, etc., say, "Give me three." Then, your child must stop and give you three good reasons to support his or her opinion.
Math	Solve problems with money amounts.	• Complete Practice Pages 327–328. • Help your child search online to find a restaurant menu that includes prices. Then, give several math challenges to be solved with the menu. For example, ask your child to come up with a lunch order for two people that is under $15 or to create a dinner order for one person that is more than $50.
Bonus: Science		• The pupil is an opening that lets light into the eye. Have your child cover his or her eyes for two minutes, uncover them, and observe the pupils in a mirror. Then, have your child gaze at a light for one minute and look at the pupils again. What changed? Why?

Parts of a Paragraph

A **paragraph** is a group of sentences that all tell about the same thing. Most paragraphs have three parts: a **beginning**, a **middle** and an **end**.

Write **beginning**, **middle** or **end** next to each sentence in the scrambled paragraphs below. There can be more than one middle sentence.

Example:

___middle___ We took the tire off the car.

___beginning___ On the way to Aunt Louise's, we had a flat tire.

___middle___ We patched the hole in the tire.

___end___ We put the tire on and started driving again.

_____ I took all the ingredients out of the cupboard.

_____ One morning, I decided to bake a pumpkin pie.

_____ I forgot to add the pumpkin!

_____ I mixed the ingredients together, but something was missing.

_____ The sun was very hot and our throats were dry.

_____ We finally decided to turn back.

_____ We started our hike very early in the morning.

_____ It kept getting hotter as we walked.

Topic Sentences

A **topic sentence** is usually the first sentence in a paragraph. It tells what the story will be about.

Read the following sentences. Circle the topic sentence that should go first in the paragraph that follows.

Rainbows have seven colors.

There's a pot of gold.

I like rainbows.

The colors are red, orange, yellow, green, blue, indigo and violet. Red forms the outer edge, with violet on the inside of the rainbow.

He cut down a cherry tree.

His wife was named Martha.

George Washington was a good president.

He helped our country get started. He chose intelligent leaders to help him run the country.

Mark Twain was a great author.

Mark Twain was unhappy sometimes.

Mark Twain was born in Missouri.

One of his most famous books is *Huckleberry Finn*. He wrote many other great books.

Middle Sentences

Middle sentences support the topic sentence. They tell more about it. Underline the middle sentences that support each topic sentence below.

Topic Sentence:

Penguins are birds that cannot fly.

Pelicans can spear fish with their sharp bills.

Many penguins waddle or hop about on land.

Even though they cannot fly, they are excellent swimmers.

Pelicans keep their food in a pouch.

Topic Sentence:

Volleyball is a team sport in which the players hit the ball over the net.

There are two teams with six players on each team.

My friend John would rather play tennis with Lisa.

Players can use their heads or their hands.

I broke my hand once playing handball.

Topic Sentence:

Pikes Peak is the most famous of all the Rocky Mountains.

Some mountains have more trees than other mountains.

Many people like to climb to the top.

Many people like to ski and camp there, too.

The weather is colder at the top of most mountains.

Ending Sentences

Ending sentences are sentences that tie the story together.

Choose the correct ending sentence for each story from the sentences below. Write it at the end of the paragraph.

I got a new pair of shoes!
I got all the corn on the cob I could eat!
I got a new eraser!

Corn on the Cob

Corn on the cob used to be my favorite food. That is, until I lost my four front teeth. For one whole year, I had to sit and watch everyone else eat my favorite food without me. Mom gave me creamed corn, but it just wasn't the same. When my teeth finally came in, Dad said he had a surprise for me. I thought I was going to get a bike or a new MP3 player or something. I was just as happy to get what I did.

_____

I would like to take a train ride every year.
Trains move faster than I thought they would.
She had brought her new gerbil along for the ride.

A Train Ride

When our family took its first train ride, my sister brought along a big box. She would not tell anyone what she had in it. In the middle of the trip, we heard a sound coming from the box. "Okay, Jan, now you have to open the box," said Mom. When she opened the box, we were surprised.

_____

What's It All About?

Underline the **topic sentence**—the sentence that most completely tells what the paragraph is all about—in each paragraph. Then, **write** two phrases that are **supporting details**—sentences that explain or tell about the topic sentence.

1. Rabbits like to live together in a group. They dig their burrows like underground apartments where they will always have lots of neighbors. They help each other take care of the young. When the weather turns cold, they snuggle up together to keep each other warm.

   Supporting detail: _____

   _____

   Supporting detail: _____

   _____

2. Rahm and Silla scratched a hole in the sandy wall of the burrow with their front feet. Then, they used their back feet to push the loose ground back into the tunnel. Silla smoothed down the walls and then pulled wool out of her fur to line the floor. They both worked hard to prepare a nursery for the babies who were soon to be born.

   Supporting detail: _____

   _____

   Supporting detail: _____

   _____

3. It happened exactly as Silla said it would. She gave birth to seven beautiful, healthy rabbits at the next full moon. The kits had small mouse-like ears and were completely deaf. Their eyes were closed tight, and they couldn't see a thing. Their bodies were bare and they needed the warmth provided by the nest their mother had prepared.

   Supporting detail: _____

   _____

   Supporting detail: _____

   _____

Add Ons

Cut out these puzzle pieces and fit them together. Glue them on a separate sheet of paper. When correctly placed, the three topic sentences (*) will be on top and the supporting sentences for each will be listed below.

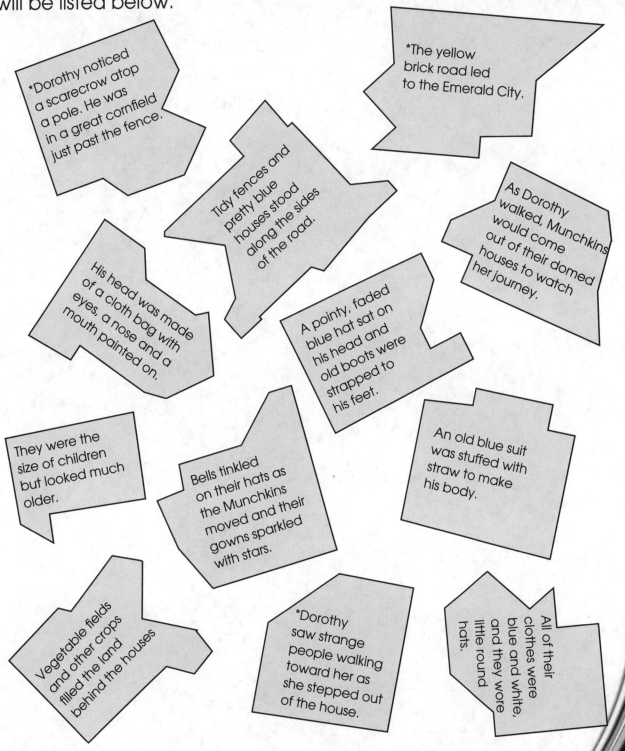

*Dorothy noticed a scarecrow atop a pole. He was in a great cornfield just past the fence.

*The yellow brick road led to the Emerald City.

Tidy fences and pretty blue houses stood along the sides of the road.

As Dorothy walked, Munchkins would come out of their domed houses to watch her journey.

His head was made of a cloth bag with eyes, a nose and a mouth painted on.

A pointy, faded blue hat sat on his head and old boots were strapped to his feet.

They were the size of children but looked much older.

Bells tinkled on their hats as the Munchkins moved and their gowns sparkled with stars.

An old blue suit was stuffed with straw to make his body.

Vegetable fields and other crops filled the land behind the houses

*Dorothy saw strange people walking toward her as she stepped out of the house.

All of their clothes were blue and white, and they wore little round hats.

Pizza "Dough" Business

The number of pieces tells you how many coins to use. Write in the amounts to equal the total price of these pizzas.

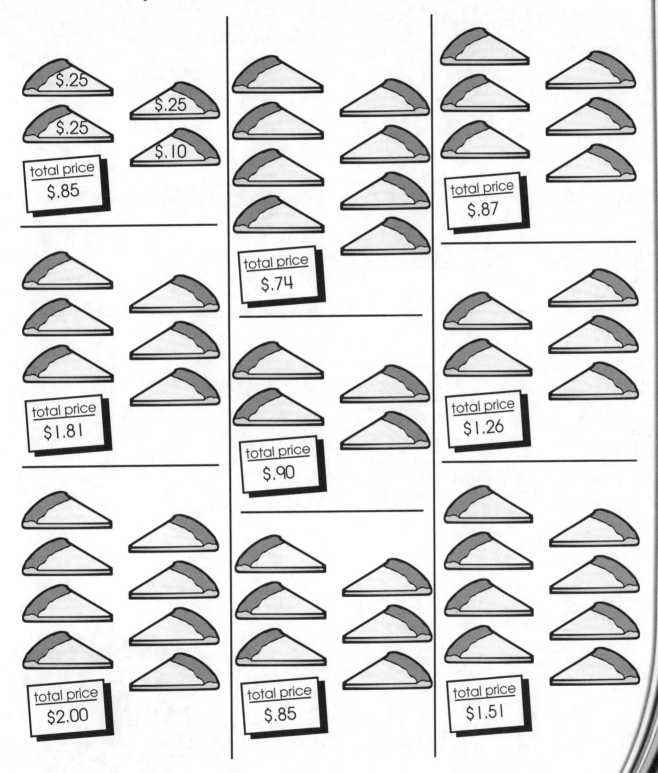

Monetary Message

What's the smartest thing to do with your money? To find out, use the key at the bottom of the page to match the letters with the sums in the blanks provided.

$\overline{\text{\$42.71}}$ $\overline{\text{\$33.94}}$ $\overline{\text{\$50.42}}$ $\overline{\text{\$100.73}}$ $\overline{\text{\$45.70}}$ $\overline{\text{\$2.39}}$,

$\overline{\text{\$33.94}}$ $\overline{\text{\$26.13}}$ $\overline{\text{\$88.02}}$ $\overline{\text{\$45.70}}$ $\overline{\text{\$2.39}}$ $\overline{\text{\$51.12}}$ $\overline{\text{\$45.70}}$ $\overline{\text{\$11.01}}$ $\overline{\text{\$11.01}}$

$\overline{\text{\$33.94}}$ $\overline{\text{\$88.02}}$ $\overline{\text{\$88.02}}$ $\overline{\text{\$55.76}}$ $\overline{\text{\$42.79}}$!

$$V = \begin{array}{r} \$42.13 \\ +\ 8.29 \\ \hline \end{array}$$

$$A = \begin{array}{r} \$\ 4.56 \\ +\ 29.38 \\ \hline \end{array}$$

$$N = \begin{array}{r} \$\ 4.65 \\ +\ 21.48 \\ \hline \end{array}$$

$$P = \begin{array}{r} \$\ 9.31 \\ +\ 33.48 \\ \hline \end{array}$$

$$L = \begin{array}{r} \$\ 6.73 \\ +\ 4.28 \\ \hline \end{array}$$

$$E = \begin{array}{r} \$81.49 \\ +\ 19.24 \\ \hline \end{array}$$

$$U = \begin{array}{r} \$50.84 \\ +\ 4.92 \\ \hline \end{array}$$

$$I = \begin{array}{r} \$\ 7.49 \\ +\ 38.21 \\ \hline \end{array}$$

$$S = \begin{array}{r} \$23.46 \\ +\ 19.25 \\ \hline \end{array}$$

$$D = \begin{array}{r} \$\ 3.04 \\ +\ 84.98 \\ \hline \end{array}$$

$$W = \begin{array}{r} \$\ 1.89 \\ +\ 49.23 \\ \hline \end{array}$$

$$T = \begin{array}{r} \$\ .42 \\ 1.94 \\ +\ .03 \\ \hline \end{array}$$

Week 31 Skills

Subject	Skill	Multi-Sensory Learning Activities
Reading and Language Arts	Use context clues to complete a story.	• Complete Practice Page 330. • Have your child use a dictionary to look up a new word such as **prudent**. Then, he or she should write a sentence using the word. Look at the sentence together to find context clues to the word's meaning.
	Find the main idea.	• Complete Practice Pages 331–333. • Have your child search for and examine an image of the painting *Washington Crossing the Delaware* by Emanuel Gottlieb Leutze. Challenge him or her to write a main idea for the image along with three supporting details.
	Choose the best reference works to answer questions.	• Complete Practice Page 334. • Brainstorm with your child different reference works available in your home, such as a dictionary, atlas, calendar, online encyclopedia, or nonfiction books. Talk about times when family members use these resources to help answer questions.
Math	Use money amounts to solve problems, including word problems.	• Complete Practice Pages 335–338. • Put different amounts of real or pretend money in several envelopes. On the front of each, tape a picture of an item from a catalog along with its price. Ask your child to determine how much change would be received if the item shown on each envelope were paid for with the amount of money inside.

Completing a Story

Use verbs to complete the story below. The verbs that tell about things that happened in the past will end in **ed**.

Last week, Amy and I _____ a contest. We were supposed to make a card to give to a child in a hospital. First, we _____ a big sheet of white paper in half to make the card. Then we _____ to draw a rainbow on the front. Amy started coloring the rainbow all by herself.

"Wait!" I said. "We both _____ the contest. Let me help!"

"Okay," Amy said. "Let's _____. You _____ a color, and then I'll _____ a color." It was more fun when we _____. When we finished making the rainbow, we _____ to _____ a sun to the picture. I cut one out of yellow paper. Then Amy _____ it just above the rainbow. Well, our card didn't win the contest, but it did make a little boy with a broken leg smile. Amy and I felt so happy! We _____ to go right home and make some more cards!

It's Major

For each paragraph, circle the sentence that tells the main idea. Underline the sentences with supporting details.

Chapter 1
Just before breakfast one day, Fern saved a pig from being killed and ended up making a new friend. She shouted at her mother and ran outdoors to her father. Though Fern did not understand barnyard life, her father gave her the pig as a pet. She named him Wilbur.

Chapter 2
Fern began caring for Wilbur every day. He would gaze at her with loving eyes as she fed him the bottle. Mr. Arable fixed a special box under an apple tree for Wilbur. Each day Wilbur walked Fern to the bus and stayed in the yard while she was at school.

Chapter 3
Wilbur started to meet other animals in the barnyard. The goose suggested he explore the farm. So he escaped from the barnyard for an afternoon of adventure. He ran, dug up ground and sniffed the afternoon smells. Soon, all the adults on the farm started chasing after Wilbur.

Chapter 5
Charlotte finally introduced herself to Wilbur. She talked to him through his dreams. In the morning, after breakfast, Wilbur located Charlotte. He was eager to know all about her. Wilbur was amazed at how smart Charlotte was.

Main Idea: Your Lungs

Imagine millions of teeny, tiny balloons joined together. That is what your lungs are like. When you breathe, the air goes to your two lungs. One lung is located on each side of your chest. The heart is located between the two lungs. The lungs are soft, spongy and delicate. That is why there are bones around the lungs. These bones are called the rib cage. The rib cage protects the lungs so they can do their job. The lungs bring oxygen (ox-i-gin) into the body. They also take waste out of the body. This waste is called carbon dioxide. We could not live without our lungs!

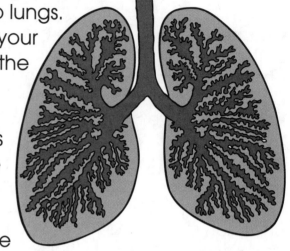

Answer these questions about your lungs.

1. Circle the main idea:

   The lungs are spongy and located in the chest. They are like small balloons.

   The lungs bring in oxygen and take out carbon dioxide. We could not live without our lungs.

2. What is the name of the bones around your lungs?

   _____

3. What is located between the lungs?

   _____

4. What goes into your lungs when you breathe?

   _____

5. Why are there bones around your lungs?

   _____

Main Idea: Venus

For many years, no one knew much about Venus. When people looked through telescopes, they could not see past Venus's clouds. Long ago, people thought the clouds covered living things. Spacecraft radar has shown this is not true. Venus is too hot for life as we know it to exist. The temperature on Venus is about 900 degrees! Remember how hot you were the last time it was 90 degrees? Now imagine it being 10 times hotter. Nothing could exist in that heat. It is also very dry on Venus. For life to exist, water must be present. Because of the heat and dryness, we know there are probably no people, plants or other life on Venus.

Answer these questions about Venus.

1. Circle the main idea:

    We cannot see past Venus's clouds to know what the planet is like.

    Spacecraft radar shows it is too hot and dry for life to exist on Venus.

2. What is the temperature on Venus? _____

3. This temperature is how many times hotter than a hot day on Earth?

    6 times hotter

    10 times hotter

4. In the past, why did people think life might exist on Venus?

    _____

    _____

References — Bat Research

Lucille the bat is always looking up information in reference books because she loves to learn new things. Below is a list of some common references.

1. Atlas
2. Card Catalog
3. Dictionary
4. Encyclopedia
5. Newspaper
6. Telephone Directory
7. Who's Who
8. World Almanac

Help Lucille match the topics below with the reference material where she is most likely to find the information.

1. Area codes and phone numbers _____

2. The subject of a book _____

3. The correct pronunciation of the word "radar" _____

4. Different types of bats _____

5. The weather forecast for the next year _____

6. The life story of a famous bat leader _____

7. A certain bat's address _____

8. A map of Transylvania _____

9. Her bat horoscope _____

10. How many full moons for the year _____

11. The definition of the word "cave" _____

12. The author and title of a book _____

13. Batball and soccer scores _____

14. Batman's birthday _____

Making Change

When you do not have the exact change to buy something at a store, the clerk must give you change. The first amount of money is what you give the clerk. The second amount is what the thing costs. In the box, list the least amount of coins and bills you will receive in change.

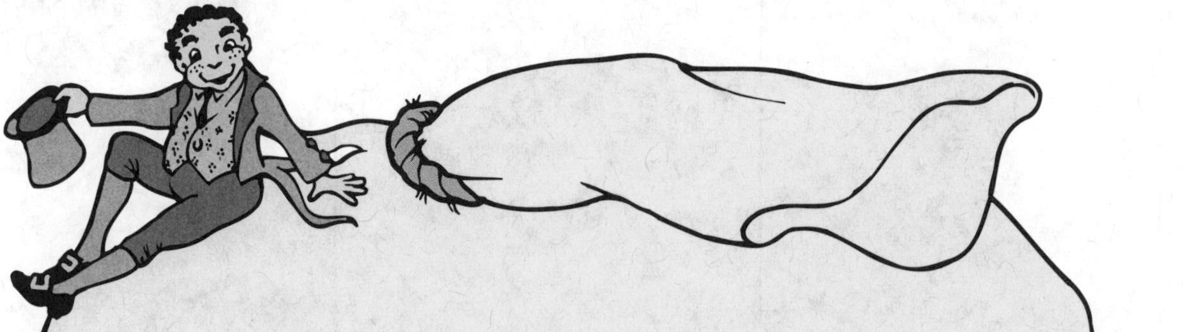

	Amount I Have	Cost of Item	Change
1	$3.75	$3.54	
2	$10.00	$5.63	
3	$7.00	$6.05	
4	$7.25	$6.50	
5	$7.50	$6.13	
6	$0.75	$0.37	
7	$7.00	$6.99	
8	$15.00	$12.75	

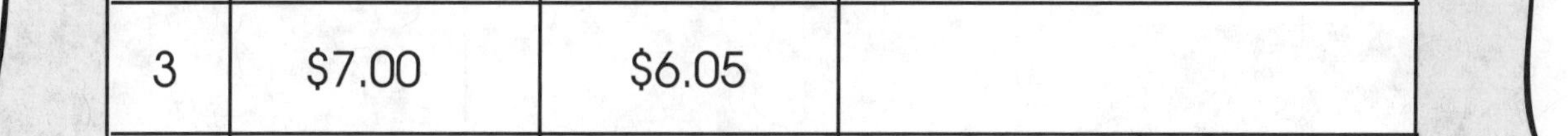

How Many Coins?

Draw the fewest coins possible to equal the amount shown in each box.

17¢

98¢

24¢

63¢

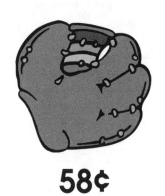

58¢

35¢

Review

Read and solve each of the problems.

The baker sets out 9 baking pans with 6 rolls on each one.
How many rolls are there in all? _____

A dozen brownies cost $1.29. James pays for a dozen
brownies with a five-dollar bill. How much change does
he receive? _____

Theresa has four quarters, a nickel and three pennies. How
much more money does she need to buy brownies? _____

The baker made 24 loaves of bread. At the end of the day,
he has one-fourth left. How many did he sell? _____

Two loaves of bread weigh a pound. How many loaves
are needed to make five pounds? _____

The bakery opens at 8:30 a.m. It closes nine and a half
hours later. What time does it close? _____

Mind-Bogglers

These problems will boggle your mind. Don't give up. Try different problem-solving strategies to help you find the answers.

1. Marta receives an allowance of $2.25 a week. This week, her mom pays her in nickels, dimes and quarters. She received more dimes than quarters. What coins did her mom use to pay her? _____
Strategy I used _____

2. Your dad wants to deposit money in his bank account. The bank is a very busy place. He has to stand in line. There are 6 people in front of him and 8 people behind him. How many people are standing in line? _____
Strategy I used _____

3. A jogger can jog 1 mile in 12 minutes. He jogged for 30 minutes today. How far did he jog? _____
Strategy I used _____

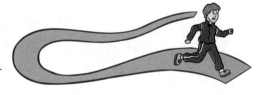

4. Your parents are trying to save money to buy something very special. If they save $2 in January, $4 in February, $8 in March, and so on, how much money will they save in a year? _____
Strategy I used _____

COMPLETE YEAR GRADE 3

Week 32 Skills

Subject	Skill	Multi-Sensory Learning Activities
Reading and Language Arts	Understand nonfiction texts.	• Complete Practice Pages 340–344. • Encourage your child to read a wide variety of nonfiction texts, including books and articles, related to his or her interests. You may wish to ask a children's librarian to explain how nonfiction books are classified and arranged at your local library. Before reading a nonfiction text, ask your child to think about what he or she already knows about the topic and what questions he or she would like to have answered.
Math	Measure length in inches.	• Complete Practice Pages 345 and 346. • Help your child measure a body part, such as a hand or forearm, to gain an understanding of how long an inch really is. Periodically, name a measurement in inches, such as three inches, and ask your child to look around for something about that length. Confirm the estimate by measuring with a ruler.
	Measure length in centimeters.	• Complete Practice Pages 347 and 348. • Make sure your child has access to a ruler with centimeter markings. Ask your child to measure the length of several small items, such as coins or pieces of candy, in both inches and centimeters and ask which unit was more precise and convenient to use.

What Kind of Community?

Read the definitions of three different types of communities below.

Rural Community	Urban Community	Suburban Community
country; large amount of open space; mostly farm land and woods.	big city or town; often at least 50,000 people; crowded with buildings and people; business center.	largely residential; often near a large city.

Read the sentences. Underline only the sentences that describe your community. Then, answer this: In what kind of a community do you live?

1. All that can be seen from a rooftop is land criss-crossed by dirt roads and fences.

2. People may sometimes wake their neighbors if they mow their lawns too early in the morning.

3. There is a feeling of open space, and yet there are shopping malls, supermarkets, schools, etc., nearby.

4. The sounds of elevated trains and honking horns are heard almost twenty-four hours a day.

5. Many people who work in the city live here because it is quieter, and the commute to the city every day is not too long.

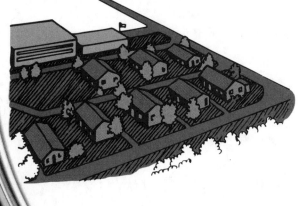

6. During the summer, neighborhood children set up lemonade stands, and families have picnics and barbecues in their backyards.

7. Homes are very close together. Many are stacked one on top of one another in buildings called apartments.

What Kind of Community?

8. Streets and sidewalks are crowded with workers going to and from work and shoppers looking in storefront windows.

9. Many people work at farming.

10. Mailboxes are often very far from the houses.

11. Neighbors are often miles apart.

12. It is on the outskirts of a city.

13. Residents of the community seldom see one another, so a dinner and dance at someone's barn is a real social event.

14. Hotels provide a place for visitors who come for meetings at the convention center.

15. The population is over 50,000.

16. The high school's students come from several outlying communities and must ride the bus because distances are great.

17. Nights are quiet except for the occasional sound of an animal.

18. Children play in parks rather than in backyards.

19. There is a feeling of country with the conveniences of a city.

Yum-Yum

Without the sense of taste, many things in life would not be as pleasant. What would it be like if all of your favorite foods had no taste at all?

Your sense of taste is found mainly in the tiny tastebuds on your tongue. To taste food, it must be chewed and mixed with saliva. The taste message is sent to the brain by nerves.

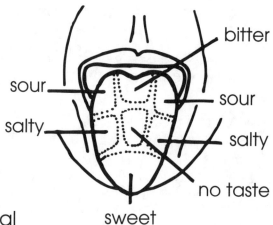

Each of the four tastes has a special center on the tongue. In each center, one of the main tastes is tasted more strongly.

1. Look at the map of the tongue. **List** the four main tastes. Next to each taste, **write** a food that is tasted in that taste center.

Taste _____   Food _____

_____   _____

_____   _____

_____   _____

2. Which taste center tastes an ice-cream cone?_____

3. Why is it more enjoyable to lick an ice-cream cone with the tip of your tongue? _____

Something Special

Where will each of these foods be tasted most strongly? Draw a line from the symbol for each food to its taste center on the tongue.

candy

vinegar

saltine cracker

lemon

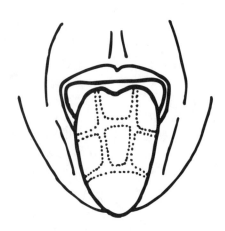

Labels

Labels give us all kinds of information about the foods we eat. The ingredients of a food are listed in a special order. The ingredient with the largest amount is listed first, the one with the next largest amount is listed second, and so on.

Complete the "Breakfast Table Label Survey" using information from the cereal label on this page.

Breakfast Table Label Survey

1. What does R.D.A. mean?

   _____

2. Calories per serving with milk

   _____

3. Calories per serving without milk

   _____

4. Calories per $\frac{1}{2}$ cup serving of milk

   _____

5. Protein per serving with milk

   _____

6. Protein per serving without milk

   _____

7. Protein in $\frac{1}{2}$ cup serving of milk

   _____

8. Percentage U.S. R.D.A. of Vitamin C

   _____

9. First ingredient

   _____

10. In what place is sugar listed?

    _____

Nutrition Information Per Serving

Serving size: 1 oz. (About $\frac{1}{3}$ Cup) (28.35 g)

Servings Per Package: 14

	1 oz. (28.35 g) Cereal	with $\frac{1}{2}$ Cup (118mL) Vitamin D Fortified Whole Milk
Calories	110	190
Protein	1 g	5 g
Carbohydrate	25 g	31 g
Fat	1 g	5 g
Sodium	195 mg	255 mg

Percentages Of U.S. Recommended Daily Allowances (U.S. RDA)

Protein	2%	8%
Vitamin A	25%	30%
Vitamin C	*	*
Thiamine	25%	30%
Riboflavin	25%	35%
Niacin	25%	25%
Calcium	*	15%
Iron	10%	10%
Vitamin D	10%	25%
Vitamin B$_6$	25%	30%
Folic Acid	25%	25%
Vitamin B$_{12}$	25%	30%
Phosphorus	2%	10%
Magnesium	2%	6%
Zinc	10%	15%
Copper	2%	4%

*Contains less than 2% of the U.S. RDA for these nutrients.

Ingredients: Corn Flour, Sugar, Oat Flour, Salt, Hydrogenated Coconut and/or Palm Kernel Oil, Corn Syrup, Honey and Fortified with the following nutrients: Vitamin A, Palmitate, Niacinamide, Iron, Zinc Oxide (Source of Zinc), Vitamin B$_6$, Riboflavin (Vitamin B$_2$), Thiamine Mononitrate (Vitamin B$_1$), Vitamin B$_{12}$ Folic Acid and Vitamin D$_2$. BHA added to packaging material to preserve freshness.

Carbohydrate Information

	1 oz. (28.35 g) Cereal	with $\frac{1}{2}$ Cup (118 mL) Whole Milk
Starch and related carbohydrates	14 g	14 g
Sucrose and other sugars	11 g	17 g
Total carbohydrates	25 g	31 g

Framework

What gives you your **shape**? Like a house's frame, your body also has a frame. It is called your skeleton. Your **skeleton** is made of more than two hundred bones.

Your skeleton helps your body move. It does this by giving your **muscles** a place to attach. Your skeleton also **protects** the soft organs inside your body from injury.

Bones have a hard, outer layer made of **calcium**. Inside each bone is a soft, **spongy** layer that looks like a honeycomb. The hollow spaces in the honeycomb are filled with **marrow**. Every minute, millions of **blood** cells die. But the bone marrow works like a little factory, making new blood cells.

Use the words in **bold** to finish the sentences.

1. Your skeleton __ __ __ __ __ __ __ __ your soft organs.
                      5

2. Bone __ __ __ __ __ __ makes new blood cells.
         2

3. Inside the bone is a soft, __ __ __ __ __ __ layer.
                                3

4. Millions of __ __ __ __ __ cells die every minute.
               4

5. The hard outer layer of bone is made from __ __ __ __ __ __ __.
                                              1

6. There are more than two hundred bones in your __ __ __ __ __ __ __ __.
                                                                        6

7. Your skeleton is a place for __ __ __ __ __ __ __ to attach.
                                              7

8. Your skeleton gives your body its __ __ __ __ __.
                                      8

Something Special
Use the numbered letters above to solve the riddle.
What do you call a skeleton that won't get out of bed?

__ __ __z__ __ __ __ __ __ __
 1 2   3   4 5 6 7 8

Measuring Length

Using a yardstick, measure and write the following lengths.
Remember to label inches, feet or yards.

1. How long is the biggest step you can take? _____

2. How far can your favorite paper airplane fly? _____

3. From start to finish, how much distance is covered when you do a
   somersault? _____

4. How far can you throw a feather? _____

5. How wide is your driveway? _____

6. How far you can walk balancing a book on your head? _____

7. How high can you stack wooden blocks before they fall over?

   _____

8. How high can you jump (measure against the wall)? _____

9. What is the distance you can hit a softball? _____

10. How much distance is covered if you skip 10 times? _____

11. How far can you jump (start with your feet together)? _____

Measurement: Inches

An inch is a unit of length in the standard measurement system.

Use a ruler to measure each object to the nearest $\frac{1}{4}$ inch.
Write **in.** to stand for inch.

Example:

1 in.

$2\frac{1}{2}$ in.

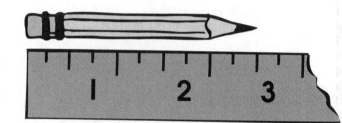

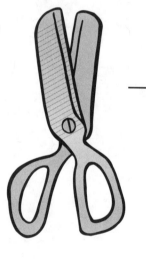

_____

_____

_____

_____   _____

Sawing Logs

Measure the logs to the nearest centimeter.

Example:

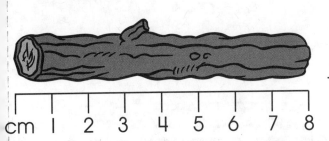

8 cm

cm 1 2 3 4 5 6 7 8

_____

_____

_____

_____

_____

_____

Measurement: Centimeter

A centimeter is a unit of length in the metric system. There are 2.54 centimeters in an inch.

Use a centimeter ruler to measure each object to the nearest half of a centimeter. Write **cm** to stand for centimeter.

Example:

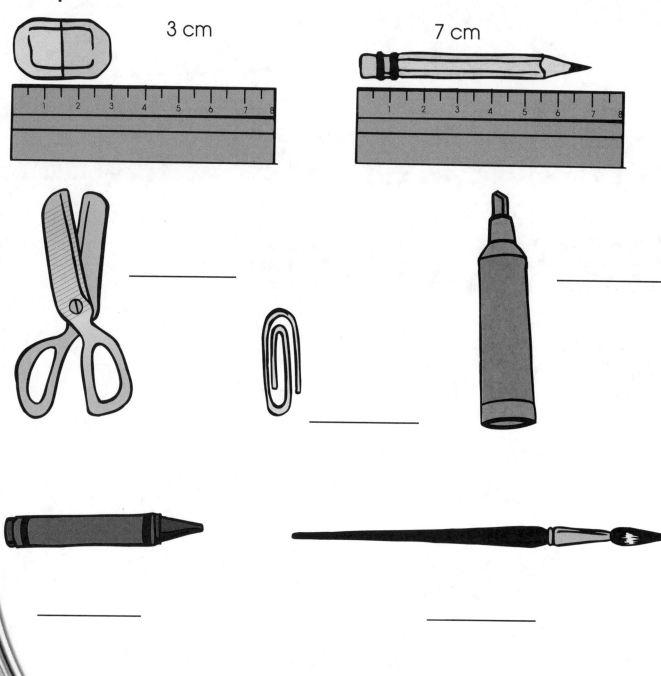

3 cm

7 cm

Week 33 Skills

Subject	Skill	Multi-Sensory Learning Activities
Reading and Language Arts	Understand nonfiction texts.	• Complete Practice Pages 350–354. • Is your child interested in sports, horses, shipwrecks, or robots? Find a nonfiction article about whatever interests your child. Encourage your child to read it, talk about what he or she liked best, and then create a related diagram, map, chart, time line, or other visual aid.
Math	Measure distances using feet, yards, and miles.	• Complete Practice Page 355. • Help your child make a scale drawing to show places that are 100 feet, 100 yards, and 100 miles away from your home.
	Measure distances using meters and kilometers.	• Complete Practice Page 356. • Has your child ever run a 100-meter dash? Ask him or her to convert 100 meters into centimeters, kilometers, inches, feet, yards, and miles.
	Explore volume.	• Complete Practice Page 357. • Ask your child to check food packages in your kitchen for measurements of volume given in milliliters or liters. How many liters does your child think your kitchen sink will hold? Test to find out.
	Explore weight.	• Complete Practice Page 358. • Have your child experiment with a bathroom scale and cans of food or other products whose weight is given in ounces. How many ounces make one pound? Five pounds?

Windows

"Oh, what beautiful brown eyes you have!" Whether you know it or not, those eyes are not totally brown. Only the **iris** is colored brown.

Your eye is shaped like a ball. It has a clear, round window in front called the **cornea**. The colored iris controls the amount of light that enters the eye. Light enters through an opening called the **pupil**. In bright light, your pupil is a small dot. In dim light, it is much larger. Behind the pupil is the **lens**. It focuses the light onto the back wall of your eye. This back wall is called the retina. The retina changes the light into nerve messages. These messages are sent to the brain along the **optic nerve**. Close your eyes. Gently touch them. They are firm because they are filled with a clear jelly called **vitreous humor**.

Label the parts of the eye using the words in bold from above.

What am I?

I focus the light. __ __ __ __
                   2   4

I become smaller in bright light. __ __ __ __ __
                                  11   1

I am the clear window. __ __ __ __ __ __
                          3   6

I am the colored part of the eye. __ __ __ __
                                      10

I send pictures to the brain. __ __ __ __ __ __ __ __ __ __
                                 12 5   7

I am the clear jelly. __ __ __ __ __ __ __ __ __ __ __ __
                               9 13 8

Use the numbered letters to solve the riddle. *What did the teacher say when his glass eye went down the drain?*

__ __ __ __ __   __ __ __ __ __ __ __   __ __ __ __ __ !
1   2 3 4 5   6 7 3 5 8 9 10   11 13 12 1 2

Tortillas, Anyone?

Juan lives in Mexico. The main food crop grown there is corn. Even though it is grown on half of Mexico's cultivated land, corn is still imported because the demand for it is so high. Since ancient times, corn has been used to make flat pancakes called **tortillas**. Sometimes they are folded and stuffed with different foods to make tacos. Throughout Mexico, you will see stands on the street serving tortillas and tacos. Juan's mother folds the tortillas and fills them with meat, goat cheese, beans, hot sauce and lettuce.

Scientists have been unable to trace the ancestry of modern corn directly to a wild plant. But they do know that people living in what is now central or southern Mexico gathered corn from wild plants about 10,000 years ago. About 5000 B.C., the Indians learned how to grow their own corn. That is how it came to be called Indian corn.

The **bold** words below make each of the sentences untrue. Rewrite the sentences so they are true.

1. Tacos are made from **wheat bread**. _____

_____

2. The Indians that gathered corn from wild plants lived in **northern Mexico**. _____

_____

3. Tortillas are made from **wheat**. _____

4. Corn is often called **Italian** corn. _____

_____

5. About **10,000** B.C., people learned to grow corn themselves. _____

_____

6. Much corn is **exported** to Mexico. _____

_____

Life in the Village

Juan's house is made of clay. The clay was mixed together with straw and water and shaped into bricks. His roof is made of red tiles that are sloped to let the rain run off easily.

In the back of Juan's house is a shady patio. It has a wall around it to form a courtyard. At night, the cow and burro join the chickens and turkeys there.

The house has a hard-packed dirt floor. Juan's mother or father builds a cooking fire on the floor. It is built near the door so that the smoke can go out the door and windows on either side of the door. That is where Juan's mother makes the tortillas that he loves. It is 10-year-old Maria's job to sweep the floor and bring cool water to drink from the village fountain. She helps her mother wash the family's clothes in the river.

Juan helps his father make the clay animals to sell at the village market during fiestas. Some day Juan wants to be a potter like his father. Juan has already sold some vases at the market.

Draw a picture of Juan's house and yard below. Reread the paragraphs above to include as much detail as possible. When you draw the front door, draw what you can see inside of it.

Landforms and Physical Features

Notice different landforms and physical features found in the picture.

Label the ten landforms on the picture. Then, write the name of each one next to its definition below.

1. mountain   3. lake   5. peninsula   7. basin   9. canyon
2. plain   4. plateau   6. hill   8. island   10. river

A large area of flat or gently sloping land _____

A body of land completely surrounded by water _____

A deep valley with steep sides _____

A body of land surrounded by water on three sides _____

An area of flat land that is higher than the surrounding land _____

A low region surrounded by higher land _____

A large stream of water that flows into a larger body of water _____

A natural elevation smaller than a mountain _____

A body of water that is completely surrounded by land _____

A very high hill _____

Nature's Creations

Match each formation with its definition by writing a number in each blank.

_____ river   1. Land rising high above the land around it.

_____ bay   2. Land surrounded completely by water.

_____ island   3. Piece of land surrounded by water on all but one side.

_____ gulf   4. Inlet of a large body of water that extends into the land; smaller than a gulf.

_____ mountain   5. Earth opening that spills lava, rock and gases.

_____ plain   6. Large inland body of water.

_____ lake   7. Lowland between hills or mountains.

_____ peninsula   8. Long narrow body of water.

_____ valley   9. Large area of flat grasslands.

_____ volcano   10. Vast body of salt water.

_____ ocean   11. Large area of a sea or ocean partially enclosed by land.

Measurement: Foot, Yard, Mile

Decide whether you would use feet, yards or miles to measure each object.

I foot = 12 inches
I yard = 36 inches or 3 feet
I mile = 1,760 yards

length of a river ___miles___

height of a tree _____

width of a room _____

length of a football field _____

height of a door _____

length of a dress _____

length of a race _____

height of a basketball hoop _____

width of a window _____

distance a plane travels _____

Solve the problem.

Tara races Tom in the 100-yard dash. Tara finishes
10 yards in front of Tom. How many feet did Tara finish
in front of Tom?   _____

Measurement: Meter and Kilometer

Meters and **kilometers** are units of length in the metric system. A meter is equal to 39.37 inches. A kilometer is equal to about $\frac{5}{8}$ of a mile.

Decide whether you would use meters or kilometers to measure each object.

I meter = 100 centimeters
I kilometer = 1,000 meters

length of a river ___kilometer___

height of a tree _____

width of a room _____

length of a football field _____

height of a door _____

length of a dress _____

length of a race _____

height of a basketball pole _____

width of a window _____

distance a plane travels _____

Solve the problem.

Tara races Tom in the 100-meter dash. Tara finishes 10 meters in front of Tom. How many centimeters did Tara finish in front of Tom?

_____

Discovering Capacity

Discover the capacity of different objects and containers around your house.

You will need:
measuring cup (2-cup capacity),
tablespoon, pie tin, cake pan,
I cup of salt, I cup of ice,
bathroom sink, a large baking pan,
I gallon plastic jug,
I gallon freezer bag,
2-liter plastic jug

Activities:

1. How many cups of water are in a I-gallon plastic jug? _____

2. How many tablespoons of salt does it takes to fill up I cup? _____
   How many tablespoons of water does it take to fill up $\frac{1}{4}$ cup? _____

3. Pull up the drain stopper in your bathroom sink. How many cups of water
   will your sink hold? _____ How many gallons is that? _____

4. Measure out I cup of ice. Let it melt. How much water do you now
   have? _____ How do you explain this? _____

5. How many cups of water does it takes to fill up a pie tin? _____

6. How many cups of water does it take to fill up a 2-liter plastic jug? _____

7. How many cups of water does it take to fill up a large baking pan from
   your kitchen? _____

8. Does a I-gallon-size plastic freezer bag really hold a gallon of
   something? How many cups of water can you fit inside one. _____
   Is that a gallon? _____

9. Fill up a cake pan with water. Count how many cups it takes. _____
   If 2 cups = I pint, how many pints does it hold? _____
   If 2 pints = I quart, what is the quart capacity of your cake pan? _____

Comparing Solid and Liquid Weights

The **net weight** listed on products you buy in the store refers to the actual weight of the product you are buying. This does not include the weight of the container it is packaged in. To include the container would be its **gross weight**.

Use a balance scale to compare the weights of different solid objects with equivalent liquids.

You will need:
different small objects from around the house, such as a container of pepper, a container of glue, a pair of scissors, etc.
a scale
a 12-ounce plastic jar with a lid
orange juice
water
milk
other liquids
measuring cup

1. Place a small object on the scale.
2. While measuring, slowly add a cup of liquid at a time to the container on the other side of the scale until you find equal weight. Record your findings below.
3. As an alternative, use the same object but use different liquids.

Object	Liquid Equivalent

Week 34 Skills

Subject	Skill	Multi-Sensory Learning Activities
Reading and Language Arts	Read, write, and follow directions.	• Complete Practice Pages 360–364. • Cook something special. Let your child read the recipe aloud and make sure you are following the directions exactly. • Decide on a simple procedure, such as buttoning a shirt or making toast. Both you and your child should write step-by-step directions for it. Then, each writer should read his or her directions aloud while the other tries to carry them out. Which directions were easier to follow? Why?
Math	Find the perimeter of shapes.	• Complete Practice Pages 365–368. • Ask your child to measure the perimeter of his or her mattress in feet and inches. What would the perimeter of a blanket need to be in order to extend six inches beyond the mattress all the way around?
Bonus: Science		• Ask your child to choose an insect that can be easily found near your home and spend some time observing it. Then, encourage your child to do some research about the insect and to make a diagram of its body with labeled parts. Title the diagram with the insect's common name, genus name, and species name.

Directions

A **direction** is a sentence written as a command.

Write the missing directions for these pictures. Begin each direction with one of the verbs below.

glue	enter	share	add	decide	fold

How To Make a Peanut Butter and Jelly Sandwich:

1. Spread peanut butter on bread.

2. _____

3. Cut the sandwich in half.

4. _____

How To Make a Valentine:

1. _____

2. Draw half a heart.

3. Cut along the line you drew.

4. _____

Following Directions

Learning to follow directions is very important. Use the map to find your way to different houses.

1. Color the start house yellow.
2. Go north 2 houses, and east two houses.
3. Go north 2 houses, and west 4 houses.
4. Color the house green.

5. Start at the yellow house.
6. Go east 1 house, and north 3 houses.
7. Go west 3 houses, and south 3 houses.
8. Color the house blue.

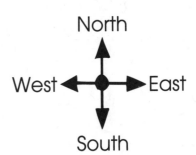

Following Directions

Read each sentence and do what it says to do.

1. Count the syllables in each word. Write the number on the line by the word.
2. Draw a line between the two words in each compound word.
3. Draw a circle around each name of a month.
4. Draw a box around each food word.
5. Draw an **X** on each noise word.
6. Draw a line under each day of the week.
7. Write the three words from the list you did not mark.

Draw a picture of each of those words.

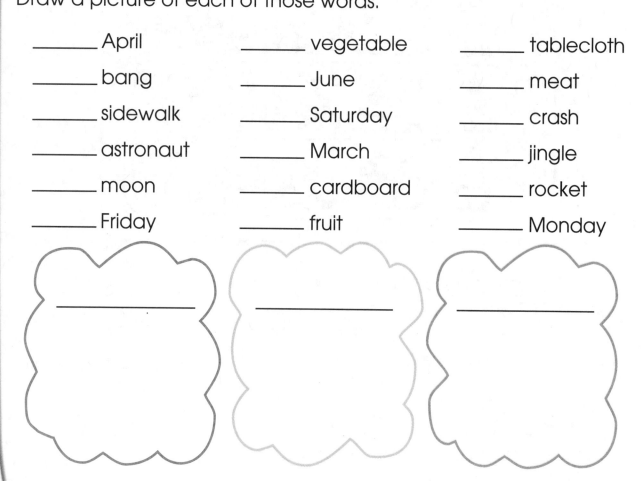

_____ April	_____ vegetable	_____ tablecloth
_____ bang	_____ June	_____ meat
_____ sidewalk	_____ Saturday	_____ crash
_____ astronaut	_____ March	_____ jingle
_____ moon	_____ cardboard	_____ rocket
_____ Friday	_____ fruit	_____ Monday

Following Directions: A Recipe

Following directions means doing what the directions say to do. Following directions is an important skill to know. When you are trying to find a new place, build a model airplane or use a recipe, you should follow the directions given.

Read the following recipe. Then, answer the questions on page 364.

Fruit Salad

1 fresh pineapple	2 oranges
1 cantaloupe	1 pear
2 bananas	1 cup seedless grapes
1 cup strawberries	lemon juice

- Cut the pineapple into chunks.

- Use a small metal scoop to make balls of the cantaloupe.

- Slice the pear, bananas and strawberries.

- Peel the oranges and divide them into sections. Cut each section into bite-sized pieces.

- Dip each piece of fruit in lemon juice, then combine them in a large bowl.

- Cover and chill.

- Pour fruit dressing of your choice over the chilled fruit, blend well and serve cold.

  Makes 4 large servings.

Following Directions: A Recipe

Using the recipe on page 363, answer the questions below.

1. How many bananas does the recipe require? _____

2. Does the recipe explain why you must dip the fruit in lemon juice? ____

   Why would it be important to do this? _____

   _____

3. Would your fruit salad be as good if you did not cut the pineapple or

   section the oranges? Why or why not? _____

   _____

4. Which do you do first?

   (Check one.)

   ____ Pour dressing over the fruit.

   ____ Slice the pear.

   ____ Serve the fruit salad.

5. Which three fruits do you slice?

   _____

   _____

   _____

Geometry: Perimeter

The perimeter is the distance around an object. Find the perimeter by adding the lengths of all the sides.

Find the perimeter for each object (ft. = feet).

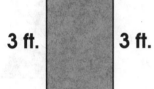

2 ft.

3 ft. **3 ft.**

2 ft.

10 ft.

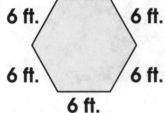

6 ft.

6 ft. **6 ft.**

6 ft. **6 ft.**

6 ft.

_____

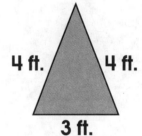

4 ft. **4 ft.**

3 ft.

_____

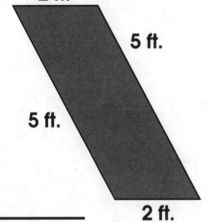

2 ft.

5 ft.

5 ft.

2 ft.

_____

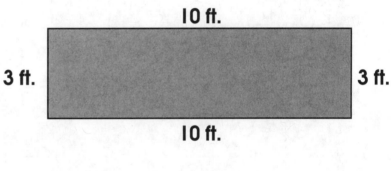

10 ft.

3 ft. **3 ft.**

10 ft.

_____

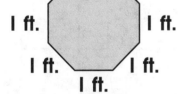

I ft.

I ft. **I ft.**

I ft. **I ft.**

I ft. **I ft.**

I ft.

_____

7 ft. **5 ft.**

5 ft.

_____

3 ft.

I ft. **I ft.**

5 ft.

_____

Perimeter Problems

Perimeter is the distance around a figure. Find the perimeter for the figures below.

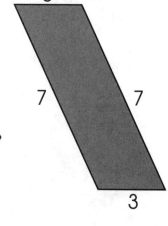

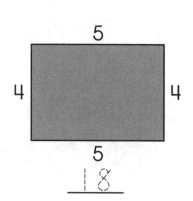

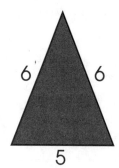

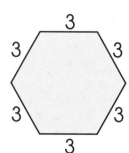

18 _____   _____   _____   _____

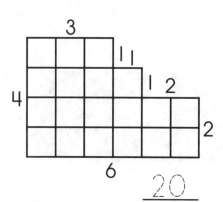

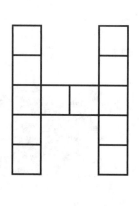

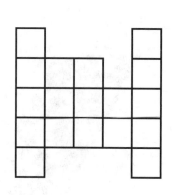

20 _____   _____   _____

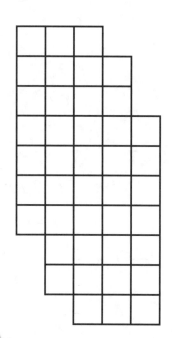

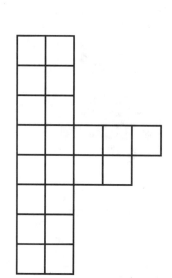

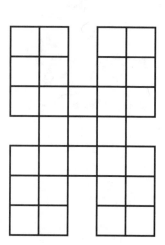

_____   _____   _____

Measurement: Perimeter

Perimeter is calculated by adding the lengths of the sides of a figure.

Examples:

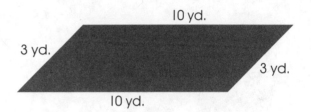

2 + 2 + 2 + 2 + 6 + 6 = 20
The perimeter of this hexagon is 20 ft.

10 + 10 + 3 + 3 = 26
The perimeter of this parallelogram is 26 yd.

Find the perimeter of the following figures.

_____ Perimeter

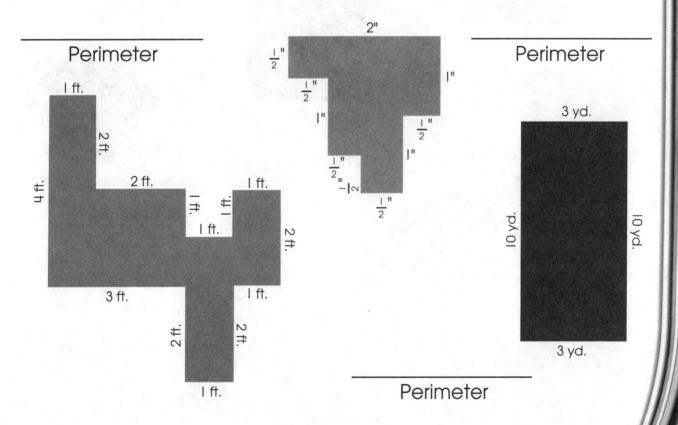

_____ Perimeter

Metric Measurement: Perimeter

Calculate the perimeter of each figure.

Example:

$4 + 5 + 4 + 1 + 2 + 3 + 2 = 21$ meters

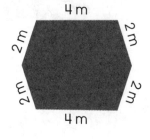

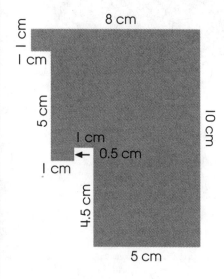

_____

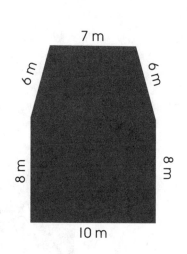

_____

_____

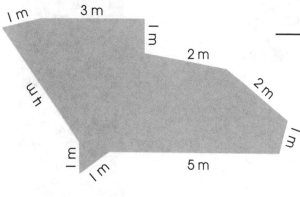

_____

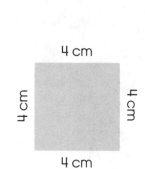

_____

COMPLETE YEAR GRADE 3

Week 35 Skills

Subject	Skill	Multi-Sensory Learning Activities
Reading and Language Arts	Read, write, and follow directions.	• Complete Practice Pages 370–374. • Give your child a series of written directions. The directions may be silly (such as collecting an assortment of unusual items), or serious (such as doing household chores). When your child has completed all the directions successfully, reward him or her with a special outing or treat.
Math	Find the perimeter and area of shapes.	• Complete Practice Pages 375–377. • Using a free Web site, print a sheet of graph paper with one-inch squares. Draw some shapes on the page and ask your child to find their area. Then ask, "Why do we measure area in square units?"
	Use a graph to show information.	• Complete Practice Page 378. • Using the graph on page 378 as a model, challenge your child to make a bar graph showing the number of different types of items (books, stuffed animals, etc.) in his or her bedroom.
Bonus: Social Studies		• Encourage your child to learn the names of your state's governor, your state's U.S. senators, your district's U.S. congressional representative, and your town's mayor. Then, have your child write a letter about an issue that is important to him or her and mail it to one official.

Animals in the Rainforest

Brazil is located in South America. This country is partially covered by rainforests in which thousands of different plants and animals live. However, many of these animals could become extinct because of the destruction of the rainforests for lumber. Follow the directions below to discover some of the animals that live in the rainforest.

1. Draw a jungle pig (called a tapir) hiding in the leaves.

2. Draw a jaguar lying on the ground.

3. Draw a parrot in the trees.

4. Draw an anaconda snake on the riverbank.

5. Draw spiders on the trees and on the ground.

6. Draw fish in the river.

7. Draw a caiman (alligator-like animal) in the river.

8. Draw butterflies in the air.

9. Color your rainforest and its animals.

A Journey to Japan

Follow the directions to complete the map of Japan.

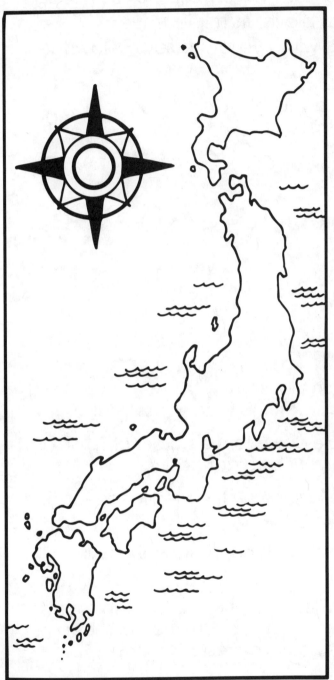

1. Add the four directional letters to the compass rose.
2. Label the islands in capital letters:
   KYUSHU - southernmost
   HOKKAIDO - northernmost
   HONSHU - south of Hokkaido
   SHIKOKU - north of Kyushu
3. Add a red ★ and label the capital city, **Tokyo**.
4. Draw a mountain at **Mount Fuji's** location.
5. Label **Nagasaki** by the dot on Kyushu Island.
6. Label the **Sea of Japan** and the **Pacific Ocean**. Add blue waves.
7. Label **Osaka** by the dot on Honshu Island.
8. Outline the islands in these colors:
   Hokkaido—orange
   Honshu—green
   Shikoku—red
   Kyushu—yellow
9. Along the northern edge of the box, label the map **JAPAN**, using a different color for each letter.
10. Draw the flag of Japan.

Tour de France

The Tour de France is a 2,000-mile bicycle race that winds around France for over 3 weeks in July. The route changes from year to year. The map of France below shows the principal cities through which more than 100 professional bicyclists might travel. Pretend you are a rider striving to win a yellow jersey. Follow the directions below.

1. You live in Luxembourg. You and your bicycle fly from Luxembourg across Belgium to Lille on July 1st. Draw a solid line from Luxembourg to Lille. You begin the race here.

2. Next, travel to St. Malo. Draw a solid blue line from Lille to St. Malo.

3. Continue on to Tours. Draw a red line from St. Malo to Tours.

4. From Tours, you travel to Bordeaux. Draw a solid red line from Tours to Bordeaux.

5. Draw a blue dotted line from Bordeaux to Agen. This takes you about halfway through the race. What a relief!

6. From Agen, you ride your bicycle down to the border of Spain and back up to Toulouse. Continue your blue dotted line.

7. From Toulouse, you go east to Marseille on the Mediterranean Sea. Draw your route in red and label the sea.

8. Draw a wiggly red line from Marseille through the French Alps to Alpe d'Huez.

9. Your climb to Alpe d'Huez is 9 miles long and has 21 hairpin turns. Thousands of spectators are watching you. On another sheet of paper, draw what you look like when you reach the top.

10. From there, you cycle to just a few miles outside of Paris. Draw a blue dotted line to that point. You are first to cross the finish line! Draw and decorate your yellow T-shirt on construction paper.

A Picture from Above

A floor plan looks like a picture someone drew looking down from the sky. It shows you where things are.

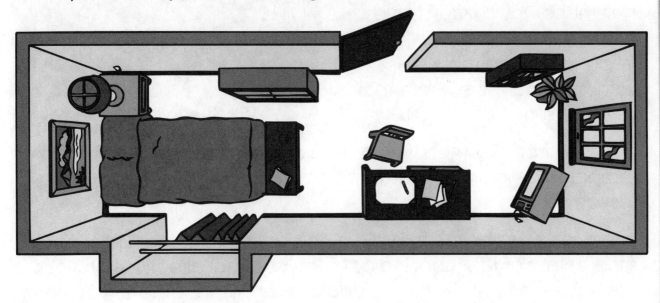

Circle the word which correctly completes each statement.

1. The TV is near the . . .   a. door   b. window   c. bed
2. The dresser is near the . . .   a. window   b. door   c. TV
3. Next to the bed is a . . .   a. TV   b. window   c. table
4. The bench is at the end of the . . . a. bed   b. bookshelf   c. closet
5. The plant is by the . . .   a. dresser   b. bed   c. window
6. The bookshelf is next to the . . .   a. bed   b. closet   c. door
7. The lamp is on the . . .   a. table   b. TV   c. dresser

Follow these directions.

1. Draw a red circle around the TV.
2. Draw a black **X** on the desk.
3. Draw an oval rug in front of the bench using a color of your choice.
4. Draw a stuffed animal in the center of the bed.

Drawing a Compass Rose

The maps of the early explorers were beautiful pieces of art. Their maps would often have pictures of fire-breathing dragons and sea monsters warning of dangers where they were traveling.

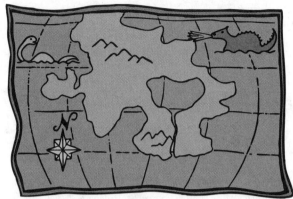

In a corner of their map would be a beautiful **compass rose**. The compass rose indicates the four cardinal directions—north, south, east and west.

Follow the steps below to draw a compass rose in the upper right-hand corner of the map. Indicate the cardinal directions on your rose. After completing the compass rose, draw a map of your own make-believe land.

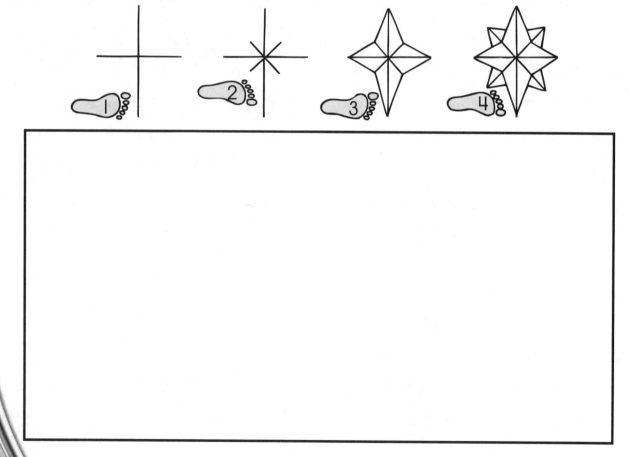

A Square Activity

Area is the number of square units contained in a surface. Find the area by counting the square units.

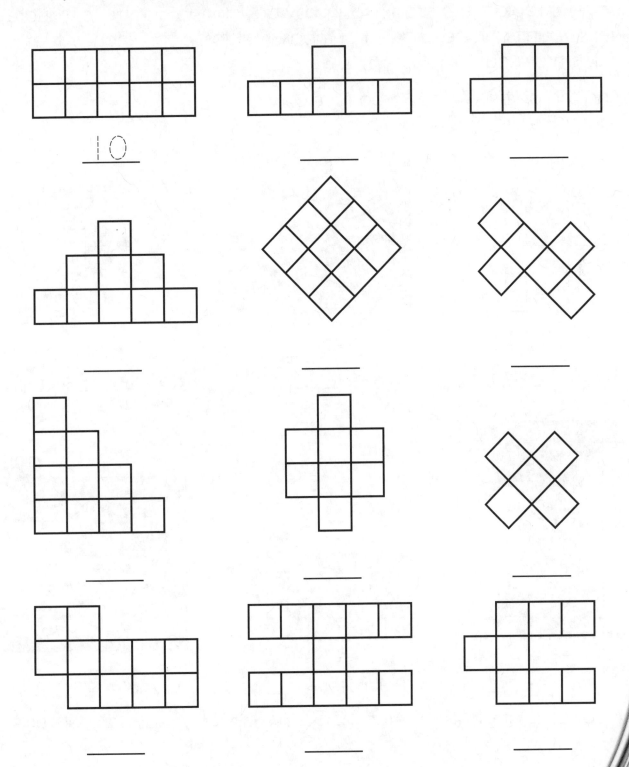

10

Measurement: Perimeter and Area

Perimeter is the distance around a figure. It is found by adding the lengths of the sides. **Area** is the number of square units needed to cover a region. The area is found by adding the number of square units. A unit can be any unit of measure. Most often, inches, feet or yards are used.

Find the perimeter and area for each figure. The first one is done for you.

☐ = 1 square unit

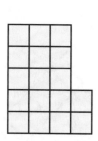

Perimeter = **18** units

Area = **17** sq. units

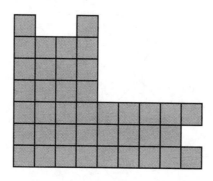

Perimeter = _____ units

Area = _____ sq. units

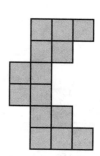

Perimeter = _____ units

Area = _____ sq. units

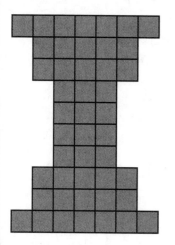

Perimeter = _____ units

Area = _____ sq. units

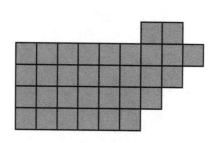

Perimeter = _____ units

Area = _____ sq. units

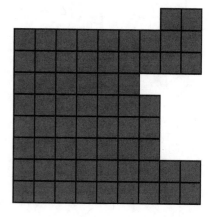

Perimeter = _____ units

Area = _____ sq. units

Measurement: Perimeter and Area

Area is also calculated by multiplying the length times the width of a square or rectangular figure. Use the formula: A = l x w.

Calculate the perimeter of each figure.

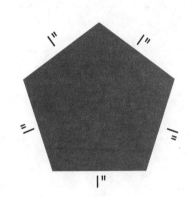

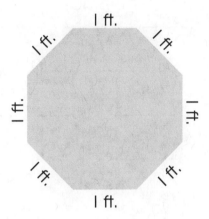

_____

_____

_____

Calculate the area of each figure.

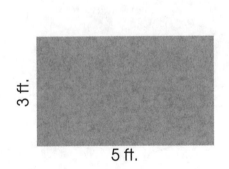

_____

_____

_____

Graphs

A **graph** is a drawing that shows information about numbers.

Color the picture. Then, tell how many there are of each object by completing the graph.

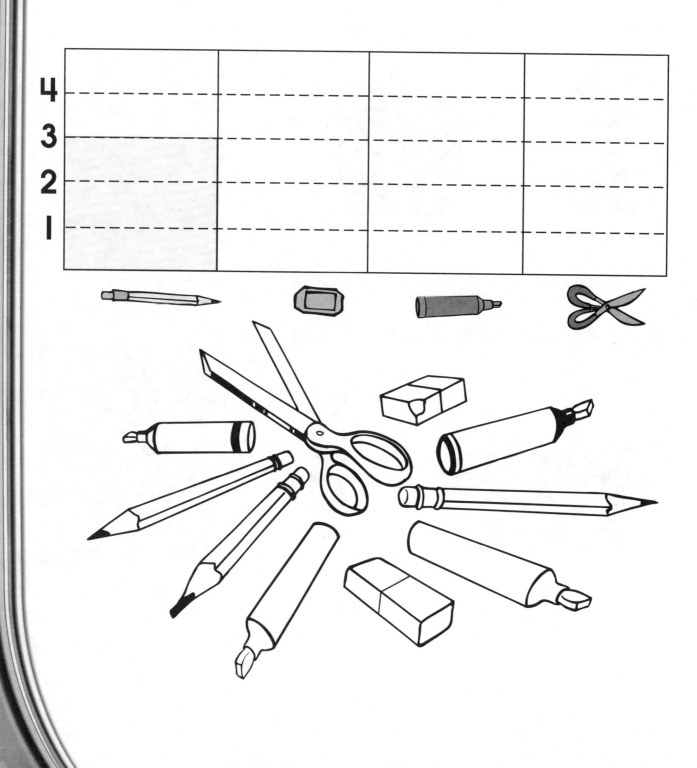

Week 36 Skills

Subject	Skill	Multi-Sensory Learning Activities
Reading and Language Arts	Read and understand maps and other visual aids in nonfiction text.	• Complete Practice Pages 380–384. • Look through a print or online newspaper with your child. Notice what information is given in sentences and paragraphs and what facts are presented in charts, graphs, maps, or other formats. Talk about how to read graphics and why they are useful.
Math	Read and interpret graphs.	• Complete Practice Pages 385 and 386. • Ask your child to use information from weather.gov or another source to make a graph showing precipitation amounts in your area for the last month. What are three questions that can be answered by reading the graph?
	Understand scale drawings.	• Complete Practice Pages 387 and 388. • Challenge your child to make a scale drawing of his or her bedroom and its furnishings using a scale of one foot: one inch.

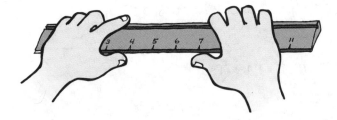

Using a Grid

A **map grid** helps people locate places easily. Use the numbers and letters to help you answer the questions.

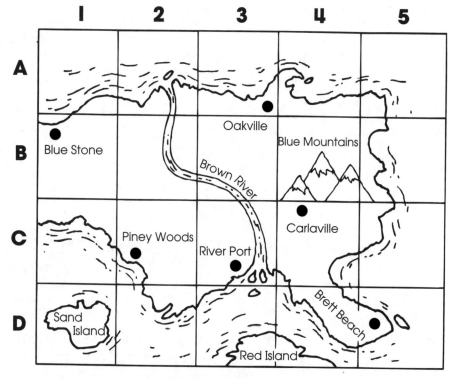

1. In which space is Brett Beach?_____

2. In which two spaces is Red Island? _____

3. In which four spaces is Brown River?_____

4. In which space is Carlaville? _____

5. In which two spaces are the Blue Mountains? _____

6. Name the town located in A3._____

7. Name the two islands found on the map. _____

8. Name the city directly north of D4._____

9. In C5, add a town to the map.

10. In B2, add some trees.

11. In A5, add an island and name the island.

12. Draw a boat in D2.

Connect-A-Dot

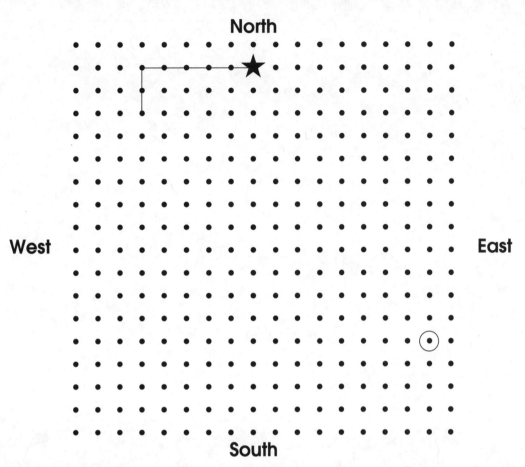

Follow these directions to complete a drawing. Begin at the star.
The first two steps are done for you.

Draw a straight line . . .

1. Five spaces west.
2. Two spaces south.
3. Four spaces east.
4. Nine spaces south.
5. Two spaces east.

6. Nine spaces north.
7. Four spaces east.
8. Two spaces north.
9. Five spaces west.

What letter did you draw? _____

Begin at the circle to complete another drawing.

Draw a straight line . . .

1. Four spaces south.
2. One space west.
3. Three spaces north.

4. One space west.
5. One space north.
6. Two spaces east.

What number did you draw? _____

What Do Hikers See?

Follow the directions to complete this area map.

1. Draw a west of the .

2. Draw 6 south of the .

3. Draw an in the middle of the .

4. Draw 10 south of the 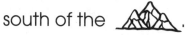.

5. Draw a between the and the .

6. Draw 2 on the east side of the .

7. Draw 2  south of the 6 .

8. Draw 3 south of the .

Products in the United States

Use the map and the legend to answer the questions below.

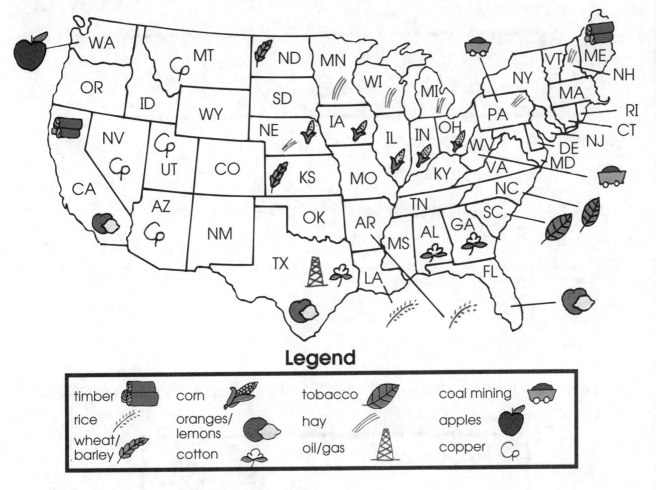

Legend

timber	corn	tobacco	coal mining
rice	oranges/lemons	hay	apples
wheat/barley	cotton	oil/gas	copper

1. Which state grows apples?_____

2. How many states on this map grow oranges and lemons? _____

3. Both Arkansas and Louisiana grow _____.

4. Wheat and barley are grown in _____.

5. North and South Carolina both grow _____.

6. _____ is produced in Maine.

7. Name the product grown in Alabama and Georgia. _____

8. Coal is mined in the states of _____.

9. Name the states that grow corn. _____

_____

Cartographers Use Symbols

On another sheet of paper, draw a map using the symbols and directions given below.

1. Draw a compass rose in the lower right-hand corner of the page.

2. Draw a ⎰⎰ in the center of your paper from west to east.

3. Draw 6 ⌂ in the southwest corner of the map.

4. Draw 4 🌲 east of the ⌂.

5. Draw a G north of the ⎰⎰.

6. Draw a C west of the G.

7. Draw a T south of the ⎰⎰.

On another sheet of paper, draw another map using the symbols and directions given below.

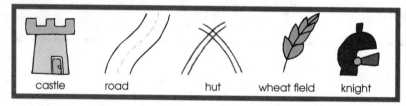

1. Draw a compass rose in the lower right-hand corner of the page.

2. Draw a castle in the center of the page.

3. Draw a road from the castle door southeast to the bottom of the page.

4. Draw 4 huts west of the castle.

5. Draw a knight on the east and west sides of the castle door.

6. Draw a wheat field east of the castle.

7. Draw a road east from the huts to the castle road.

"Oh My, How You Have Grown!"

What makes your body grow? Your body is made up of about 50 trillion cells. One of the most important jobs of a cell is to make you grow. One cell divides and forms two cells. Two cells divide and form four cells, and so on.

Not all your cells keep dividing. Some cells die. Other cells are dividing and replacing those that died. There are even a few left over to help you grow.

Amanda kept a record of her growth. You can take your own measurements, too. Then, fill in the chart and compare your growth with Amanda's growth. You may need a friend to help you.

1. Who is taller, Amanda or you? _____

   _____

   By how many inches? _____

2. Measure your arms from your shoulder to your wrist.

   Who has longer arms? _____

   By how many inches? _____

Personal history
Ask your parents what your height and weight were when you were born. How much have you grown?

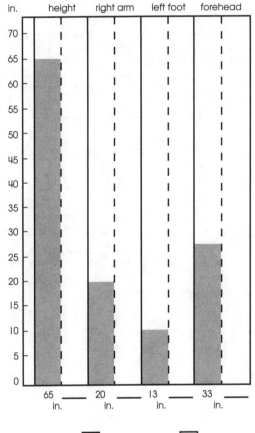

Amanda   You

Fun Fact
Your fastest growing stage happened before you were born. During the first week, when you were still inside your mother, you grew from one cell into billions of cells!

Potato Face

Read the line graphs to draw the potato faces.

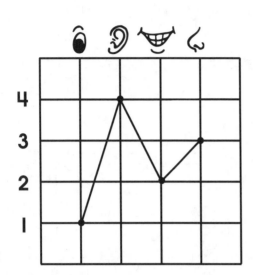

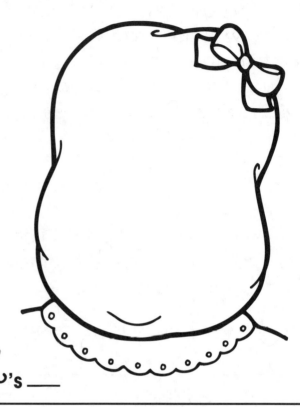

How many?

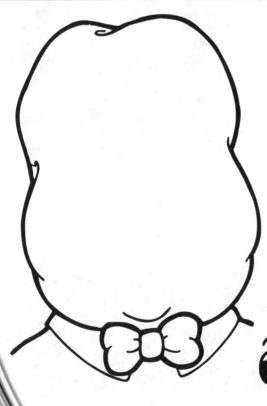

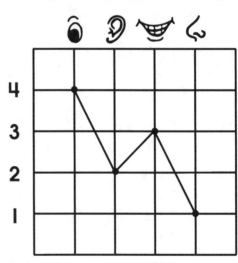

How many?

COMPLETE YEAR GRADE 3

Measuring Distance on a Map

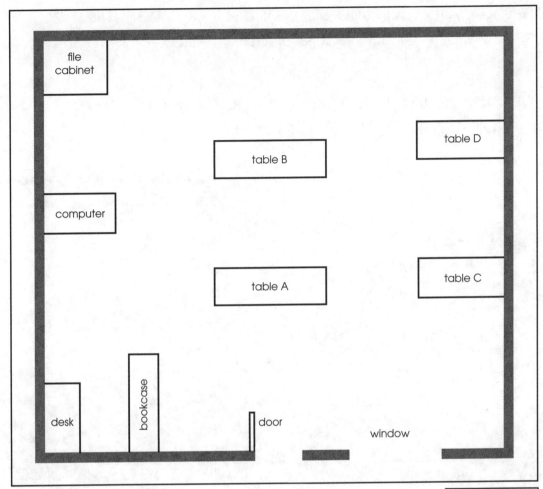

1 inch = 10 feet

Use a ruler to help you answer these questions.

1. According to the scale, how many feet equal 1 inch? _____

2. How many feet is table A from the door? _____

3. How far is the file cabinet from the desk? _____

4. How far is table B from table D? _____

5. How many feet long is the classroom from the west wall to the east wall? _____

6. How far is the door from the window? _____

7. How wide is the window? _____

8. How far is the computer from the desk? _____

Map Skills: Scale

A **map scale** shows how far one place is from another. This map scale shows that 1 inch on this page equals 1 mile at the real location.

Use a ruler and the map scale to find out how far it is from Ann's house to other places. Round to the nearest inch.

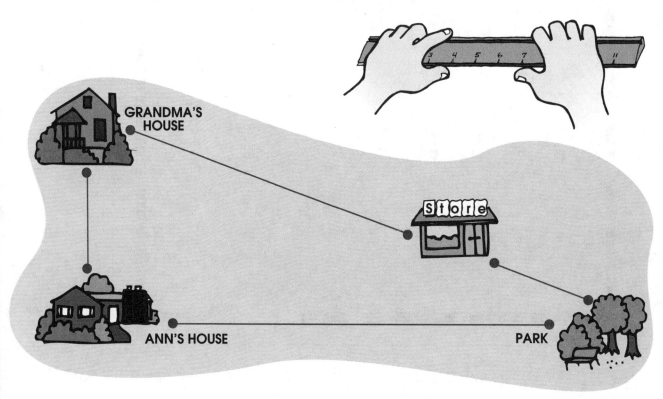

1. How far is it from Ann's house to the park? _____

2. How far is it from Ann's house to Grandma's house? _____

3. How far is it from Grandma's house to the store? _____

4. How far did Ann go when she went from her house to Grandma's and then to the store? _____

Fourth Quarter Check-Up

Reading and Language Arts

❑ I can sequence story events in a logical order.

❑ I know how to write a paragraph with a main idea and supporting details.

❑ I can find the main idea of a reading passage.

❑ I can use reference works to help answer questions.

❑ I can read and understand fiction and nonfiction texts.

❑ I can read, write, and follow directions.

❑ I can find information by reading maps, graphs, and other visual aids.

Math

❑ I can tell time using digital and analog clocks.

❑ I can solve problems about money amounts.

❑ I can measure length with standard and metric units.

❑ I understand measures of volume.

❑ I understand measures of weight.

❑ I can find the perimeter of a shape.

❑ I can find the area of a shape.

❑ I can make graphs and use them to answer questions.

❑ I can make a scale drawing.

Final Project

Use a computer or art supplies to make a travel brochure about an interesting place that is close to your home or an interesting place far away that you would like to visit. Include a map of the place drawn to scale; a graph, pie chart, or other visual aid that provides information about the place; a drawing or photo of the place; and a paragraph that gives fun facts about the place. You may wish to ask your school librarian to display the brochure at the library.

Student Reference

Word Parts

	Examples
Word Roots	
aster, astro: "star"	asteroid, astronaut
dic: "say, tell"	dictionary, predict
port: "carry"	export, support
scrib, scrip: "write"	describe, scribble
vac: "empty"	evacuate, vacuum
Prefixes	
counter–	counterattack, countermeasure
mis–	mistake, misstep
over–	overcharge, overpopulate
un–	undo, unsafe
Suffixes	
–able	readable, achievable
–ed	created, hopped
–ish	babyish, greenish
–ment	announcement, argument

Homophones

ate, eight	cent, scent	hour, our	tail, tale
bare, bear	choose, chews	made, maid	their, there, they're
be, bee	dear, deer	nose, knows	threw, through
been, bin	eye, I	one, won	wait, weight
blew, blue	grown, groan	pair, pear	weak, week
board, bored	hear, here	read, red	wood, would
break, brake	high, hi	sea, see	
buy, by	hole, whole	sell, cell	

The United States of America

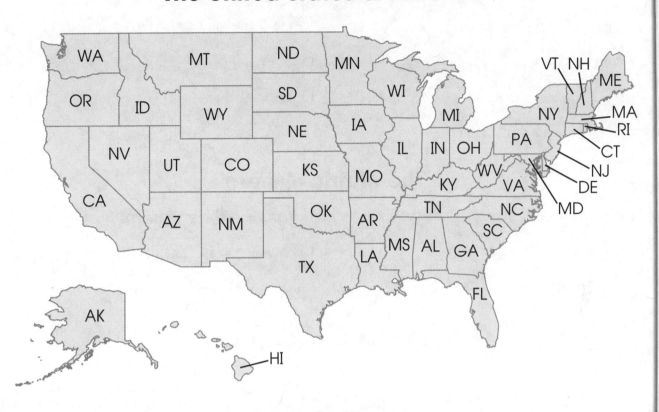

World Map

Student Reference, cont.

U.S. Customary System of Measurement

I foot = 12 inches

I yard = 3 feet

I mile = 5,280 feet

I pound = 16 ounces

I pint = 2 cups

I quart = 2 pints

I gallon = 4 quarts

The Metric System

I centimeter = 10 millimeters

I meter = 100 centimeters

I kilometer = 1,000 meters

I gram = 100 centigrams

I kilogram = 1,000 grams

I liter = 100 centiliters

Two-Dimensional Shapes

Circle

Square

Triangle

Rectangle

Oval

Rhombus

Hexagon

Octagon

Three-Dimensional Shapes

Cube

Cone

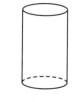
Cylinder

Sphere

Multiplication Chart

X	1	2	3	4	5	6	7	8	9	10	11	12
1	1	2	3	4	5	6	7	8	9	10	11	12
2	2	4	6	8	10	12	14	16	18	20	22	24
3	3	6	9	12	15	18	21	24	27	30	33	36
4	4	8	12	16	20	24	28	32	36	40	44	48
5	5	10	15	20	25	30	35	40	45	50	55	60
6	6	12	18	24	30	36	42	48	54	60	66	72
7	7	14	21	28	35	42	49	56	63	70	77	84
8	8	16	24	32	40	48	56	64	72	80	88	96
9	9	18	27	36	45	54	63	72	81	90	99	108
10	10	20	30	40	50	60	70	80	90	100	110	120
11	11	22	33	44	55	66	77	88	99	110	121	132
12	12	24	36	48	60	72	84	96	108	120	132	144

Recommended Read-Alouds for Grade 3

The Golden Dream of Carlo Chuchio by Lloyd Alexander

Gilda Joyce, Psychic Investigator by Jennifer Allison

The American Story: 100 True Tales from American History by Jennifer Armstrong

Freddy the Detective by Walter Brooks

The Wonderful Flight to the Mushroom Planet by Eleanor Cameron

Because of Winn-Dixie by Kate Camillo

Frindle by Andrew Clements

Morning Girl by Michael Dorris

Dexter the Tough by Margaret Peterson Haddix

Girl Wonder: A Baseball Story in Nine Innings by Deborah Hopkinson

Living Color by Steve Jenkins

Animals in the House: A History of Pets and People by Sheila Keenan

The Facts and Fictions of Minna Pratt by Patricia MacLachlan

Homer Price by Robert McCloskey

The Penguin's Peril: Taylor-Made Tales #4 by Ellen Miles

Paint the Wind by Pam Muñoz Ryan

Knights of the Kitchen Table by Jon Scieszka

Storms by Seymour Simon

Loser by Jerry Spinelli

My Curious Uncle Dudley by Barry Yourgrau

Answer Key

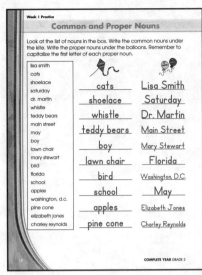

Week 1 Practice

Common and Proper Nouns

Look at the list of nouns in the box. Write the common nouns under the kite. Write the proper nouns under the balloons. Remember to capitalize the first letter of each proper noun.

lisa smith	
cats	
shoelace	
saturday	
dr. martin	
whistle	
teddy bears	
main street	
may	
boy	
lawn chair	
mary stewart	
bird	
florida	
school	
apples	
washington, d.c.	
pine cone	
elizabeth jones	
charley reynolds	

cats — Lisa Smith
shoelace — Saturday
whistle — Dr. Martin
teddy bears — Main Street
boy — Mary Stewart
lawn chair — Florida
bird — Washington, D.C.
school — May
apples — Elizabeth Jones
pine cone — Charley Reynolds

COMPLETE YEAR GRADE 3

18

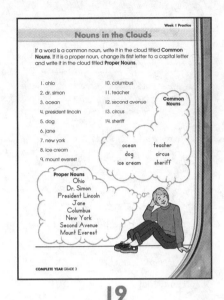

Week 1 Practice

Nouns in the Clouds

If a word is a common noun, write it in the cloud titled **Common Nouns**. If it is a proper noun, change its first letter to a capital letter and write it in the cloud titled **Proper Nouns**.

1. ohio
2. dr. simon
3. ocean
4. president lincoln
5. dog
6. jane
7. new york
8. ice cream
9. mount everest
10. columbus
11. teacher
12. second avenue
13. circus
14. sheriff

Common Nouns
ocean   teacher
dog   circus
ice cream   sheriff

Proper Nouns
Ohio
Dr. Simon
President Lincoln
Jane
Columbus
New York
Second Avenue
Mount Everest

COMPLETE YEAR GRADE 3

19

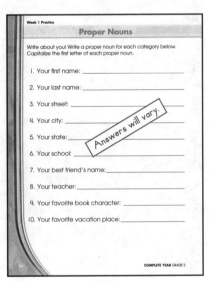

Week 1 Practice

Proper Nouns

Write about you! Write a proper noun for each category below. Capitalize the first letter of each proper noun.

1. Your first name: _____
2. Your last name: _____
3. Your street: _____
4. Your city: _____
5. Your state: _____
6. Your school: _____
7. Your best friend's name: _____
8. Your teacher: _____
9. Your favorite book character: _____
10. Your favorite vacation place: _____

Answers will vary.

COMPLETE YEAR GRADE 3

20

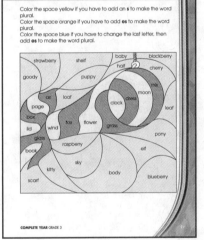

Week 1 Practice

Bright and Beautiful

Color the space yellow if you have to add an **s** to make the word plural.
Color the space orange if you have to add **es** to make the word plural.
Color the space blue if you have to change the last letter, then add **es** to make the word plural.

COMPLETE YEAR GRADE 3

21

Week 1 Practice

Plurals

A word that names one thing is **singular**, like **house**. A word that names more than one thing is **plural**, like **houses**.

To make a word plural, we usually add **s**.

Examples: one book — two book**s**   one tree — four tree**s**

To make plural words that end in **s, ss, x, sh** and **ch**, we add **es**.

Examples: one fox — two fox**es**   one bush — three bush**es**

Write the word that is missing from each pair below. Add **s** or **es** to make the plural words. The first one is done for you.

Singular	Plural
table	tables
beach	beaches
class	classes
ax	axes
brush	brushes
crash	crashes

COMPLETE YEAR GRADE 3

22

Week 1 Practice

Add 'Em Up!

Addition is "putting together" or adding two or more numbers to find the sum.

Add the following problems as quickly and as accurately as you can.

3 +2 5	6 +4 10	5 +4 9	2 +9 11
6 +2 8	4 +1 5	9 +6 15	7 +6 13	8 +7 15	8 +9 17
9 +4 13	1 +8 9	4 +7 11	7 +9 16	5 +6 11	5 +3 8
6 +6 12	8 +8 16	7 +7 14	4 +4 8
2 +8 10	5 +2 7	3 +6 9	8 +5 13

How quickly did you complete this page? *Answers will vary.*

COMPLETE YEAR GRADE 3

23

Answer Key

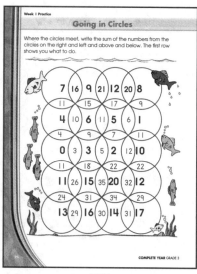

24

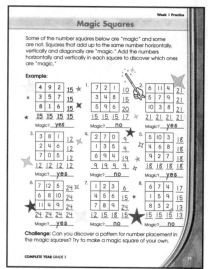

25

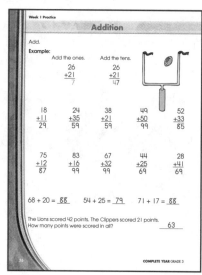

26

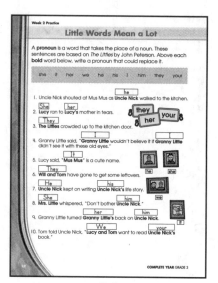

28

29

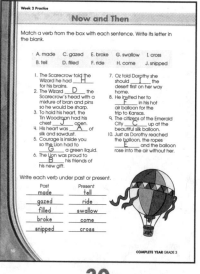

30

Answer Key

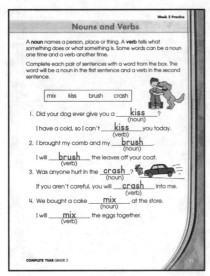

31

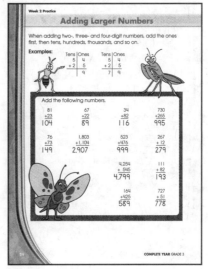

32

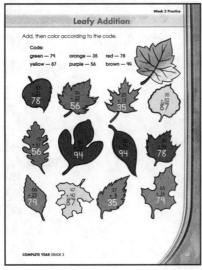

33

34

35

36

Answer Key

398

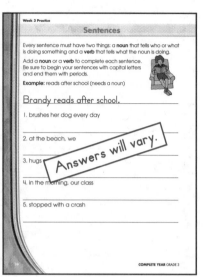

Week 3 Practice

Sentences

Every sentence must have two things: a **noun** that tells who or what is doing something and a **verb** that tells what the noun is doing.

Add a **noun** or a **verb** to complete each sentence. Be sure to begin your sentences with capital letters and end them with periods.

Example: reads after school. (needs a noun)

Brandy reads after school.

1. brushes her dog every day

2. at the beach, we

3. hugs

4. in the morning, our class

5. stopped with a crash

Answers will vary.

COMPLETE YEAR GRADE 3

38

Week 3 Practice

Helping Verbs

A **helping verb** is a word used with an action verb.

Examples: might, shall and **are**

Write a helping verb from the box with each action verb.

can	could	must	might
may	would	should	will
shall	did	does	do
had	have	has	am
are	were	is	
be	being	been	

Possible Answers:

Example:
Tomorrow, I ___might___ play soccer.

1. Mom ___may___ buy my new soccer shoes tonight.
2. Yesterday, my old soccer shoes ___were___ ripped by the cat.
3. I ___am___ going to ask my brother to go to the game.
4. He usually ___does___ not like soccer.
5. But, he ___will___ go with me because I am his sister.
6. He ___has___ promised to watch the entire soccer game.
7. He has ___been___ helping me with my homework.
8. I ___can___ spell a lot better because of his help.
9. Maybe I ___could___ finish the semester at the top of my class.

COMPLETE YEAR GRADE 3

39

Week 3 Practice

Helping Verbs

A **verb phrase** contains a **main verb** and a **helping verb**. The helping verb usually comes before the main verb. **Has** and **have** can be used as helping verbs.

Example: We **have learned** about dental health.
helping main
verb   verb

Underline the helping verb and circle the main verb in each sentence.

1. A dental hygienist has come to talk to our class.
2. We have written questions ahead of time to ask her.
3. I have wondered if it is really necessary to brush after every meal.
4. We have waited to be shown the proper way to floss our teeth.
5. We have learned the names of all the different kinds of teeth.
6. We have listed incisors, cuspids and molars as names of teeth.
7. Most of us have known the parts of a tooth for a long time.
8. The teacher has given us a list of snack foods that may cause cavities.
9. Nearly half the class has eaten too much sugar today.
10. I have experimented with different kinds of toothpaste to see which ones clean teeth best.

COMPLETE YEAR GRADE 3

40

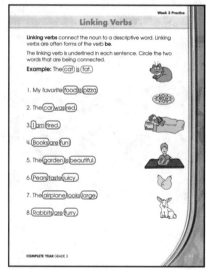

Week 3 Practice

Linking Verbs

Linking verbs connect the noun to a descriptive word. Linking verbs are often forms of the verb **be**.

The linking verb is underlined in each sentence. Circle the two words that are being connected.

Example: The (cat) is (fat).

1. My favorite (food) is (pizza)
2. The (car) was (red)
3. (I) am (tired)
4. (Books) are (fun)
5. The (garden) is (beautiful)
6. (Pears) taste (juicy)
7. The (airplane) looks (large)
8. (Rabbits) are (furry)

COMPLETE YEAR GRADE 3

41

Week 3 Practice

Linking Verbs

A **linking verb** does not show action. Instead, it links the subject of the sentence with a noun or adjective in the predicate. **Am. is. are. was** and **were** are linking verbs.

Example:
Thomas Jefferson **was** president of the United States.

Write a linking verb in each blank.

1. The class's writing assignment ___is___ a report on U.S. presidents.
2. The reports ___are___ due tomorrow.
3. I ___am___ glad I chose to write about Thomas Jefferson, the third president of our country.
4. Early in his life, he ___was___ the youngest delegate to the First Continental Congress.
5. The colonies ___were___ angry at England.
6. Thomas Jefferson ___was___ a great writer, so he was asked to help write the Declaration of Independence.
7. The signing of that document ___was___ a historical event.
8. Later, as president, Jefferson ___was___ responsible for the Louisiana Purchase.
9. He ___was___ the first president to live in the White House.
10. Americans ___are___ fortunate today for the part Thomas Jefferson played in our country's history.

COMPLETE YEAR GRADE 3

42

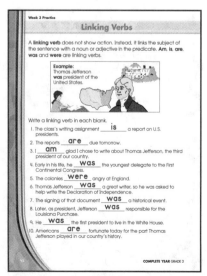

Week 3 Practice

Addition: Regrouping

Study the example. Add using regrouping.

Examples:

Add the ones. Regroup.	Add the tens. Regroup.	Add the hundreds.
1	1 11	11
156 6	5 156	156
+267 +7	+6 +267	+267
3 13	12 23	423

29	81	52	49	162
46	78	67	37	+349
+12	+33	+23	+19	511
87	192	142	105	

273	655	783	385	428
+198	+297	+148	+169	+122
471	952	931	554	550

Sally went bowling. She had scores of 115, 129 and 103. What was her total score for three games? ___347___

COMPLETE YEAR GRADE 3

43

Page 44

Week 3 Practice

Addition: Regrouping

Add using regrouping. Then, use the code to discover the name of a United States president.

348 +752 1,100	642 +277 919	386 +787 1,173	184 +875 1,059	578 +874 1,452
653 +768 1,421	653 +359 1,012	946 +239 1,185	393 +257 650	199 +843 1,042
721 +679 1,400				

G W A S H I N G T O N

1012	1173	1059	1421	919	650	1452	1042	1100	1400	1185
N	A	S	I	W	T	H	O	G	N	G

COMPLETE YEAR GRADE 3

44

Page 45

Week 3 Practice

Addition: Regrouping

Study the example. Add using regrouping.

Example:

5,356
 +3,976
 9,332

Steps:
1. Add the ones.
2. Regroup the tens. Add the tens.
3. Regroup the hundreds. Add the hundreds.
4. Add the thousands.

6,849 +3,276 10,125	1,846 +8,384 10,230	9,221 +6,769 15,990
2,758 +3,663 6,421	5,299 +8,764 14,063	7,932 +6,879 14,811

A plane flew 1,838 miles on the first day. It flew 2,347 miles on the second day. How many miles did it fly in all? __4,185__

COMPLETE YEAR GRADE 3

45

Page 46

Week 3 Practice

Addition: Mental Math

Try to do these addition problems in your head without using paper and pencil.

7 +4 11	6 +3 9	8 +1 9	10 +2 12	2 +9 11	6 +6 12
10 +20 30	40 +20 60	80 +100 180	60 +30 90	50 +70 120	100 +40 140
350 +150 500	300 +500 800	400 +800 1,200	450 +10 460	680 +100 780	900 +70 970
1,000 +200 1,200	4,000 400 +30 4,430	300 200 +80 580	8,000 500 +60 8,560	9,800 +150 9,950	7,000 300 +30 7,330

COMPLETE YEAR GRADE 3

46

Page 48

Week 4 Practice

Irregular Verbs

Irregular verbs are verbs that do not change from the present tense to the past tense in the regular way with **d** or **ed**.

Example: sing, sang

Read the sentence and underline the verb. Choose the past-tense form from the box and write it next to the sentence.

blow — blew	fly — flew
come — came	give — gave
take — took	wear — wore
make — made	sing — sang
grow — grew	

Example:

Dad will <u>make</u> a cake tonight. __made__

1. I will probably <u>grow</u> another inch this year. __grew__
2. I will <u>blow</u> out the candles. __blew__
3. Everyone will <u>give</u> me presents. __gave__
4. I will <u>wear</u> my favorite red shirt. __wore__
5. My cousins will <u>come</u> from out of town. __came__
6. It will <u>take</u> them four hours. __took__
7. My Aunt Betty will <u>fly</u> in from Cleveland. __flew__
8. She will <u>sing</u> me a song when she gets here. __sang__

COMPLETE YEAR GRADE 3

48

Page 49

Week 4 Practice

Irregular Verbs

Circle the verb that completes each sentence.

1. Scientists will try to (find, found) the cure.
2. Eric (brings, brought) his lunch to school yesterday.
3. Every day, Betsy (sings, sang) all the way home.
4. Jason (breaks, broke) the vase last night.
5. The ice had (freezes, frozen) in the tray.
6. Mitzi has (swims, swum) in that pool before.
7. Now I (choose, chose) to exercise daily.
8. The teacher has (rings, rung) the bell.
9. The boss (speaks, spoke) to us yesterday.
10. She (says, said) it twice already.

COMPLETE YEAR GRADE 3

49

Page 50

Week 4 Practice

Irregular Verbs

The verb **be** is different from all other verbs. The present-tense forms of **be** are **am**, **is** and **are**. The past-tense forms of **be** are **was** and **were**. The verb **to be** is written in the following ways:

singular: I am, you are, he is, she is, it is
plural: we are, you are, they are

Choose the correct form of **be** from the words in the box and write it in each sentence.

are	am	is	was

Example:

I __am__ feeling good at this moment.

1. My sister __is__ a good singer.
2. You __are__ going to the store with me.
3. Sandy __was__ at the movies last week.
4. Rick and Tom __are__ best friends.
5. He __is__ happy about the surprise.
6. The cat __is__ hungry.
7. I __am__ going to the ball game.
8. They __are__ silly.
9. I __am__ glad to help my mother.

COMPLETE YEAR GRADE 3

50

Answer Key

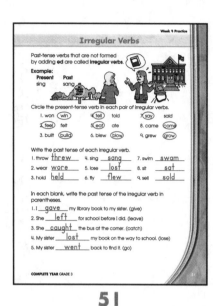

51

53

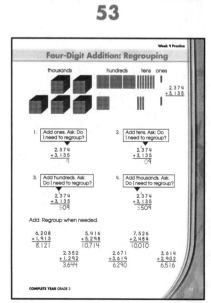

55

52

54

56

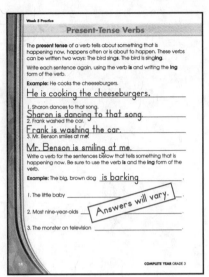

Week 5 Practice

Present-Tense Verbs

The **present tense** of a verb tells about something that is happening now, happens often or is about to happen. These verbs can be written two ways: The bird sings. The bird is singing.

Write each sentence again, using the verb **is** and writing the **ing** form of the verb.

Example: He cooks the cheeseburgers.

He is cooking the cheeseburgers.

1. Sharon dances to that song.
Sharon is dancing to that song.
2. Frank washed the car.
Frank is washing the car.
3. Mr. Benson smiles at me.
Mr. Benson is smiling at me.

Write a verb for the sentences below that tells something that is happening now. Be sure to use the verb **is** and the **ing** form of the verb.

Example: The big, brown dog __is barking__

1. The little baby _____
2. Most nine-year-olds _____
3. The monster on television _____

Answers will vary.

COMPLETE YEAR GRADE 3

58

Week 5 Practice

Present-Tense Verbs

When something is happening right now, it is in the **present tense**. There are two ways to write verbs in the present tense:

Examples: The dog **walks**. The cats **play**.
The dog **is walking**. The cats **are playing**.

Write each sentence again, writing the verb a different way.

Example:
He lists the numbers.
He is listing the numbers.

1. She is pounding the nail.
She pounds the nail.
2. My brother toasts the bread.
He is toasting the bread.
3. They search for the robber.
They are searching for the robber.
4. The teacher lists the pages.
The teacher is listing the pages.
5. They are spilling the water.
They spill the water.
6. Ken and Amy load the packages.
They are loading the packages.

COMPLETE YEAR GRADE 3

59

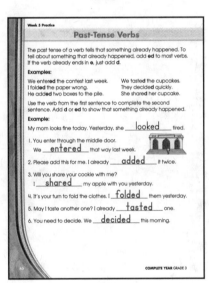

Week 5 Practice

Past-Tense Verbs

The past tense of a verb tells that something already happened. To tell about something that already happened, add **ed** to most verbs. If the verb already ends in **e**, just add **d**.

Examples:

We entered the contest last week.   We tasted the cupcakes.
I folded the paper wrong.   They decided quickly.
He added two boxes to the pile.   She shared her cupcake.

Use the verb from the first sentence to complete the second sentence. Add **d** or **ed** to show that something already happened.

Example:
My mom looks fine today. Yesterday, she __looked__ tired.

1. You enter through the middle door.
We __entered__ that way last week.
2. Please add this for me. I already __added__ it twice.
3. Will you share your cookie with me?
I __shared__ my apple with you yesterday.
4. It's your turn to fold the clothes. I __folded__ them yesterday.
5. May I taste another one? I already __tasted__ one.
6. You need to decide. We __decided__ this morning.

COMPLETE YEAR GRADE 3

60

Week 5 Practice

Past-Tense Verbs

When you write about something that already happened, you add **ed** to most verbs. For some verbs that have a short vowel and end in one consonant, you double the consonant before adding **ed**.

Examples:

He hugged his pillow.   The dog grabbed the stick.
She stirred the carrots.   We planned to go tomorrow.
They clapped for me.   They dragged their bags on the ground.

Use the verb from the first sentence to complete the second sentence. Change the verb in the second part to the past tense. Double the consonant and add **ed**.

Example:
We skip to school. Yesterday, we __skipped__ the whole way.

1. It's not nice to grab things. When you __grabbed__ my cookie, I felt angry.
2. Did anyone hug you today? Dad __hugged__ me this morning.
3. We plan our vacations every year. Last year, we __planned__ to go to the beach.
4. Is it my turn to stir the pot? You __stirred__ it last time.
5. Let's clap for Andy, just like we __clapped__ for Amy.
6. My sister used to drag her blanket everywhere.
Once, she __dragged__ it to the store.

COMPLETE YEAR GRADE 3

61

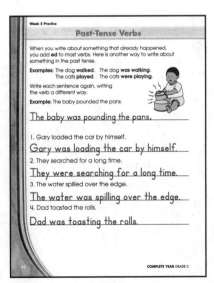

Week 5 Practice

Past-Tense Verbs

When you write about something that already happened, you add **ed** to most verbs. Here is another way to write about something in the past tense.

Examples: The dog **walked**. The dog **was walking**.
The cats **played**. The cats **were playing**.

Write each sentence again, writing the verb a different way.

Example: The baby pounded the pans.
The baby was pounding the pans.

1. Gary loaded the car by himself.
Gary was loading the car by himself.
2. They searched for a long time.
They were searching for a long time.
3. The water spilled over the edge.
The water was spilling over the edge.
4. Dad toasted the rolls.
Dad was toasting the rolls.

COMPLETE YEAR GRADE 3

62

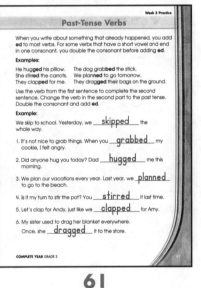

Week 5 Practice

Subtraction

Subtraction means "taking away" or subtracting one number from another to find the difference. For example, 10 – 3 = 7.

Subtract.

Example: Subtract the ones.   Subtract the tens.

$$\begin{array}{r} 39 \\ -24 \\ \hline 5 \end{array} \qquad \begin{array}{r} 39 \\ -24 \\ \hline 15 \end{array}$$

$$\begin{array}{r} 48 \\ -35 \\ \hline 13 \end{array} \qquad \begin{array}{r} 95 \\ -22 \\ \hline 73 \end{array} \qquad \begin{array}{r} 87 \\ -16 \\ \hline 71 \end{array} \qquad \begin{array}{r} 55 \\ -43 \\ \hline 12 \end{array}$$

$$\begin{array}{r} 37 \\ -14 \\ \hline 23 \end{array} \qquad \begin{array}{r} 69 \\ -57 \\ \hline 12 \end{array} \qquad \begin{array}{r} 44 \\ -23 \\ \hline 21 \end{array} \qquad \begin{array}{r} 99 \\ -78 \\ \hline 21 \end{array}$$

66 – 44 = 22   57 – 33 = 24

The yellow car traveled 87 miles per hour. The orange car traveled 66 miles per hour. How much faster was the yellow car traveling? __21 m.p.h.__

COMPLETE YEAR GRADE 3

63

Page 64

Week 5 Practice

Subtraction: Regrouping

Subtraction means "taking away" or subtracting one number from another to find the difference. For example, 10 – 3 = 7. To regroup is to use 1 ten to form 10 ones, 1 hundred to form 10 tens and so on.

Study the example. Subtract using regrouping.

Example:
$$32 = 2 \text{ tens} + 12 \text{ ones}$$
$$-13 = 1 \text{ ten} + 3 \text{ ones}$$
$$19 = 1 \text{ ten} + 9 \text{ ones}$$

33 −28 = 5	86 −59 = 27	92 −37 = 55	71 −48 = 23
63 −47 = 16	45 −18 = 27	31 −22 = 9	55 −39 = 16

82 − 69 = 13   73 − 36 = 37

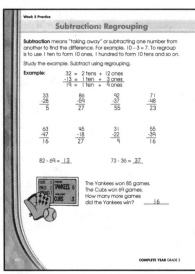

The Yankees won 85 games. The Cubs won 69 games. How many more games did the Yankees win? __16__

COMPLETE YEAR GRADE 3

Page 65

Week 5 Practice

Subtraction: Regrouping

Regrouping for subtraction is the opposite of regrouping for addition. Study the example. Subtract using regrouping. Then, use the code to color the flowers.

Example:
647
−453
194

Steps:
1. Subtract ones.
2. Subtract tens. Five tens cannot be subtracted from 4 tens.
3. Regroup tens by regrouping 6 hundreds (5 hundreds + 10 tens).
4. Add the 10 tens to the 4 tens.
5. Subtract 5 tens from 14 tens.
6. Subtract the hundreds.

If the answer has:
1 one, color it red;
8 ones, color it pink;
5 ones, color it yellow.

COMPLETE YEAR GRADE 3

Page 66

Week 5 Practice

Subtraction: Regrouping

Study the example. Follow the steps. Subtract using regrouping.

Example:
634
− 455
179

Steps:
1. Subtract ones. You cannot subtract 5 ones from 4 ones.
2. Regroup ones by regrouping 3 tens to 2 tens + 10 ones.
3. Subtract 5 ones from 14 ones.
4. Regroup tens by regrouping hundreds (5 hundreds + 10 tens).
5. Subtract 5 tens from 12 tens.
6. Subtract hundreds.

635 −169 = 466	553 −174 = 379	832 −563 = 269	944 −578 = 366
423 −268 = 155	941 −872 = 69	733 −498 = 235	266 −197 = 69
387 −198 = 189	594 −385 = 209	960 −759 = 201	887 −598 = 289

Sue goes to school 185 days a year. Yoko goes to school 313 days a year. How many more days of school does Yoko attend each year? __128__

COMPLETE YEAR GRADE 3

Page 68

Week 6 Practice

Past-Tense Verbs

Write sentences that tell about each picture using the words **was** and **were**. Use words from the box as either nouns or verbs.

pound	spill	toast	list	load	search

Answers will vary.

COMPLETE YEAR GRADE 3

Page 69

Week 6 Practice

Past-Tense Verbs

The **past tense** of a verb tells about something that has already happened. We add a **d** or an **ed** to most verbs to show that something has already happened.

Use the verb from the first sentence to complete the second sentence.

Example:
Please **walk** the dog.   I already __walked__ her.

1. The flowers look good.   They __looked__ better yesterday.
2. Please accept my gift.   I __accepted__ it for my sister.
3. I wonder who will win.   I __wondered__ about it all night.
4. He will saw the wood.   He __sawed__ some last week.
5. Fold the paper neatly.   She __folded__ her paper.
6. Let's cook outside tonight.   We __cooked__ outside last night.
7. Do not block the way.   They __blocked__ the entire street.
8. Form the clay this way.   He __formed__ it into a ball.
9. Follow my car.   We __followed__ them down the street.
10. Glue the pages like this.   She __glued__ the flowers on.

COMPLETE YEAR GRADE 3

Page 70

Week 6 Practice

Future-Tense Verbs

The **future tense** of a verb tells about something that has not happened yet but will happen in the future. **Will** or **shall** are usually used with future tense.

Change the verb tense in each sentence to future tense.

Example: She cooks dinner.
__She will cook dinner.__

1. He plays baseball.
__He will play baseball.__
2. She walks to school.
__She will walk to school.__
3. Bobby talks to the teacher.
__Bobby will talk to the teacher.__
4. I remember to vote.
__I will remember to vote.__
5. Jack mows the lawn every week.
__Jack will mow the lawn every week.__
6. We go on vacation soon.
__We will go on vacation soon.__

COMPLETE YEAR GRADE 3

Answer Key

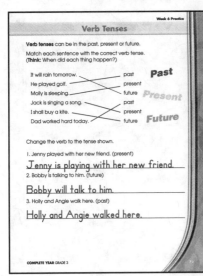

Week 6 Practice

Verb Tenses

Verb tenses can be in the past, present or future.

Match each sentence with the correct verb tense.
(Think: When did each thing happen?)

It will rain tomorrow. — past **Past**
He played golf. — present
Molly is sleeping. — future **Present**
Jack is singing a song. — past
I shall buy a kite. — present **Future**
Dad worked hard today. — future

Change the verb to the tense shown.

1. Jenny played with her new friend. (present)
   Jenny is playing with her new friend.
2. Bobby is talking to him. (future)
   Bobby will talk to him.
3. Holly and Angie walk here. (past)
   Holly and Angie walked here.

COMPLETE YEAR GRADE 3

71

Week 6 Practice

Subject-Verb Agreement

The subject and verb in a sentence must agree in number.

Examples:
An adult **plant makes** seeds.
  singular singular
  noun   verb
Adult **plants make** seeds.
  plural plural
  noun   verb

If the subject and verb agree, circle the letter under **Yes** at the end of the sentence. If they do not, circle the letter under **No**.

	Yes	No
1. Seeds travel in many ways.	(A)	R
2. Sometimes, seeds falls in the water.	T	(D)
3. Then, they may floats a long distance.	S	(L)
4. Animals gather seeds in the fall.	(O)	E
5. Squirrels digs holes to bury their seeds.	M	(A)
6. Cardinals likes to eat sunflower seeds.	J	(N)
7. The wind scatters seeds, too.	(E)	G
8. Dogs carries seeds that are stuck in their fur.	L	(I)
9. Some seeds stick to people's clothing.	(I)	N
10. People plants seeds to grow baby plants.	R	(D)

Write the circled letters on the lines above the matching numbers to spell the answer to this question: *Which lion scatters seeds?*

A   D A N D E L I O N
1   10 5 8 2 7 3 9 4 6

COMPLETE YEAR GRADE 3

72

Week 6 Practice

Subtraction: Regrouping

Study the example. Follow the steps. Subtract using regrouping. If you have to regroup to subtract ones and there are no tens, you must regroup twice.

Example:

```
 300    Steps:
-182    1. Subtract ones. You cannot subtract 2 ones from 0
─────       ones.
 118    2. Regroup. No tens. Regroup hundreds
           (2 hundreds + 10 tens).
        3. Regroup tens (9 tens + 10 ones).
        4. Subtract 2 ones from 10 ones.
        5. Subtract 8 tens from 9 tens.
        6. Subtract 1 hundred from 2 hundreds.
```

602	306	600	807	703
-423	-128	-263	-499	-328
179	178	337	308	375

800	206	400	508	909
-557	-137	-224	-379	-769
243	69	176	129	140

207	604	308	700	900
-138	-397	-199	-531	-278
69	207	109	169	622

COMPLETE YEAR GRADE 3

73

Week 6 Practice

Subtraction: Regrouping

Subtract. Regroup when necessary. The first one is done for you.

7,354	4,214	8,437	6,837
-5,295	-3,185	-5,338	-4,318
2,059	1,029	3,099	2,519

5,735	1,036	6,735	3,841
-3,826	-947	-6,646	-1,953
1,909	89	89	1,888

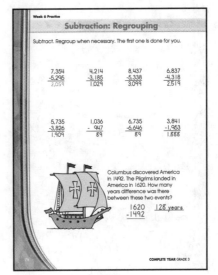

Columbus discovered America in 1492. The Pilgrims landed in America in 1620. How many years difference was there between these two events?

```
 1620     128 years
-1492
```

COMPLETE YEAR GRADE 3

74

Week 6 Practice

Mountaintop Getaway

Solve the problems. Find a path to the cabin by shading in all the answers that have a **3** in them.

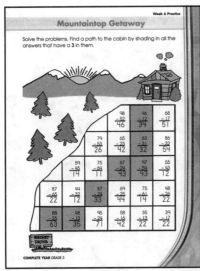

98	46	68
-52	-12	-17
46	34	51

79	65	63	86
-53	-23	-31	-32
26	42	32	54

59	75	67	55
-45	-64	-24	-43
14	11	43	12

87	44	57	69	48
-65	-32	-24	-25	-26
22	12	33	44	22

88	48	95	58	35	39
-25	-13	-16	-16	-13	-17
63	35	71	42	22	22

SECRET PATHS

COMPLETE YEAR GRADE 3

75

Week 6 Practice

Subtraction: Mental Math

Try to do these subtraction problems in your head without using paper and pencil.

9	12	7	5	15	2
-3	-6	-6	-1	-5	-0
6	6	1	4	10	2

40	90	100	20	60	70
-20	-80	-50	-20	-10	-40
20	10	50	0	50	30

450	500	250	690	320	900
-250	-300	-20	-100	-20	-600
200	200	230	590	300	300

1,000	8,000	7,000	4,000	9,500	5,000
-400	-500	-900	-2,000	-4,000	-2,000
600	7,500	6,100	2,000	5,500	3,000

COMPLETE YEAR GRADE 3

76

Answer Key

Page 78

Adjectives

Use the words in the box to answer the questions below. Use each word only once.

| polite careless neat shy selfish thoughtful |

1. Someone who is quiet and needs some time to make new friends is **shy**.

2. A person who says "please" and "thank you" is **polite**

3. Someone who always puts all the toys away is **neat**

4. A person who won't share with others is being **selfish**

5. A person who leaves a bike out all night is being **careless**

6. Someone who thinks of others is **thoughtful**

COMPLETE YEAR GRADE 3

78

Page 79

Adjectives

Use the adjectives in the box to answer the questions below.

| polite careless neat shy selfish thoughtful |

1. Change a letter in each word to make an adjective.

near **neat**

why **shy**

2. Write the word that rhymes with each of these.

fell dish **selfish**

not full **thoughtful**

hair mess **careless**

3. Find these words in the adjectives. Write the adjective.

at **neat**

are **careless**

it **polite**

COMPLETE YEAR GRADE 3

79

Page 80

Adjectives: Explaining Sentences

Use a word from the box to tell about a person in each picture below. Then, write a sentence that explains why you chose that word.

| polite neat careless shy selfish thoughtful |

The word I picked: **shy**

I think so because . . .

the girl is standing alone and looks sad

The word I picked: **thoughtful**

I think so because . . .

it is thoughtful to give someone flowers.

The word I picked: **selfish**

I think so because . . .

the boy is not sharing his cookies.

COMPLETE YEAR GRADE 3

80

Page 81

Adjectives

Look at each picture. Then, add adjectives to the sentences. Use colors, numbers, words from the box and any other words you need to describe each picture.

| polite neat careless shy selfish thoughtful |

Example:
The boy shared his pencil.

The polite boy shared his red pencil.

The girl dropped her coat.

The boy _____

Answers will vary.

The boy put books away.

COMPLETE YEAR GRADE 3

81

Page 82

Marvelous Modifiers

Words that describe are called **adjectives**. Circle the adjectives in the sentences below.

WET PAINT

1. Lucas stared at the (cool) (white) paint in the can.
2. The (green) grass was marked with bits of (white) paint.
3. The (naughty) twins needed a (warm) (soapy) bath.
4. The painters worked with (large) rollers.
5. Lucas thought it was a (great) joke.

For each noun below, write two descriptive adjectives. Then, write a sentence using all three words. *Answers may include:*

1. marshmallows **soft** **white**
Andy ate the soft white marshmallows.

2. airplane **big** **silver**
He is flying to Texas in the big silver airplane.

3. beach **broad** **sandy**
They were playing on the broad sandy beach.

4. summer **hot** **dry**
This year we had a hot, dry summer.

COMPLETE YEAR GRADE 3

82

Page 83

Proper Adjectives

A **proper adjective** is a word that describes a noun or a pronoun. A proper adjective always begins with a capital letter.

Example:
The **American** flag waves proudly over the **United States** capital.

Underline the proper adjective in each sentence.

1. Spanish music is beautiful.
2. Some Americans buy Japanese cars.
3. I saw the Canadian flag flying.
4. Have you ever eaten Irish stew?
5. The Russian language is hard to learn.
6. Did you say you like French fries?
7. My favorite dog is a German shepherd.
8. Dad fished for Alaskan salmon.

Rewrite each phrase, changing the proper noun into a proper adjective.

1. the mountains of Colorado **the Colorado mountains**
2. skyline of Chicago **the Chicago skyline**

COMPLETE YEAR GRADE 3

83

Answer Key

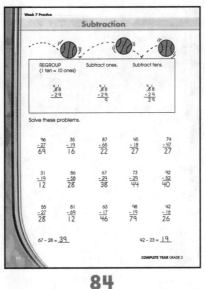

Subtraction

REGROUP
(1 ten = 10 ones)   Subtract ones.   Subtract tens.

Solve these problems.

96 − 27 = 69	35 − 19 = 16	87 − 65 = 22	45 − 18 = 27	74 − 47 = 27
31 − 19 = 12	86 − 58 = 28	67 − 29 = 38	73 − 29 = 44	92 − 52 = 40
55 − 27 = 28	81 − 69 = 12	63 − 17 = 46	98 − 19 = 79	42 − 16 = 26

67 − 28 = 39   42 − 23 = 19

COMPLETE YEAR GRADE 3

84

Round and Round She Goes...

Take a ride around this wheel. Solve the subtraction problems.

800 − 736 = 64
406 − 243 = 163
200 − 82 = 118
900 − 623 = 277
800 − 744 = 56
700 − 543 = 157
600 − 432 = 168
400 − 278 = 122
500 − 248 = 252
400 − 324 = 76
400 − 365 = 35
300 − 284 = 16

COMPLETE YEAR GRADE 3

85

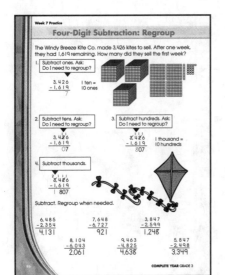

Four-Digit Subtraction: Regroup

The Windy Breeze Kite Co. made 3,426 kites to sell. After one week, they had 1,619 remaining. How many did they sell the first week?

1. Subtract ones. Ask: Do I need to regroup?

3,426 − 1,619 = 7   1 ten = 10 ones

2. Subtract tens. Ask: Do I need to regroup?

3,426 − 1,619 = 07

3. Subtract hundreds. Ask: Do I need to regroup?

3,426 − 1,619 = 807   1 thousand = 10 hundreds

4. Subtract thousands.

3,426 − 1,619 = 1,807

Subtract. Regroup when needed.

6,485 − 2,354 = 4,131	7,648 − 6,727 = 921	3,847 − 2,599 = 1,248
8,104 − 6,043 = 2,061	9,463 − 4,825 = 4,638	5,847 − 2,498 = 3,349

COMPLETE YEAR GRADE 3

86

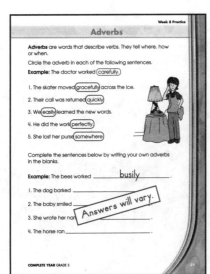

Adjectives That Compare

Add **er** to most **adjectives** when comparing two nouns. Add **est** to most adjectives when comparing three or more nouns.

Example: The forecaster said this winter is **colder** than last winter.
It is the **coldest** winter on record.

Write the correct form of the adjective in parentheses.

1. The weather map showed that the **coldest** place of all was Fargo, North Dakota. (cold)
2. The **warmest** city of all was Needles, California. (warm)
3. Does San Diego get **hotter** than San Francisco? (hot)
4. The **deepest** snow of all fell in Buffalo, New York. (deep)
5. That snowfall was two inches **deeper** than in Syracuse. (deep)
6. The **windiest** place in the country was Wichita, Kansas. (windy)
7. The **strongest** winds of all blew there. (strong)
8. The **foggiest** city in the U.S. was Chicago. (foggy)
9. Seattle was the **rainiest** of all the cities listed on the map. (rainy)
10. It is usually **rainier** in Seattle than in Portland. (rainy)

COMPLETE YEAR GRADE 3

88

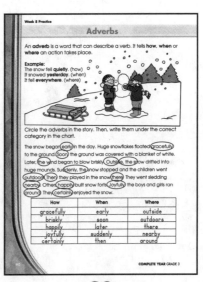

Adverbs

Adverbs are words that describe verbs. They tell where, how or when.

Circle the adverb in each of the following sentences.

Example: The doctor worked (carefully.)

1. The skater moved (gracefully) across the ice.
2. Their call was returned (quickly.)
3. We (easily) learned the new words.
4. He did the work (perfectly.)
5. She lost her purse (somewhere.)

Complete the sentences below by writing your own adverbs in the blanks.

Example: The bees worked ____busily____.

1. The dog barked ____
2. The baby smiled ____
3. She wrote her nam ____   Answers will vary.
4. The horse ran ____

COMPLETE YEAR GRADE 3

89

Adverbs

An **adverb** is a word that can describe a verb. It tells **how**, **when** or **where** an action takes place.

Example:
The snow fell **quietly**. (how)
It snowed **yesterday**. (when)
It fell **everywhere**. (where)

Circle the adverbs in the story. Then, write them under the correct category in the chart.

The snow began (early) in the day. Huge snowflakes floated (gracefully) to the ground. (Soon) the ground was covered with a blanket of white. Later, the wind began to blow (briskly.) (Outside,) the snow drifted into huge mounds. (Suddenly,) the snow stopped and the children went (outdoors.) (Then) they played in the snow (there.) They went sledding (nearby.) Other (happily) built snow forts (joyfully) the boys and girls ran (around.) They (certainly) enjoyed the snow.

How	When	Where
gracefully	early	outside
briskly	soon	outdoors
happily	later	there
joyfully	suddenly	nearby
certainly	then	around

COMPLETE YEAR GRADE 3

90

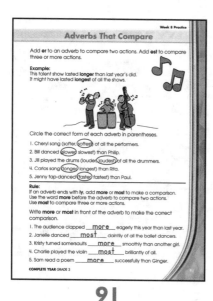

Adverbs That Compare

Add **er** to an adverb to compare two actions. Add **est** to compare three or more actions.

Example:
This talent show lasted **longer** than last year's did.
It might have lasted **longest** of all the shows.

Circle the correct form of each adverb in parentheses.

1. Cheryl sang (softer, (softest)) of all the performers.
2. Bill danced ((slower) slowest) than Philip.
3. Jill played the drums (louder, (loudest)) of all the drummers.
4. Carlos sang ((longer) longest) than Rita.
5. Jenny tap-danced ((faster) fastest) than Paul.

Rule:
If an adverb ends with **ly**, add **more** or **most** to make a comparison. Use the word **more** before the adverb to compare two actions. Use **most** to compare three or more actions.

Write **more** or **most** in front of the adverb to make the correct comparison.

1. The audience clapped ___more___ eagerly this year than last year.
2. Janelle danced ___most___ daintily of all the ballet dancers.
3. Kristy turned somersaults ___more___ smoothly than another girl.
4. Charlie played the violin ___most___ brilliantly of all.
5. Sam read a poem ___more___ successfully than Ginger.

COMPLETE YEAR GRADE 3

91

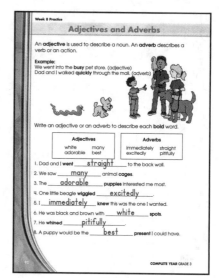

Adjectives and Adverbs

An **adjective** is used to describe a noun. An **adverb** describes a verb or an action.

Example:
We went into the **busy** pet store. (adjective)
Dad and I walked **quickly** through the mall. (adverb)

Write an adjective or an adverb to describe each **bold** word.

Adjectives		Adverbs	
white	many	immediately	straight
adorable	best	excitedly	pitifully

1. Dad and I went ___straight___ to the back wall.
2. We saw ___many___ animal cages.
3. The ___adorable___ puppies interested me most.
4. One little beagle wiggled ___excitedly___.
5. I ___immediately___ knew this was the one I wanted.
6. He was black and brown with ___white___ spots.
7. He whined ___pitifully___.
8. A puppy would be the ___best___ present I could have.

COMPLETE YEAR GRADE 3

92

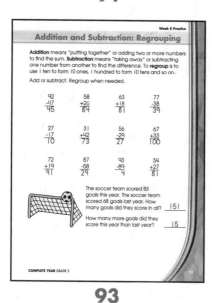

Addition and Subtraction: Regrouping

Addition means "putting together" or adding two or more numbers to find the sum. **Subtraction** means "taking away" or subtracting one number from another to find the difference. To **regroup** is to use 1 ten to form 10 ones, 1 hundred to form 10 tens and so on.

Add or subtract. Regroup when needed.

```
  92      58      63      77
 -17     +26     +18     -38
  75      84      81      39

  27      31      56      67
 -17     +42     -29     +33
  10      73      27     100

  72      87      93      54
 +19     -58     -89     +27
  91      29       4      81
```

The soccer team scored 83 goals this year. The soccer team scored 68 goals last year. How many goals did they score in all? ___151___

How many more goals did they score this year than last year? ___15___

COMPLETE YEAR GRADE 3

93

Addition and Subtraction

Add or subtract using regrouping.

```
   28       82       33       67
   56       49       75       94
  +93      +51     +128     +248
  177      182      236      409

  683      756      818      956
 -495     +139     -387     +267
  188      895      431    1,223

1,588    4,675    8,732    2,938
 -989   -2,976   -5,664   +3,459
  599    1,699    3,068    6,397
```

To drive from New York City to Los Angeles is 2,832 miles. To drive from New York City to Miami is 1,327 miles. How much farther is it to drive from New York City to Los Angeles than from New York City to Miami?

```
  2,832
 -1,327
  1,505
```

COMPLETE YEAR GRADE 3

94

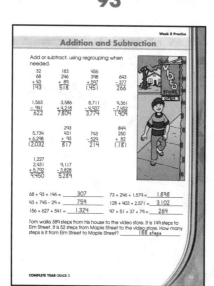

Addition and Subtraction

Add or subtract, using regrouping when needed.

```
   32      183      466
   68      246      398      643
  +43      +89     +597     -377
  143      518    1,451      266

1,563    3,586    8,711    9,361
 -941   +4,218   -4,937   -7,452
  622    7,804    3,774    1,909

5,734      293      743      849
+6,298     431              250
12,032     +93     -529      +82
           817      214    1,181

1,227
2,431    9,117
+5,792  -3,828
 9,450   5,289
```

68 + 93 + 146 = ___307___   73 + 246 + 1,579 = ___1,898___
43 + 745 - 29 = ___759___   128 + 403 + 2,571 = ___3,102___
156 + 627 + 541 = ___1,324___   97 + 51 + 37 + 79 = ___264___

Tom walks 389 steps from his house to the video store. It is 149 steps to Elm Street. It is 52 steps from Maple Street to the video store. How many steps is it from Elm Street to Maple Street? ___188 steps___

COMPLETE YEAR GRADE 3

95

Addition and Subtraction

Add or subtract, using regrouping when needed.

```
   38    1,269    5,792      629    4,647
   43    2,453   -4,814      491   -2,988
  +21   +8,219      978     +308    1,709
  102   11,941            1,428

5,280       68      197    7,321      456
-3,147      27     +213   -2,789     +974
 2,133     +42      816    4,532    1,430
           137

3,932      492    9,873    4,978    6,235
+4,681     863    +5,483  +2,131   +2,986
 8,613     +57   15,356    7,109    9,221
         1,412
```

Sue stocked her pond with 263 bass and 187 trout. 97 fish swam away in a flood. How many fish are left? ___353 fish___

COMPLETE YEAR GRADE 3

96

Answer Key

98

Week 9 Practice

Parts of Speech

Nouns, pronouns, verbs, adjectives, adverbs and prepositions are all **parts of speech**.

Label the words in each sentence with the correct part of speech.

Example: The cat is fat.
article noun verb adjective

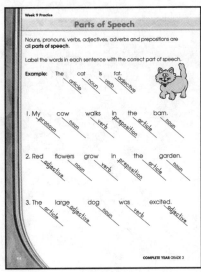

1. My cow walks in the barn.
pronoun noun verb preposition article noun

2. Red flowers grow in the garden.
adjective noun verb preposition article noun

3. The large dog was excited.
article adjective noun verb adjective

COMPLETE YEAR GRADE 3

99

Week 9 Practice

Parts of Speech

Ask someone to give you nouns, verbs, adjectives and pronouns where shown. Write them in the blanks. Read the story to your friend when you finish.

The _____ Adventure
(adjective)

I went for a _____. I found a really big _____.
(noun)   (noun)

It was so _____ that I _____ all the
(adjective)   (verb)

way home. I put it in my _____ ...ment, it
(noun)

began to _____ ... t to my
(verb)

I decid... _____ it in a box and wrap it up with
(verb)

_____ paper. I gave it to _____ for a
(adjective)   (person)

present. When _____ opened it, _____
(pronoun)   (pronoun)

_____ _____ shouted, "Thank you!
(past-tense verb) (pronoun)

This is the best _____ I've ever had!"
(noun)

Answers will vary.

COMPLETE YEAR GRADE 3

100

Week 9 Practice

Parts of Speech

Write the part of speech of each underlined word.

NOUN PRONOUN VERB ADJECTIVE ADVERB PREPOSITION

There <u>are</u> many <u>different</u> kinds of animals. Some animals <u>live</u> in the wild. Some animals live in the <u>zoo</u>. And still others live in homes. The animals that <u>live</u> in homes are called pets.

There are many types of pets. Some pets without fur are fish, turtles, snakes and hermit crabs. Trained birds can fly <u>around</u> <u>your</u> house. Some <u>furry</u> animals are cats, dogs, rabbits, ferrets, gerbils or hamsters. Some animals can <u>successfully</u> learn tricks that <u>you</u> teach them. Whatever your favorite animal is, animals can be <u>special</u> friends!

1. verb   4. verb
2. adjective   5. preposition   7. adjective   9. pronoun
3. noun   6. pronoun   8. adverb   10. adjective

COMPLETE YEAR GRADE 3

101

Week 9 Practice

Sentence Building

A **sentence** can tell more and more. Read the sentence parts. Write a word on each line to make each sentence tell more.

Answers will vary.

1. Mrs. Brown bought a sweater.
   Who?

2. Mrs. Brown bought a sweater and two shirts.
   Who?   What?

3. Mrs. Brown bought a sweater and two shirts
   Who?   What?
   before leaving the store.
   Where?

4. Mrs. Brown bought a sweater and two shirts
   Who?   What?
   before leaving the store to pick up Sally
   Where?   Who?

5. Mrs. Brown bought a sweater and two shirts
   Who?   What?
   before leaving the store to pick up Sally
   Where?   Who?
   at 3:00 p.m.
   When?

COMPLETE YEAR GRADE 3

102

Week 9 Practice

Kinds of Sentences

Remember: a **statement** tells something, a **question** asks something and a **command** tells someone to do something.

On each line, write a statement, question or command. Use a word from the box in each sentence.

| glue | share | decide |
| enter | add | fold |

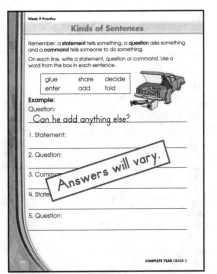

Example:
Question:
Can he add anything else?

1. Statement:
_____

2. Question:
_____

3. Comm...

4. State...

Answers will vary.

5. Question:
_____

COMPLETE YEAR GRADE 3

103

Week 9 Practice

Kinds of Sentences

Use the group of words below to write three sentences: a **statement**, a **question** and a **command**.

add can these he quickly numbers

Example:
Statement:
He can add these numbers quickly.

Question:
Can he add these numbers quickly?

Command:
Add these numbers quickly.

fold here should we it

1. Statement:
_____

2. Question:
_____

Answers will vary.

3. Com...

COMPLETE YEAR GRADE 3

104

Week 9 Practice

Problem-Solving: Addition, Subtraction

Read and solve each problem. The first one is done for you.

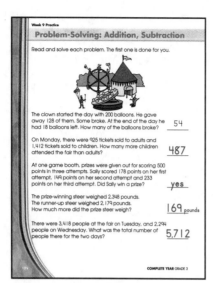

The clown started the day with 200 balloons. He gave away 128 of them. Some broke. At the end of the day he had 18 balloons left. How many of the balloons broke? **54**

On Monday, there were 925 tickets sold to adults and 1,412 tickets sold to children. How many more children attended the fair than adults? **487**

At one game booth, prizes were given out for scoring 500 points in three attempts. Sally scored 178 points on her first attempt, 149 points on her second attempt and 233 points on her third attempt. Did Sally win a prize? **yes**

The prize-winning steer weighed 2,348 pounds. The runner-up steer weighed 2,179 pounds. How much more did the prize steer weigh? **169** pounds

There were 3,418 people at the fair on Tuesday, and 2,294 people on Wednesday. What was the total number of people there for the two days? **5,712**

COMPLETE YEAR GRADE 3

105

Week 9 Practice

Wacky Waldo's Animal Circus

Wacky Waldo has trained a very unusual animal circus. He taught sharks to ride tricycles. He trained mice to scare tigers and snakes to be as cuddly as kittens. He even trained donkeys to fly like sparrows.

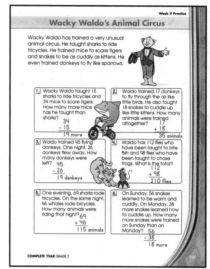

1. Wacky Waldo taught 15 sharks to ride tricycles and 34 mice to scare tigers. How many more mice has he taught than sharks?
34
− 15
19 more

2. Waldo trained 17 donkeys to fly through the air like little birds. He also taught 18 snakes to cuddle up like little kittens. How many animals were trained altogether?
17
+ 18
35 animals

3. Waldo trained 45 flying donkeys. One night, 26 donkeys flew away. How many donkeys were left?
45
− 26
19 donkeys

4. Waldo has 112 flies who have been taught to bite fish and 98 flies who have been taught to chase frogs. What is the total?
112
+ 98
210 flies

5. One evening, 69 sharks rode tricycles. On the same night, 46 whales rode bicycles. How many animals were riding that night?
69
+ 46
115 animals

6. On Sunday, 56 snakes learned to be warm and cuddly. On Monday, 38 more snakes learned how to cuddle up. How many more snakes were trained on Sunday than on Monday?
56
− 38
18 more

COMPLETE YEAR GRADE 3

106

Week 9 Practice

Lizzy the Lizard

Lizzy the Lizard has a great collection of insects. She is always on the lookout for new and different types of bugs.

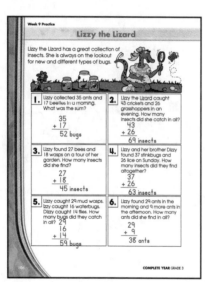

1. Lizzy collected 35 ants and 17 beetles in a morning. What was the sum?
35
+ 17
52 bugs

2. Lizzy the Lizard caught 43 crickets and 26 grasshoppers in an evening. How many insects did she catch in all?
43
+ 26
69 insects

3. Lizzy found 27 bees and 18 wasps on a tour of her garden. How many insects did she find?
27
+ 18
45 insects

4. Lizzy and her brother Dizzy found 37 stinkbugs and 26 lice on Sunday. How many insects did they find altogether?
37
+ 26
63 insects

5. Lizzy caught 29 mud wasps. Izzy caught 16 waterbugs. Dizzy caught 14 flies. How many bugs did they catch in all?
29
16
+ 14
59 bugs

6. Lizzy found 29 ants in the morning and 9 more ants in the afternoon. How many ants did she find in all?
29
+ 9
38 ants

COMPLETE YEAR GRADE 3

112

Week 10 Practice

Statements

A **statement** is a sentence that tells something.

Use the words in the box to complete the statements below. Write the words on the lines.

| glue | decide | add |
| share | enter | fold |

1. It took ten minutes for Kayla to **add** the numbers.

2. Ben wants to **share** his cookies with me.

3. "I can't **decide** which color to choose," said Rocky.

4. **Glue** can be used to make things stick together.

5. "This is how you **fold** your paper in half," said Mrs. Green.

6. The opposite of **leave** is **enter**.

Write your own statement on the line.

Answers will vary.

COMPLETE YEAR GRADE 3

113

Week 10 Practice

Questions

Questions are asking sentences. They begin with a capital letter and end with a question mark. Many questions begin with the words **who**, **what**, **why**, **when**, **where** and **how**. Write six questions using the question words below. Make sure to end each question with a question mark.

1. Who
2. What
3. Why
4. When
5. Where
6. How

Answers will vary.

COMPLETE YEAR GRADE 3

114

Week 10 Practice

Statements and Questions

Statements are sentences that tell about something. Statements begin with a capital letter and end with a period. **Questions** are sentences that ask about something. Questions begin with a capital letter and end with a question mark.

Rewrite the sentences using capital letters and either a period or a question mark.

Example: walruses live in the Arctic
Walruses live in the Arctic.

1. are walruses large sea mammals or fish
Are walruses large sea mammals or fish?

2. they spend most of their time in the water and on ice
They spend most of their time in the water and on ice.

3. are floating sheets of ice called ice floes
Are floating sheets of ice called ice floes?

4. are walruses related to seals
Are walruses related to seals?

5. their skin is thick, wrinkled and almost hairless
Their skin is thick, wrinkled and almost hairless.

COMPLETE YEAR GRADE 3

Answer Key

Statements and Questions

Change the statements into questions and the questions into statements.

Example: Jane is happy. Is Jane happy?
Were you late? You were late.

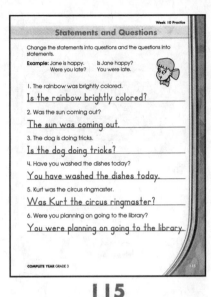

1. The rainbow was brightly colored.
Is the rainbow brightly colored?

2. Was the sun coming out?
The sun was coming out.

3. The dog is doing tricks.
Is the dog doing tricks?

4. Have you washed the dishes today?
You have washed the dishes today.

5. Kurt was the circus ringmaster.
Was Kurt the circus ringmaster?

6. Were you planning on going to the library?
You were planning on going to the library.

COMPLETE YEAR GRADE 3

115

Word Order in Sentences

You can often make a question out of a statement by changing the word order of the sentence.

Examples:
My family is going on a camping trip. (statement)
Is my family going on a camping trip? (question)

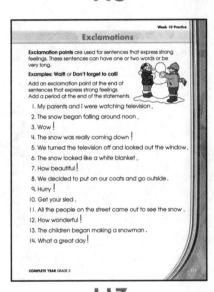

Change the word order to make each statement a question and each question a statement. Write the new sentence on the line.

1. Mom and Dad are going to take turns driving.
Are Mom and Dad going to take turns driving?
2. Ellen is getting the gear together.
Is Ellen getting the gear together?
3. James is packing the car trunk.
Is James packing the car trunk?
4. Will it be dark when we arrive at the lake?
It will be dark when we arrive at the lake.
5. Joey's job is to put up the tent.
Is it Joey's job to put up the tent?
6. Will we sit around the fire and tell stories.
We will sit around the fire and tell stories.

COMPLETE YEAR GRADE 3

116

Exclamations

Exclamation points are used for sentences that express strong feelings. These sentences can have one or two words or be very long.

Examples: Wait! or **Don't forget to call!**

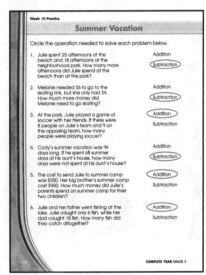

Add an exclamation point at the end of sentences that express strong feelings.
Add a period at the end of the statements.

1. My parents and I were watching television.
2. The snow began falling around noon.
3. Wow!
4. The snow was really coming down!
5. We turned the television off and looked out the window.
6. The snow looked like a white blanket.
7. How beautiful!
8. We decided to put on our coats and go outside.
9. Hurry!
10. Get your sled.
11. All the people on the street came out to see the snow.
12. How wonderful!
13. The children began making a snowman.
14. What a great day!

COMPLETE YEAR GRADE 3

117

Summer Vacation

Circle the operation needed to solve each problem below.

1. Julie spent 25 afternoons at the beach and 18 afternoons at the neighborhood park. How many more afternoons did Julie spend at the beach than at the park? Addition **(Subtraction)**

2. Melanie needed $6 to go to the skating rink, but she only had $4. How much more money did Melanie need to go skating? Addition **(Subtraction)**

3. At the park, Julie played a game of soccer with her friends. If there were 8 people on Julie's team and 9 on the opposing team, how many people were playing soccer? **(Addition)** Subtraction

4. Cody's summer vacation was 94 days long. If he spent 68 summer days at his aunt's house, how many days were not spent at his aunt's house? Addition **(Subtraction)**

5. The cost to send Julie to summer camp was $350. Her big brother's summer camp cost $450. How much money did Julie's parents spend on summer camp for their two children? **(Addition)** Subtraction

6. Julie and her father went fishing at the lake. Julie caught only 6 fish, while her dad caught 18 fish. How many fish did they catch altogether? **(Addition)** Subtraction

COMPLETE YEAR GRADE 3

118

Movie Inventory

Janice helped her mother keep track of movies at the library. Write the answer to each problem on the line.

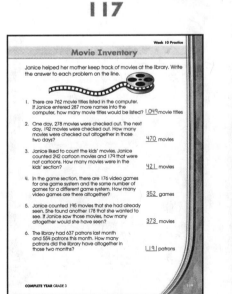

1. There are 762 movie titles listed in the computer. If Janice entered 287 more names into the computer, how many movie titles would be listed? 1,049 movie titles

2. One day, 278 movies were checked out. The next day, 192 movies were checked out. How many movies were checked out altogether in those two days? 470 movies

3. Janice liked to count the kids' movies. Janice counted 242 cartoon movies and 179 that were not cartoons. How many movies were in the kids' section? 421 movies

4. In the game section, there are 176 video games for one game system and the same number of games for a different game system. How many video games are there altogether? 352 games

5. Janice counted 195 movies that she had already seen. She found another 178 that she wanted to see. If Janice saw those movies, how many altogether would she have seen? 373 movies

6. The library had 637 patrons last month and 554 patrons this month. How many patrons did the library have altogether in those two months? 1,191 patrons

COMPLETE YEAR GRADE 3

119

Building a House

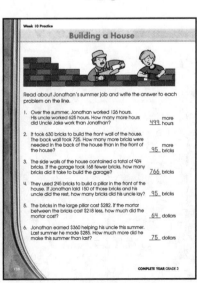

Read about Jonathan's summer job and write the answer to each problem on the line.

1. Over the summer, Jonathan worked 126 hours. His uncle worked 625 hours. How many more hours did Uncle Jake work than Jonathan? 499 more hours

2. It took 630 bricks to build the front wall of the house. The back wall took 725. How many more bricks were needed in the back of the house than in the front of the house? 95 more bricks

3. The side walls of the house contained a total of 934 bricks. If the garage took 168 fewer bricks, how many bricks did it take to build the garage? 766 bricks

4. They used 245 bricks to build a pillar in the front of the house. If Jonathan laid 150 of those bricks and his uncle did the rest, how many bricks did his uncle lay? 95 bricks

5. The bricks in the large pillar cost $282. If the mortar between the bricks cost $218 less, how much did the mortar cost? 64 dollars

6. Jonathan earned $360 helping his uncle this summer. Last summer he made $285. How much more did he make this summer than last? 75 dollars

COMPLETE YEAR GRADE 3

120

Answer Key

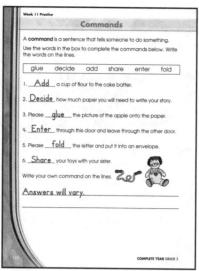

Week 11 Practice

Commands

A **command** is a sentence that tells someone to do something.
Use the words in the box to complete the commands below. Write the words on the lines.

| glue | decide | add | share | enter | fold |

1. **Add** a cup of flour to the cake batter.
2. **Decide** how much paper you will need to write your story.
3. Please **glue** the picture of the apple onto the paper.
4. **Enter** through this door and leave through the other door.
5. Please **fold** the letter and put it into an envelope.
6. **Share** your toys with your sister.

Write your own command on the lines.

Answers will vary.

COMPLETE YEAR GRADE 3

122

Week 11 Practice

Commands

A **command** is a sentence that tells someone to do something. It ends with a **period**.

The kids at Camp Lagoona have not cleaned their cabin. Their leader is telling them what they have to do. Write eight commands that will tell the campers things they must do to clean the cabin.

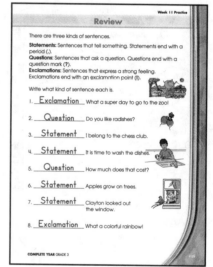

Answers may include:

1. Make the beds.
2. Empty the trash.
3. Put your clothes away.
4. Close the dresser drawers.
5. Put the shade back on the lamp.
6. Pick things up off the floor.
7. Straighten the mirror.
8. Put the hairbrush away.

COMPLETE YEAR GRADE 3

123

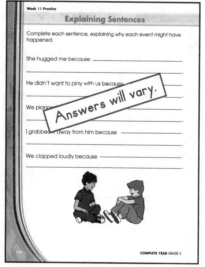

Week 11 Practice

Explaining Sentences

Complete each sentence, explaining why each event might have happened.

She hugged me because _____

_____

He didn't want to play with us because _____

We planned _____

I grabbed it away from him because _____

We clapped loudly because _____

_____

Answers will vary.

COMPLETE YEAR GRADE 3

124

Week 11 Practice

Review

There are three kinds of sentences.

Statements: Sentences that tell something. Statements end with a period (.).
Questions: Sentences that ask a question. Questions end with a question mark (?).
Exclamations: Sentences that express a strong feeling. Exclamations end with an exclamation point (!).

Write what kind of sentence each is.

1. **Exclamation** What a super day to go to the zoo!
2. **Question** Do you like radishes?
3. **Statement** I belong to the chess club.
4. **Statement** It is time to wash the dishes.
5. **Question** How much does that cost?
6. **Statement** Apples grow on trees.
7. **Statement** Clayton looked out the window.
8. **Exclamation** What a colorful rainbow!

COMPLETE YEAR GRADE 3

125

Week 11 Practice

Four Kinds of Sentences

Always begin a sentence with a capital letter. End a statement or a command with a period. End a question with a question mark. End an exclamation with an exclamation point.

Examples:
Grizzly bears are fascinating creatures. (statement)
Do they live in all parts of the world? (question)
Grizzly bears are huge! (exclamation)
Tell me more about bears. (command)

Rewrite each sentence using the correct capitalization and punctuation.

1. grizzly bears live in Wyoming, Montana, Idaho, Alaska and western Canada
   Grizzly bears live in Wyoming, Montana, Idaho, Alaska and western Canada.
2. some grizzlies are eight feet in length
   Some grizzlies are eight feet in length.
3. did you know that male grizzlies can weigh 800 pounds
   Did you know that male grizzlies can weigh 800 pounds?
4. these bears are huge
   These bears are huge!
5. they can run very quickly
   They can run very quickly.
6. that's incredible speed
   That's incredible speed!
7. what do grizzly bears eat?
   What do grizzly bears eat?
8. they eat acorns, roots, berries and leaves
   They eat acorns, roots, berries and leaves.
9. they also eat fish, birds, insects and small mammals
   They also eat fish, birds, insects and small mammals.

COMPLETE YEAR GRADE 3

126

Week 11 Practice

Kinds of Sentences

A **statement** is a sentence that tells something.
A **question** is a sentence that asks something.
A **command** is a sentence that tells someone to do something.

Commands usually end with a **please**. They usually end with a period. The noun is **you** but does not need to be part of the sentence.

Example: "Come here, please." means "**You** come here, please."

Examples of commands: Stand next to me.
Please give me some paper.

Write **S** in front of the statements, **Q** in front of the questions and **C** in front of the commands. End each sentence with a period or a question mark.

Example:

C Stop and look before you cross the street.
Q 1. Did you do your math homework?
S 2. I think I lost my math book.
Q 3. Will you help me find it?
S 4. I looked everywhere.
C 5. Please open your math books to page three.
Q 6. Did you look under your desk?
S 7. I looked, but it's not there.
Q 8. Who can add seven and four?
C 9. Come up and write the answer on the board.
Q 10. Chris, where is your math book?
S 11. I don't know for sure.
C 12. Please share a book with a friend.

COMPLETE YEAR GRADE 3

127

Answer Key

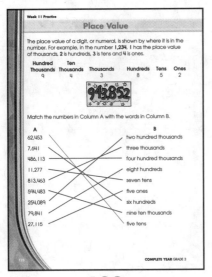

128

129

130

132

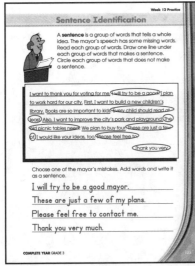

133

A Penny for Your Thoughts

Week 12 Practice

A **phrase** is an **incomplete** thought—it doesn't make sense all by itself. A **sentence** is a **complete** thought.

Circle **phrase** or **sentence** to show whether each group of words below is an incomplete or a complete thought.

1. day of feasting in the village — (phrase) / sentence
2. It was a string of blue beads — phrase / (sentence)
3. the chief was pleased — phrase / (sentence)
4. played drums and danced — (phrase) / sentence
5. he looked at the ship — phrase / (sentence)
6. pointed to the north — (phrase) / sentence
7. rowed toward the ship — (phrase) / sentence
8. we will tell the chief — phrase / (sentence)
9. she is sad — phrase / (sentence)
10. going back to England — (phrase) / sentence

Add words to the phrases above to make complete thoughts. Don't forget to start each sentence with a capital letter and end it with a period.

Answers may include:

Yesterday was a day of feasting in the village.
We played drums and danced to celebrate the occasion.
He pointed to the north to show us the direction they would travel.
They rowed toward the ship.
They were going back to England.

COMPLETE YEAR GRADE 3

134

Answer Key

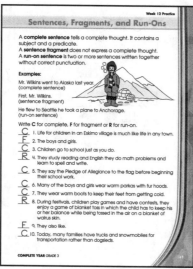

Week 12 Practice

Sentences, Fragments, and Run-Ons

A **complete sentence** tells a complete thought. It contains a subject and a predicate.
A **sentence fragment** does not express a complete thought.
A **run-on sentence** is two or more sentences written together without correct punctuation.

Examples:

Mr. Wilkins went to Alaska last year.
(complete sentence)

First, Mr. Wilkins.
(sentence fragment)

He flew to Seattle he took a plane to Anchorage.
(run-on sentence)

Write **C** for complete, **F** for fragment or **R** for run-on.

C 1. Life for children in an Eskimo village is much like life in any town.
F 2. The boys and girls.
C 3. Children go to school just as you do.
R 4. They study reading and English they do math problems and learn to spell and write.
C 5. They say the Pledge of Allegiance to the flag before beginning their school work.
C 6. Many of the boys and girls wear warm parkas with fur hoods.
C 7. They wear warm boots to keep their feet from getting cold.
R 8. During festivals, children play games and have contests, they enjoy a game of blanket toss in which the child has to keep his or her balance while being tossed in the air on a blanket of walrus skin.
F 9. They also like.
C 10. Today, many families have trucks and snowmobiles for transportation rather than dogsleds.

COMPLETE YEAR GRADE 3

135

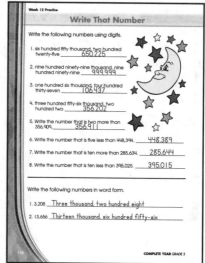

Week 12 Practice

Write That Number

Write the following numbers using digits.

1. six hundred fifty thousand, two hundred twenty-five __650,225__
2. nine hundred ninety-nine thousand, nine hundred ninety-nine __999,999__
3. one hundred six thousand, four hundred thirty-seven __106,437__
4. three hundred fifty-six thousand, two hundred two __356,202__
5. Write the number that is two more than 356,909. __356,911__
6. Write the number that is five less than 448,394. __448,389__
7. Write the number that is ten more than 285,634. __285,644__
8. Write the number that is ten less than 395,025. __395,015__

Write the following numbers in word form.

1. 3,208 __Three thousand, two hundred eight__
2. 13,656 __Thirteen thousand, six hundred fifty-six__

COMPLETE YEAR GRADE 3

136

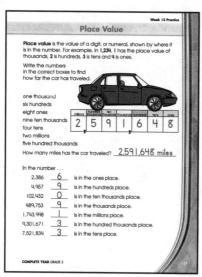

Week 12 Practice

Place Value

Place value is the value of a digit, or numeral, shown by where it is in the number. For example, in 1,234, 1 has the place value of thousands, 2 is hundreds, 3 is tens and 4 is ones.

Write the numbers in the correct boxes to find how far the car has traveled.

one thousand
six hundreds
eight ones
nine ten thousands
four tens
two millions
five hundred thousands

millions	hundred thousands	ten thousands	thousands	hundreds	tens	ones
2	5	9	1	6	4	8

How many miles has the car traveled? __2,591,648 miles__

In the number . . .

2,386 __6__ is in the ones place.
4,957 __9__ is in the hundreds place.
102,432 __0__ is in the ten thousands place.
489,753 __9__ is in the thousands place.
1,743,998 __1__ is in the millions place.
9,301,671 __3__ is in the hundred thousands place.
7,521,834 __3__ is in the tens place.

COMPLETE YEAR GRADE 3

137

Week 12 Practice

Place Value: Standard Form

For this activity, you will need a number spinner or number cube.

Roll the cube or spin the spinner the same number of times as there are spaces in each place value box. The first number rolled or spun goes in the ones place, the second number in the tens place, and so on.

Example:

thousands	hundreds	tens	ones
4	5	6	7

Standard Form
4,567

Answers will vary.

Write the number words for the numerals above.

__four thousand + five hundred + sixty + seven__

__Answers will vary.__

COMPLETE YEAR GRADE 3

138

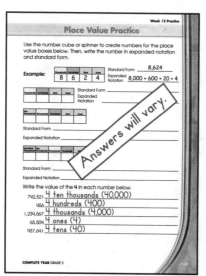

Week 12 Practice

Place Value Practice

Use the number cube or spinner to create numbers for the place value boxes below. Then, write the number in expanded notation and standard form.

Example:

thousands	hundreds	tens	ones
8	6	2	4

Standard Form __8,624__
Expanded Notation __8,000 + 600 + 20 + 4__

Answers will vary.

Write the value of the 4 in each number below.

742,521 __4 ten thousands (40,000)__
456 __4 hundreds (400)__
1,234,567 __4 thousands (4,000)__
65,504 __4 ones (4)__
937,641 __4 tens (40)__

COMPLETE YEAR GRADE 3

139

Week 12 Practice

Rounding: The Nearest Ten

If the ones number is 5 or greater, "round up" to the nearest 10. If the ones number is 4 or less, the tens number stays the same and the ones number becomes a zero.

Examples: 15 round up to 20   23 round down to 20   47 round up to 50

7 __10__   58 __60__
12 __10__   81 __80__
33 __30__   94 __90__
27 __30__   44 __40__
73 __70__   88 __90__
25 __30__   66 __70__
39 __40__   70 __70__

COMPLETE YEAR GRADE 3

140

Answer Key

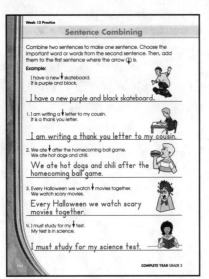

Week 13 Practice

Sentence Combining

Combine two sentences to make one sentence. Choose the important word or words from the second sentence. Then, add them to the first sentence where the arrow ⬇ is.

Example:
I have a new ⬇ skateboard.
It is purple and black.

I have a new purple and black skateboard.

1. I am writing a ⬇ letter to my cousin.
   It is a thank you letter.

I am writing a thank you letter to my cousin.

2. We ate ⬇ after the homecoming ball game.
   We ate hot dogs and chili.

We ate hot dogs and chili after the homecoming ball game.

3. Every Halloween we watch ⬇ movies together.
   We watch scary movies.

Every Halloween we watch scary movies together.

4. I must study for my ⬇ test.
   My test is in science.

I must study for my science test.

COMPLETE YEAR GRADE 3

142

Week 13 Practice

And and But

We can use **and** or **but** to make one longer sentence from two short ones.

Use **and** or **but** to make two short sentences into a longer, more interesting one. Write the new sentence on the line below the two short sentences.

Example:
The skunk has black fur. The skunk has a white stripe.

The skunk has black fur and a white stripe.

1. The skunk has a small head. The skunk has small ears.

The skunk has a small head and small ears.

2. The skunk has short legs. Skunks can move quickly.

The skunk has short legs but can move quickly.

3. Skunks sleep in hollow trees. Skunks sleep underground.

Skunks sleep in hollow trees and underground.

4. Skunks are chased by animals. Skunks do not run away.

Skunks are chased by animals but do not run away.

5. Skunks sleep during the day. Skunks hunt at night.

Skunks sleep during the day and hunt at night.

COMPLETE YEAR GRADE 3

143

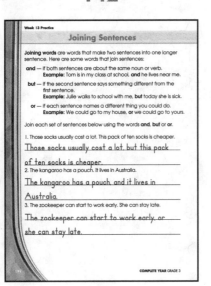

Week 13 Practice

Joining Sentences

Joining words are words that make two sentences into one longer sentence. Here are some words that join sentences:

and — if both sentences are about the same noun or verb.
Example: Tom is in my class at school, **and** he lives near me.

but — if the second sentence says something different from the first sentence.
Example: Julie walks to school with me, **but** today she is sick.

or — if each sentence names a different thing you could do.
Example: We could go to my house, **or** we could go to yours.

Join each set of sentences below using the words **and**, **but** or **or**.

1. Those socks usually cost a lot. This pack of ten socks is cheaper.

Those socks usually cost a lot, but this pack of ten socks is cheaper.

2. The kangaroo has a pouch. It lives in Australia.

The kangaroo has a pouch, and it lives in Australia.

3. The zookeeper can start to work early. She can stay late.

The zookeeper can start to work early, or she can stay late.

COMPLETE YEAR GRADE 3

144

Week 13 Practice

Joining Sentences

If and **when** can be joining words, too.

Read each set of sentences. Then, join the two sentences to make one longer sentence.

Example: The apples will need to be washed.
The apples are dirty.

The apples will need to be washed if they are dirty.

1. The size of the crowd grew. It grew when the game began.

The size of the crowd grew when the game began.

2. Be careful driving in the fog. The fog is thick.

Be careful driving in the fog if the fog is thick.

3. Pack your suitcases. Do it when you wake up in the morning.

Pack your suitcases when you wake up in the morning.

COMPLETE YEAR GRADE 3

145

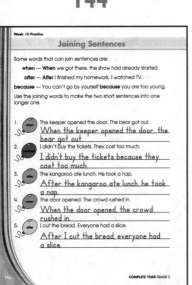

Week 13 Practice

Joining Sentences

Some words that can join sentences are:

when — When we got there, the show had already started.

after — After I finished my homework, I watched TV.

because — You can't go by yourself **because** you are too young.

Use the joining words to make the two short sentences into one longer one.

1. when — The keeper opened the door. The bear got out.
When the keeper opened the door, the bear got out.

2. because — I didn't buy the tickets. They cost too much.
I didn't buy the tickets because they cost too much.

3. after — The kangaroo ate lunch. He took a nap.
After the kangaroo ate lunch, he took a nap.

4. when — The door opened. The crowd rushed in.
When the door opened, the crowd rushed in.

5. after — I cut the bread. Everyone had a slice.
After I cut the bread, everyone had a slice.

COMPLETE YEAR GRADE 3

146

Week 13 Practice

Rounding: Tens

Rounding a number means expressing it to the nearest ten, hundred, thousand, and so on. Knowing how to round numbers makes estimating sums, differences and products easier. When rounding to the nearest ten, the key number is in the ones place. If the ones digit is 5 or larger, round up to the next highest ten. If the ones digit is 4 or less, round down to the nearest ten.

Examples:
- Round 81 to the nearest ten.
- 1 is the key digit.
- If it is less than 5, round down.
- Answer: 80

- Round 246 to the nearest ten.
- 6 is the key digit.
- If it is more than 5, round up.
- Answer: 250

Round these numbers to the nearest ten.

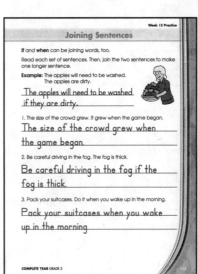

41 — 40
32 — 30
75 — 80
29 — 30
481 — 480
165 — 170
89 — 90
17 — 20
38 — 40
68 — 70
52 — 50
573 — 570
98 — 100
87 — 90
43 — 40
12 — 10

COMPLETE YEAR GRADE 3

147

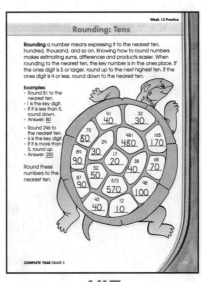

413

Answer Key

Week 13 Practice

Rounding: The Nearest Hundred

If the tens number is 5 or greater, "round up" to the nearest hundred. If the tens number is 4 or less, the hundreds number remains the same.

Remember: Look at the number directly to the right of the place you are rounding to.

Example:

230 round down to 200   470 round up to 500

150 round up to 200   732 round down to 700

456 **500**   120 **100**

340 **300**   923 **900**

867 **900**   550 **600**

686 **700**   231 **200**

770 **800**   492 **500**

COMPLETE YEAR GRADE 3

148

Week 13 Practice

Rounding: Hundreds and Thousands

When rounding to the nearest hundred, the key number is in the tens place. If the tens digit is 5 or larger, round up to nearest hundred. If the tens digit is 4 or less, round down to the nearest hundred.

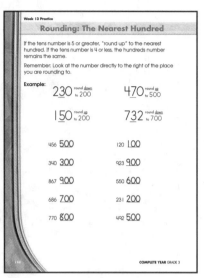

Examples:
Round 871 to the nearest hundred.
7 is the key digit.
If it is more than 5, round up.
Answer: 900

Round 421 to the nearest hundred.
2 is the key digit.
If it is less than 4, round down.
Answer: 400

Round these numbers to the nearest hundred.

255 **300**   368 **400**   443 **400**   578 **600**
562 **600**   698 **700**   99 **100**   775 **800**
812 **800**   592 **600**   124 **100**   10,235 **10,200**

When rounding to the nearest thousand, the key number is in the hundreds place. If the hundreds digit is 5 or larger, round up to the nearest thousand. If the hundreds digit is 4 or less, round down to the nearest thousand.

Examples:
Round 7,932 to the nearest thousand.
9 is the key digit.
If it is more than 5, round up.
Answer: 8,000

Round 1,368 to the nearest thousand.
3 is the key digit.
If it is less than 4, round down.
Answer: 1,000

Round these numbers to the nearest thousand.

8,631 **9,000**   1,248 **1,000**   798 **1,000**
999 **1,000**   6,229 **6,000**   8,461 **8,000**
9,654 **10,000**   4,963 **5,000**   99,923 **100,000**

COMPLETE YEAR GRADE 3

149

Week 13 Practice

Rounding

Round these numbers to the nearest ten.

18 **20**   33 **30**   82 **80**   56 **60**
24 **20**   49 **50**   91 **90**   67 **70**

Round these numbers to the nearest hundred.

243 **200**   689 **700**   263 **300**   162 **200**
389 **400**   720 **700**   351 **400**   490 **500**
463 **500**   846 **800**   928 **900**   733 **700**

Round these numbers to the nearest thousand.

2,638 **3,000**   3,940 **4,000**   8,653 **9,000**
6,238 **6,000**   1,429 **1,000**   5,061 **5,000**
7,289 **7,000**   2,742 **3,000**   9,460 **9,000**
3,109 **3,000**   4,697 **5,000**   8,302 **8,000**

Round these numbers to the nearest ten thousand.

11,368 **10,000**   38,421 **40,000**
75,302 **80,000**   67,932 **70,000**
14,569 **10,000**   49,926 **50,000**
93,694 **90,000**   81,648 **80,000**
26,784 **30,000**   87,065 **90,000**
57,843 **60,000**   29,399 **30,000**

COMPLETE YEAR GRADE 3

150

Week 14 Practice

Subjects of Sentences

The **subject** of a sentence tells who or what the sentence is about.

Example:
The buffalo provided the Plains Native Americans with many things.
(subject)

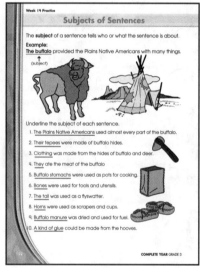

Underline the subject of each sentence.

1. The Plains Native Americans used almost every part of the buffalo.

2. Their tepees were made of buffalo hides.

3. Clothing was made from the hides of buffalo and deer.

4. They ate the meat of the buffalo

5. Buffalo stomachs were used as pots for cooking.

6. Bones were used for tools and utensils.

7. The tail was used as a flyswatter.

8. Horns were used as scrapers and cups.

9. Buffalo manure was dried and used for fuel.

10. A kind of glue could be made from the hooves.

COMPLETE YEAR GRADE 3

152

Week 14 Practice

Simple Subjects

A **simple subject** is the main noun or pronoun in the complete subject.

Draw a line between the subject and the predicate. Circle the simple subject.

Example: The black (bear) lives in the zoo.

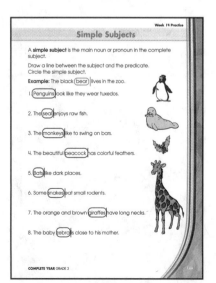

1. (Penguins) look like they wear tuxedos.

2. The (seal) enjoys raw fish.

3. The (monkeys) like to swing on bars.

4. The beautiful (peacock) has colorful feathers.

5. (Bats) like dark places.

6. Some (snakes) eat small rodents.

7. The orange and brown (giraffes) have long necks.

8. The baby (zebra) is close to his mother.

COMPLETE YEAR GRADE 3

153

Week 14 Practice

Compound Subjects

Compound subjects are two or more nouns that have the same predicate.

Combine the subjects to create one sentence with a compound subject.

Example: Jill can swing.
Whitney can swing.
Luke can swing.
Jill, Whitney and Luke can swing.

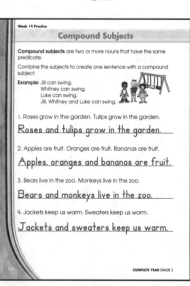

1. Roses grow in the garden. Tulips grow in the garden.

Roses and tulips grow in the garden.

2. Apples are fruit. Oranges are fruit. Bananas are fruit.

Apples, oranges and bananas are fruit.

3. Bears live in the zoo. Monkeys live in the zoo.

Bears and monkeys live in the zoo.

4. Jackets keep us warm. Sweaters keep us warm.

Jackets and sweaters keep us warm.

COMPLETE YEAR GRADE 3

154

Answer Key

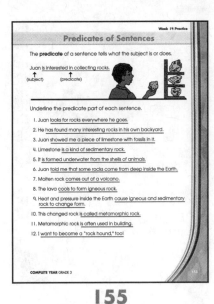

Predicates of Sentences

Week 14 Practice

The **predicate** of a sentence tells what the subject is or does.

Juan is interested in collecting rocks.
(subject) (predicate)

Underline the predicate part of each sentence.

1. Juan looks for rocks everywhere he goes.
2. He has found many interesting rocks in his own backyard.
3. Juan showed me a piece of limestone with fossils in it.
4. Limestone is a kind of sedimentary rock.
5. It is formed underwater from the shells of animals.
6. Juan told me that some rocks come from deep inside the Earth.
7. Molten rock comes out of a volcano.
8. The lava cools to form igneous rock.
9. Heat and pressure inside the Earth cause igneous and sedimentary rock to change form.
10. This changed rock is called metamorphic rock.
11. Metamorphic rock is often used in building.
12. I want to become a "rock hound," too!

COMPLETE YEAR GRADE 3

155

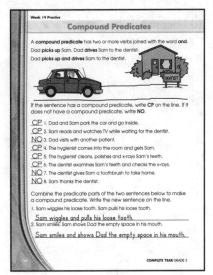

Week 14 Practice

Compound Predicates

A **compound predicate** has two or more verbs joined with the word **and**.
Dad **picks up** Sam. Dad **drives** Sam to the dentist.
Dad **picks up and drives** Sam to the dentist.

If the sentence has a compound predicate, write **CP** on the line. If it does not have a compound predicate, write **NO**.

CP 1. Dad and Sam park the car and go inside.
CP 2. Sam reads and watches TV while waiting for the dentist.
NO 3. Dad visits with another patient.
CP 4. The hygienist comes into the room and gets Sam.
CP 5. The hygienist cleans, polishes and x-rays Sam's teeth.
CP 6. The dentist examines Sam's teeth and checks the x-rays.
NO 7. The dentist gives Sam a toothbrush to take home.
NO 8. Sam thanks the dentist.

Combine the predicate parts of the two sentences below to make a compound predicate. Write the new sentence on the line.
1. Sam wiggles his loose tooth. Sam pulls his loose tooth.
   Sam wiggles and pulls his loose tooth.
2. Sam smiles. Sam shows Dad the empty space in his mouth.
   Sam smiles and shows Dad the empty space in his mouth.

COMPLETE YEAR GRADE 3

156

Week 14 Practice

Skipping Through the Tens

Skip-count by tens. Begin with the number on the first line. Write each number that follows.

0, 10, 20, 30, 40, 50, 60, 70, 80, 90, 100
3, 13, 23, 33, 43, 53, 63, 73, 83, 93, 103
1, 11, 21, 31, 41, 51, 61, 71, 81, 91, 101
8, 18, 28, 38, 48, 58, 68, 78, 88, 98, 108
6, 16, 26, 36, 46, 56, 66, 76, 86, 96, 106
4, 14, 24, 34, 44, 54, 64, 74, 84, 94, 104
2, 12, 22, 32, 42, 52, 62, 72, 82, 92, 102
5, 15, 25, 35, 45, 55, 65, 75, 85, 95, 105

What is ten more than ...
26 **36**   29 **39**
44 **54**   77 **87**
53 **63**   91 **101**
24 **34**   49 **59**

COMPLETE YEAR GRADE 3

157

Week 14 Practice

Counting to 100

Count by twos:

2	4	6	8	10	12	14	16	18	20	22	24	26	28
30	32	34	36	38	40	42	44	46	48	50	52	54	56
58	60	62	64	66	68	70	72	74	76	78	80	82	84
86	88	90	92	94	96	98	100

Count by threes:

3	6	9	12	15	18	21	24	27	30	33	36	39	42
45	48	51	54	57	60	63	66	69	72	75	78	81	84
87	90	93	96	99	102

Count by fours:

| 4 | 8 | 12 | 16 | 20 | 24 | 28 | 32 | 36 | 40 | 44 | 48 | 52 | 56 |
| 60 | 64 | 68 | 72 | 76 | 80 | 84 | 88 | 92 | 96 | 100 |

COMPLETE YEAR GRADE 3

158

Week 14 Practice

Skip-Counting

Skip-counting is a quick way to count by skipping numbers. For example, when you skip-count by 2s, you count 2, 4, 6, 8, and so on. You can skip-count by many different numbers such as 2s, 4s, 5s, 10s and 100s.

The illustration below shows skip-counting by 2s to 14.

0 1 2 3 4 5 6 7 8 9 10 11 12 13 14 15 16 17 18 19 20

Use the number line to help you skip-count by 2s from 0 to 20.
0, 2, 4, 6, 8, 10, 12, 14, 16, 18, 20
Skip-count by 3s by filling in the rocks across the pond.

3, 6, 9, 12, 15, 18, 21

COMPLETE YEAR GRADE 3

159

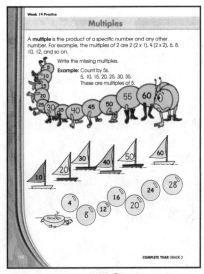

Week 14 Practice

Multiples

A **multiple** is the product of a specific number and any other number. For example, the multiples of 2 are 2 (2 x 1), 4 (2 x 2), 6, 8, 10, 12, and so on.

Write the missing multiples.

Example: Count by 5s.
5, 10, 15, 20, 25, 30, 35.
These are multiples of 5.

5, 10, 15, 20, 25, 30, 35, 40, 45, 50, 55, 60

10, 20, 30, 40, 50, 60

4, 8, 12, 16, 20, 24, 28

COMPLETE YEAR GRADE 3

160

162

Week 15 Practice

Syllables

All words can be divided into syllables. **Syllables** are word parts which have one vowel sound in each part.

Draw a line between the syllables and write the word on the correct line below. The first one is done for you.

little	bumblebee	pillow
truck	dazzle	dog
pencil	flag	angelic
rejoicing	ant	telephone

1 SYLLABLE	2 SYLLABLES	3 SYLLABLES
truck	little	rejoicing
flag	pencil	bumblebee
ant	dazzle	angelic
dog	pillow	telephone

COMPLETE YEAR GRADE 3

163

Week 15 Practice

Syllables

When the letters **le** come at the end of a word, they sometimes have the sound of **ul**, as in **raffle**.

Draw a line to match the syllables so they make words. The first one is done for you.

can	gle
fur	cle
pur	ple
cir	kle
spar	zle
raf	dle
ea	fle
siz	tle

Use the words you made to complete the sentences. One is done for you.

1. Will you buy a ticket for our school raffle?
2. The _____ turtle _____ pulled his head into his shell.
3. We could hear the bacon _____ sizzle _____ in the pan.
4. The baby had one _____ candle _____ on her birthday cake.
5. My favorite color is _____ purple _____.
6. Look at that diamond _____ sparkle _____!
7. The bald _____ eagle _____ is our national bird.
8. Draw a _____ circle _____ around the correct answer.

COMPLETE YEAR GRADE 3

164

Week 15 Practice

Quilting Bee

Follow the code to color the quilt squares.

| 1-syllable words = blue | 3-syllable words = green |
| 2-syllable words = red | 4-syllable words = yellow |

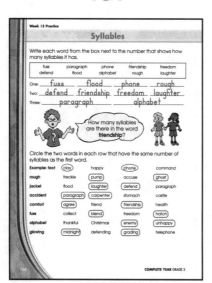

COMPLETE YEAR GRADE 3

165

Week 15 Practice

Syllables

A **syllable** is a word—or part of a word—with only one vowel sound. Some words have just one syllable, such as **cat**, **dog** and **house**. Some words have two syllables, such as **in-sist** and **be-fore**. Some words have three syllables, such as **re-mem-ber**; four syllables, such as **un-der-stand-ing**; or more. Often, words are easier to spell if you know how many syllables they have.

syl-la-bles

Write the number of syllables in each word below.

Word	Syllables		Word	Syllables
1. amphibian	4		11. want	1
2. liter	2		12. communication	5
3. guild	1		13. pedestrian	4
4. chill	2		14. kilo	2
5. vegetarian	5		15. autumn	2
6. comedian	4		16. dinosaur	3
7. warm	1		17. grammar	2
8. piano	3		18. dry	1
9. barbarian	4		19. solar	2
10. chef	1		20. wild	1

Next to each number, write words with the same number of syllables.

1.
2.
3.
4.
5.

Answers will vary.

COMPLETE YEAR GRADE 3

166

Week 15 Practice

Syllables

Write each word from the box next to the number that shows how many syllables it has.

| fuss | paragraph | phone | friendship | freedom |
| defend | flood | alphabet | rough | laughter |

One: fuss   flood   phone   rough
Two: defend   friendship   freedom   laughter
Three: paragraph   alphabet

How many syllables are there in the word **friendship**?

Circle the two words in each row that have the same number of syllables as the first word.

Example: fact — (clay) — happy — (phone) — command

rough	(freckle)	pump	accuse	(ghost)
jacket	flood	(laughter)	(defend)	paragraph
accident	(paragraph)	(carpenter)	stomach	castle
comfort	(agree)	friend	(friendship)	health
fuss	collect	(blend)	freedom	(hatch)
alphabet	thankful	Christmas	(enemy)	(unhappy)
glowing	(midnight)	defending	(grading)	telephone

COMPLETE YEAR GRADE 3

167

Week 15 Practice

Multiplication

Multiplication is a short way to find the sum of adding the same number a certain amount of times. For example, 4 x 7 = 28 instead of 7 + 7 + 7 + 7 = 28.

Study the example. Solve the problems.

Example:
3 + 3 + 3 = 9
3 threes = 9
3 x 3 = 9

7 + 7 = 14
2 sevens = 14
2 x 7 = 14

4 + 4 + 4 + 4 = 16
4 fours = 16
4 x 4 = 16

5 + 5 = 10
2 fives = 10
2 x 5 = 10

2 + 2 + 2 + 2 = 8
4 twos = 8
4 x 2 = 8

6 + 6 = 12
2 sixes = 12
2 x 6 = 12

COMPLETE YEAR GRADE 3

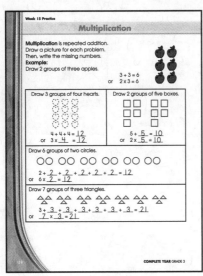

168

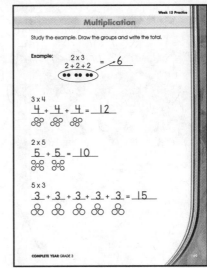

169

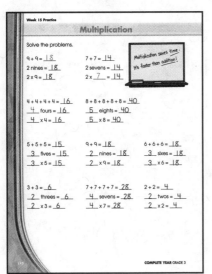

170

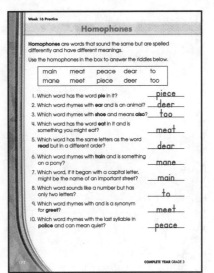

172

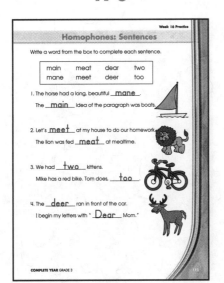

173

174

175

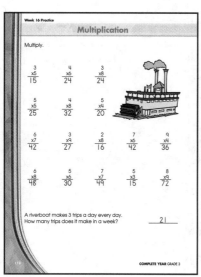

178

177

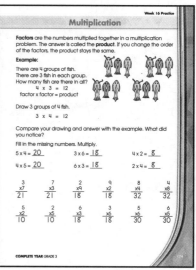

179

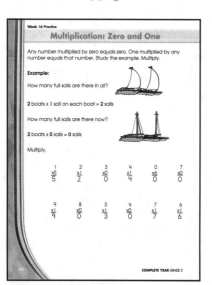

180

182

Answer Key

Page 183

Homophones

Homophones are words that sound the same but are spelled differently and have different meanings.

Example:

sew   sow   so

Read the sentences and write the correct word in the blanks.

Example:

blue blew — She has **blue** eyes.
— The wind **blew** the barn down.

eye I	He hurt his left ___**eye**___ playing ball.
	___**I**___ like to learn new things.
see sea	Can you ___**see**___ the winning runner from here?
	He goes diving for pearls under the ___**sea**___.
eight ate	The baby ___**ate**___ the banana.
	Jane was ___**eight**___ years old last year.
one won	Jill ___**won**___ first prize at the science fair.
	I am the only ___**one**___ in my family with red hair.
be bee	Jenny cried when a ___**bee**___ stung her.
	I have to ___**be**___ in bed every night at eight o'clock.
two to too	My father likes to ___**to**___ play tennis.
	I like to play, ___**too**___.
	It takes at least ___**two**___ people to play.

COMPLETE YEAR GRADE 3

183

Page 184

Homophones

Circle the correct word to complete each sentence. Then, write the word on the line.

1. I am going to ___**write**___ a letter to my grandmother. (right, **write**)
2. Draw a circle around the ___**right**___ answer. (**right**, write)
3. Wait an ___**hour**___ before going swimming. (our, **hour**)
4. This is ___**our**___ house. (**our**, hour)
5. He got a ___**beet**___ from his garden. (**beet**, beat)
6. Our football team ___**beat**___ that team. (**beat**, beet)
7. Go to the store and ___**buy**___ a loaf of bread. (by, **buy**)
8. We will drive ___**by**___ our house. (**by**, buy)
9. It will be trouble if the dog ___**sees**___ the cat. (seas, **sees**)
10. They sailed the seven ___**seas**___. (**seas**, sees)
11. We have ___**two**___ cars in the garage. (to, too, **two**)
12. I am going ___**to**___ the zoo today. (**to**, too, two)
13. My little brother is going ___**too**___. (to, **too**, two)

COMPLETE YEAR GRADE 3

184

Page 185

Homophones

Homophones are words that sound the same but have different spellings and meanings.

Complete each sentence using a word from the box.

blew	night	blue	knight	hour	in	ant	inn
our	aunt	meet	too	two	to	meat

1. A red ___**ant**___ crawled up the wall.
2. It will be one ___**hour**___ before we can go back home.
3. Will you ___**meet**___ us later?
4. We plan to stay at an ___**inn**___ during our trip.
5. The king had a ___**knight**___ who fought bravely.
6. The wind ___**blew**___ so hard that I almost lost my hat.
7. His jacket was ___**blue**___.
8. My ___**aunt**___ plans to visit us this week.
9. I will come ___**in**___ when it gets too cold outside.
10. It was late at ___**night**___ when we finally got there.
11. ___**Two**___ of us will go with you.
12. I will mail a note ___**to**___ someone at the bank.
13. Do you eat red ___**meat**___?
14. We would like to join you, ___**too**___.
15. Come over to see ___**our**___ new cat.

COMPLETE YEAR GRADE 3

185

Page 186

Homophones

Circle the words that are not used correctly. Write the correct word above the circled word. Use the words in the box to help you. The first one has been done for you.

road	see	one	be	so	I	brakes	piece	there
wait	not	some	hour	would	no	deer	you	heard

Jake and his family were getting close to Grandpa's. It had taken them nearly an **hour** (our) to get **there** (their) but Jake knew it was worth it. In his mind, he could already **see** (sea) the pond and could almost feel the cool water. It had been **so** (sew) hot this summer in the apartment. "**Would** you (Wood you) like a **piece** (peace) of my apple, Jake?" asked his big sister Clara. "**Eye** (I) can't eat any more." "**No** (Know) thank you," Jake replied. "I still have **some** (sum) of my fruit left." Suddenly, Dad slammed on the **brakes** (breaks). "Did you see that **deer** (dear) on the **road** (rode)? I always **heard** (herd) that if you see **one** (won) there might **be** (bee) more." "Good thinking, Dad. I'm glad you are a safe driver. We're **not** (know) very far from Grandpa's now. I can't **wait** (weight)!"

COMPLETE YEAR GRADE 3

186

Page 187

Hairs on Hares?

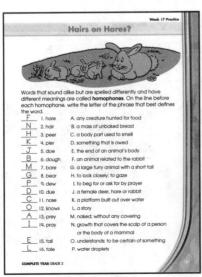

Words that sound alike but are spelled differently and have different meanings are called **homophones**. On the line before each homophone, write the letter of the phrase that best defines the word.

_F_	1. hare	A. any creature hunted for food
_N_	2. hair	B. a mass of unbaked bread
_H_	3. peer	C. a body part used to smell
_K_	4. pier	D. something that is owed
_J_	5. doe	E. the end of an animal's body
_B_	6. dough	F. an animal related to the rabbit
_M_	7. bare	G. a large furry animal with a short tail
_G_	8. bear	H. to look closely; to gaze
_P_	9. dew	I. to beg for or ask for by prayer
_D_	10. due	J. a female deer, hare or rabbit
_C_	11. nose	K. a platform built out over water
_O_	12. knows	L. a story
_A_	13. prey	M. naked; without any covering
_I_	14. pray	N. growth that covers the scalp of a person or the body of a mammal
_E_	15. tall	O. understands; to be certain of something
_L_	16. tale	P. water droplets

COMPLETE YEAR GRADE 3

187

Page 188

Multiplication

Time yourself as you multiply. How quickly can you complete this page?

3 ×2 = 6	8 ×7 = 56	1 ×0 = 0	1 ×6 = 6	3 ×4 = 12	4 ×0 = 0
4 ×1 = 4	4 ×4 = 16	2 ×5 = 10	9 ×3 = 27	9 ×0 = 0	5 ×3 = 15
0 ×0 = 0	2 ×6 = 12	9 ×6 = 54	8 ×5 = 40	7 ×3 = 21	4 ×2 = 8
3 ×5 = 15	2 ×0 = 0	4 ×6 = 24	1 ×3 = 3	0 ×1 = 0	3 ×3 = 9

COMPLETE YEAR GRADE 3

188

189

190

192

193

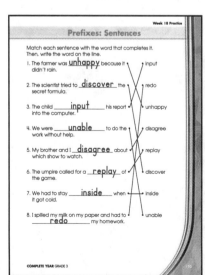

195

196

Answer Key

197

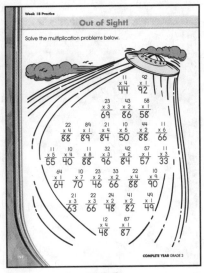

198

199

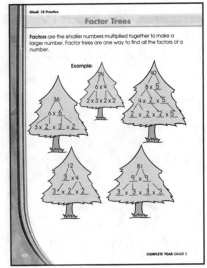

200

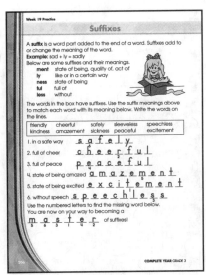

206

207

Answer Key

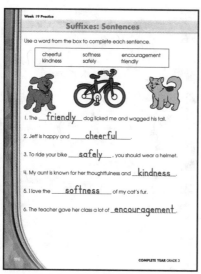

208

209

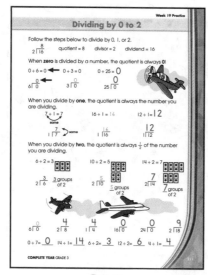

211

212

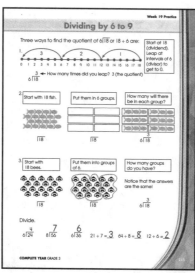

213

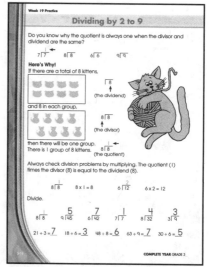

214

Answer Key

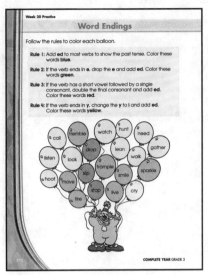

216

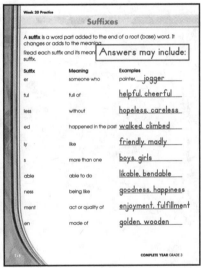

217

Suffixes

A **suffix** is a word part added to the end of a root (base) word. It changes or adds to the meaning.

Read each suffix and its meaning. | Answers may include: | suffix.

Suffix	Meaning	Examples
er	someone who	painter, _jogger_
ful	full of	_helpful, cheerful_
less	without	_hopeless, careless_
ed	happened in the past	_walked, climbed_
ly	like	_friendly, madly_
s	more than one	_boys, girls_
able	able to do	_likable, bendable_
ness	being like	_goodness, happiness_
ment	act or quality of	_enjoyment, fulfillment_
en	made of	_golden, wooden_

218

A Little More

Attach the suffixes and prefixes to as many words as possible from the list below to make new words. Many combinations are | Answers may include: | s will have to be changed slightly.

ly or lly
nesty
tower
broker
farmer
traveler

merrily
timidly
fortunately
conveniently

y
oily
woody
lucky
scary

ful
beautiful
thoughtful
thankful
graceful

un or in
inconvenient
unhappy
unfortunate

broke	grace	comfort	thought	timid	water
merry	luck	travel	thank	heart	oil
few	farm	convenient	scare	fortunate	chop
beauty	happy	correct	wood	like	most

219

Division

Division is a way to find out how many times one number is contained in another number. For example, 28 ÷ 4 = 7 means that there are seven groups of four in 28.

Study the example. Divide.

Example:

There are 6 oars.
Each canoe needs 2 oars.
How many canoes can be used?

Circle groups of 2.
There are 3 groups of 2.

$$6 \div 2 = 3$$
oars   number   =   canoes
      of oars
      needed
      per canoe

$9 \div 3 = \underline{3}$ $8 \div 2 = \underline{4}$ $16 \div 4 = \underline{4}$

$15 \div 5 = \underline{3}$ $18 \div 2 = \underline{9}$ $20 \div 4 = \underline{5}$

$21 \div 7 = \underline{3}$ $24 \div 6 = \underline{4}$ $12 \div 2 = \underline{6}$

220

Division

Divide. Draw a line from the boat to the sail with the correct answer.

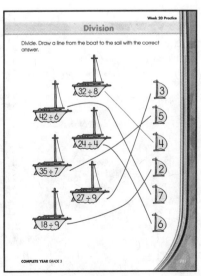

221

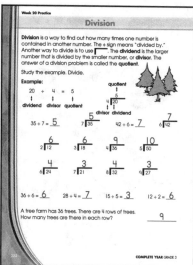

222

224

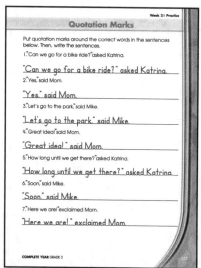

227

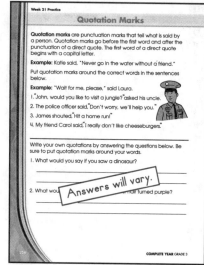

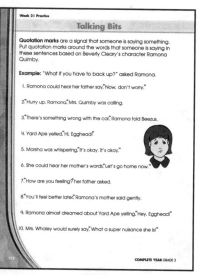

229

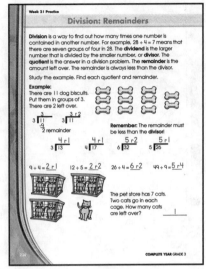

230

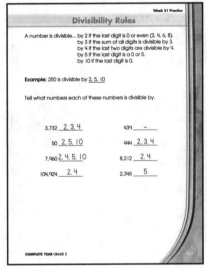

231

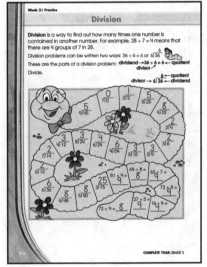

232

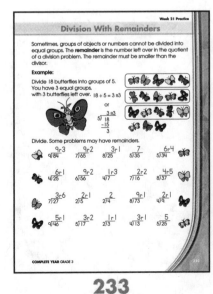

233

234

Answer Key

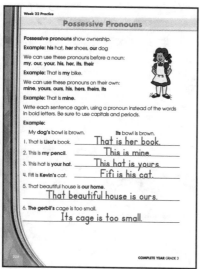

Week 22 Practice

Possessive Pronouns

Possessive pronouns show ownership.

Example: **his** hat, **her** shoes, **our** dog

We can use these pronouns before a noun:
my, our, your, his, her, its, their

Example: That is **my** bike.

We can use these pronouns on their own:
mine, yours, ours, his, hers, theirs, its

Example: That is **mine**.

Write each sentence again, using a pronoun instead of the words in bold letters. Be sure to use capitals and periods.

Example:

My **dog's** bowl is brown. **Its** bowl is brown.

1. That is **Lisa's** book. _That is her book._
2. This is **my** pencil. _This is mine._
3. This hat is **your** hat. _This hat is yours._
4. Fifi is **Kevin's** cat. _Fifi is his cat._
5. That beautiful house is **our home**.
   That beautiful house is ours.
6. **The gerbil's** cage is too small.
   Its cage is too small.

COMPLETE YEAR GRADE 3

236

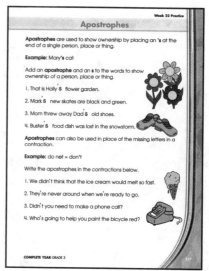

Week 22 Practice

Apostrophes

Apostrophes are used to show ownership by placing an **'s** at the end of a single person, place or thing.

Example: Mary's cat

Add an **apostrophe** and an **s** to the words to show ownership of a person, place or thing.

1. That is Holly's flower garden.
2. Mark's new skates are black and green.
3. Mom threw away Dad's old shoes.
4. Buster's food dish was lost in the snowstorm.

Apostrophes can also be used in place of the missing letters in a contraction.

Example: do not = don't

Write the apostrophes in the contractions below.

1. We didn't think that the ice cream would melt so fast.
2. They're never around when we're ready to go.
3. Didn't you need to make a phone call?
4. Who's going to help you paint the bicycle red?

COMPLETE YEAR GRADE 3

237

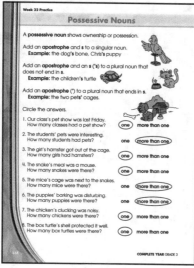

Week 22 Practice

Possessive Nouns

A **possessive noun** shows ownership or possession.

Add an **apostrophe** and **s** to a singular noun.
Example: the dog's bone, Chris's puppy

Add an **apostrophe** and an **s** ('s) to a plural noun that does not end in **s**.
Example: the children's turtle

Add an **apostrophe** (') to a plural noun that ends in **s**.
Example: the two pets' cages.

Circle the answers.

1. Our class's pet show was last Friday.
   How many classes had a pet show? (**one**) more than one
2. The students' pets were interesting.
   How many students had pets? one (**more than one**)
3. The girl's hamster got out of the cage.
   How many girls had hamsters? (**one**) more than one
4. The snake's meal was a mouse.
   How many snakes were there? (**one**) more than one
5. The mice's cage was next to the snakes.
   How many mice were there? one (**more than one**)
6. The puppies' barking was disturbing.
   How many puppies were there? one (**more than one**)
7. The chicken's clucking was noisy.
   How many chickens were there? (**one**) more than one
8. The box turtle's shell protected it well.
   How many box turtles were there? (**one**) more than one

COMPLETE YEAR GRADE 3

238

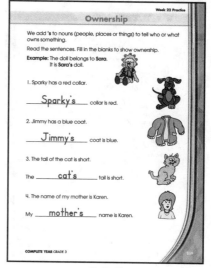

Week 22 Practice

Ownership

We add **'s** to nouns (people, places or things) to tell who or what owns something.

Read the sentences. Fill in the blanks to show ownership.

Example: The doll belongs to **Sara**.
It is **Sara's** doll.

1. Sparky has a red collar.
   Sparky's collar is red.
2. Jimmy has a blue coat.
   Jimmy's coat is blue.
3. The tail of the cat is short.
   The _cat's_ tail is short.
4. The name of my mother is Karen.
   My _mother's_ name is Karen.

COMPLETE YEAR GRADE 3

239

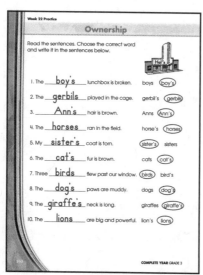

Week 22 Practice

Ownership

Read the sentences. Choose the correct word and write it in the sentences below.

1. The _boy's_ lunchbox is broken. boys (**boy's**)
2. The _gerbils_ played in the cage. gerbil's (**gerbils**)
3. _Ann's_ hair is brown. Anns (**Ann's**)
4. The _horses_ ran in the field. horse's (**horses**)
5. My _sister's_ coat is torn. (**sister's**) sisters
6. The _cat's_ fur is brown. cats (**cat's**)
7. Three _birds_ flew past our window. (**birds**) bird's
8. The _dog's_ paws are muddy. dogs (**dog's**)
9. The _giraffe's_ neck is long. giraffes (**giraffe's**)
10. The _lions_ are big and powerful. lion's (**lions**)

COMPLETE YEAR GRADE 3

240

Week 22 Practice

Division

Divide.

122R6	101R5	34R7	84R2	163R1
7)860	6)611	8)279	4)338	6)979

264	92R3	156R4	161R3	27R1
3)792	5)463	6)940	4)647	3)814

108R2	71R1	69	41	34
7)758	5)356	4)276	8)328	9)306

144R3	116R4	34	410R1	81R3
4)579	8)932	3)102	2)821	6)489

The video store has 491 DVDs.
The store sells 8 DVDs a day.
How many days will it take
to sell all of the DVDs? 61R3 → 62 days

COMPLETE YEAR GRADE 3

241

Answer Key

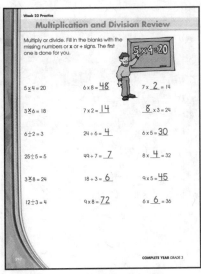

242

Week 22 Practice

Multiplication and Division Review

Multiply or divide. Fill in the blanks with the missing numbers or **x** or ÷ signs. The first one is done for you.

5 x 4 = 20   6 x 8 = __48__   7 x __2__ = 14

3 **X** 6 = 18   7 x 2 = __14__   __8__ x 3 = 24

6 ÷ 2 = 3   24 ÷ 6 = __4__   6 x 5 = __30__

25 ÷ 5 = 5   49 ÷ 7 = __7__   8 x __4__ = 32

3 **X** 8 = 24   18 ÷ 3 = __6__   9 x 5 = __45__

12 ÷ 3 = 4   9 x 8 = __72__   6 x __6__ = 36

COMPLETE YEAR GRADE 3

243

Week 22 Practice

Problem-Solving: Multiplication, Division

Read and solve each problem.

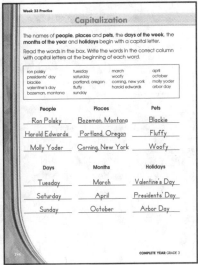

Jeff and Terry are planting a garden. They plant 3 rows of green beans with 8 plants in each row. How many green bean plants are there in the garden? __24__

There are 45 tomato plants in the garden. There are 5 rows of them. How many tomato plants are in each row? __9__

The children have 12 plants each of lettuce, broccoli and spinach. How many plants are there in all? __36__

Jeff planted 3 times as many cucumber plants as Terry. He planted 15 of them. How many did Terry plant? __5__

Terry planted 12 pepper plants. He planted twice as many green pepper plants as red pepper plants. How many green pepper plants are there? __8__

How many red pepper plants? __4__

COMPLETE YEAR GRADE 3

244

Week 22 Practice

Raising a Family

Omar and his family live a very simple life. Omar's father raises coffee plants on their one-acre farm. Omar's mother and father work very hard to earn the money to send Omar and his brother and two sisters to school. It costs $75 a year for primary school for each child. To earn more money, Omar's father works as a stonemason for $5 a day. Omar's mother works at a large farm for $2 a day.

1. How many days will Omar's father have to work as a stonemason to pay for 1 year of Omar's primary school? (**Hint:** Count by 5s.) __15 days__

2. How many days will Omar's father have to work to pay for the other three children's primary school each year? (**Hint:** Add your answer from #1 three times.) __45 days__

3. One pair of children's shoes costs $10. How many days will Omar's mother have to work to buy him a pair of shoes? __5 days__

4. How many days will Omar's mother have to work to buy the other three children new pairs of shoes? __15 days__

5. How much will it cost to buy shoes for all four children? (**Hint:** Count by 10s.) __$40.00__

COMPLETE YEAR GRADE 3

246

Week 23 Practice

Capitalization

The names of **people**, **places** and **pets**, the **days of the week**, the **months of the year** and **holidays** begin with a capital letter.

Read the words in the box. Write the words in the correct column with capital letters at the beginning of each word.

ron polsky	tuesday	march	april
presidents' day	saturday	woofy	october
blackie	portland, oregon	corning, new york	molly yoder
valentine's day	fluffy	harold edwards	arbor day
bozeman, montana	sunday		

People	Places	Pets
Ron Polsky	Bozeman, Montana	Blackie
Harold Edwards	Portland, Oregon	Fluffy
Molly Yoder	Corning, New York	Woofy

Days	Months	Holidays
Tuesday	March	Valentine's Day
Saturday	April	Presidents' Day
Sunday	October	Arbor Day

COMPLETE YEAR GRADE 3

247

Week 23 Practice

Capitalization and Commas

We capitalize the names of cities and states. We use a comma to separate the name of a city and a state.

Use capital letters and commas to write the names of the cities and states correctly.

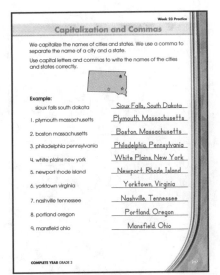

Example:
sioux falls south dakota   Sioux Falls, South Dakota

1. plymouth massachusetts   Plymouth, Massachusetts

2. boston massachusetts   Boston, Massachusetts

3. philadelphia pennsylvania   Philadelphia, Pennsylvania

4. white plains new york   White Plains, New York

5. newport rhode island   Newport, Rhode Island

6. yorktown virginia   Yorktown, Virginia

7. nashville tennessee   Nashville, Tennessee

8. portland oregon   Portland, Oregon

9. mansfield ohio   Mansfield, Ohio

COMPLETE YEAR GRADE 3

248

Week 23 Practice

Spelling

Circle the word in each sentence that is not spelled correctly. Then, write the word correctly.

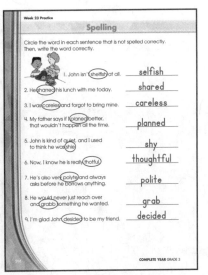

1. John isn't shelfish at all.   selfish

2. He sharred his lunch with me today.   shared

3. I was careles and forgot to bring mine.   careless

4. My father says if I planed better, that wouldn't happen all the time.   planned

5. John is kind of quiet, and I used to think he was shie.   shy

6. Now, I know he is really thotful.   thoughtful

7. He's also very polyte and always asks before he borrows anything.   polite

8. He would never just reach over and grabb something he wanted.   grab

9. I'm glad John desided to be my friend.   decided

COMPLETE YEAR GRADE 3

Answer Key

249

Spelling

Week 23 Practice

Circle the word in each sentence that is not spelled correctly. Then, write the word correctly.

1. Be sure to stopp at the red light. — **stop**
2. The train goes down the trak. — **track**
3. Please put the bred in the toaster. — **bread**
4. I need another blok to finish. — **block**
5. The beasst player won a trophy. — **best**
6. Blow out the candles and make a wish. — **wish**
7. The truk blew its horn. — **truck**

COMPLETE YEAR GRADE 3

250

Review

Week 23 Practice

Circle the words that are not spelled correctly in the story. Then, write each word correctly on the lines below.

One day, Peter and I were sitting on a bench at the park. A polise woman came and sat in the empty space beside us. "Have you seen a little dog with thik black fur?" she asked. She was very poolite. "Remember that dog?" I asked Peter. "He was just here!" Peter nodded. He was too shie to say anything.

"Give us his adress," I said. "We'll find him and take him home." She got out a pensil and wrote the adress in the senter of a piece of paper. Peter and I desided to walk down the street the way the dog had gone. There was a krowd of people at a cherch we passed, but no dog.

Then it started getting late. "We'd better go home," Peter said. "I can't see in this darkness anyway."

As we turned around to go back, there was the little dog! He had been following us! We took him to the adress. The girl who came to the door grabed him and huged him tight. "I'm sorry I let you wander away," she told me. "I'll never be so carless again." I thought she was going to kiss us, too. We left just in time!

police	space	thick
polite	shy	address
pencil	address	center
decided	crowd	church
darkness	address	grabbed
hugged	careless	kiss

COMPLETE YEAR GRADE 3

251

Review

Week 23 Practice

Circle the two words in each sentence that are not spelled correctly. Then, write the words correctly.

1. Arn't you going to shere your cookie with me?
   Aren't **share**
2. We planed a long time, but we still wern't ready.
   planned **weren't**
3. My pensil hassn't broken yet today.
   pencil **hasn't**
4. We arn't going because we don't have the correct adress.
   aren't **address**
5. Youve stired the soup too much.
   You've **stirred**
6. Weave tried to be as neet as possible.
   We've **neat**
7. She hasnt been us in this darknes.
   hasn't **darkness**

COMPLETE YEAR GRADE 3

252

Order of Operations

Week 23 Practice

When you solve a problem that involves more than one operation, this is the order to follow:

Parentheses first, then do multiplication and division in order from left to right. Finally, do all addition and subtraction steps. In order from left to right. These rules are called **Order of Operations**.

Example:
$$2 + (3 \times 5) - 2 = 15$$
$$2 + 15 - 2 = 15$$
$$17 - 2 = 15$$

Solve the problems using the correct order of operations.

$(5 - 3) + 4 \times 7 = \underline{30}$
2   28

$1 + 2 \times 3 + 4 = \underline{11}$
6

$6 \times 3 - 1 = \underline{17}$
18

$(8 \div 2) \times 4 = \underline{16}$
4

$9 \div 3 \times 3 + 0 = \underline{1}$
9

$5 - 2 \times 1 + 2 = \underline{5}$
2

COMPLETE YEAR GRADE 3

253

Order of Operations

Week 23 Practice

Use +, –, x and ÷ to complete the problems so the number sentence is true.

Example: $4 \underline{+} 2 \underline{-} 1 = 5$

$(8 \underline{\div} 2) \underline{+} 4 = 8$

$(1 \underline{+} 2) \underline{\div} 3 = 1$

$9 \underline{+} 3 \underline{-} 9 = 3$

$(7 \underline{-} 5) \underline{x} 1 = 2$

$8 \underline{x} 5 \underline{\div} 4 = 10$

$5 \underline{-} 4 \underline{\div} 1 = 1$

REMEMBER... USE THE ORDER OF OPERATIONS

COMPLETE YEAR GRADE 3

254

Perfect Symmetry

Week 23 Practice

A figure that can be separated into two matching parts is **symmetric**.

Line of Symmetry

Is the dotted line a line of symmetry?

<u>yes</u>   <u>no</u>   T <u>yes</u>   <u>no</u>

Draw the matching part.

Use letters to make symmetric words.

DECK

T
O
M

M
A
T

Make your own symmetric words.

Answers will vary.

COMPLETE YEAR GRADE 3

Answer Key

C, K, CK Words: Spelling

Write the words from the box that answer the questions.

| crowd | keeper | cost | pack | kangaroo | thick |

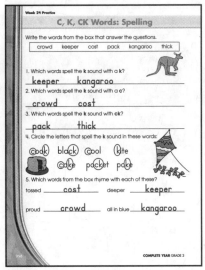

1. Which words spell the **k** sound with a **k**?
keeper   kangaroo

2. Which words spell the **k** sound with a **c**?
crowd   cost

3. Which words spell the **k** sound with **ck**?
pack   thick

4. Circle the letters that spell the **k** sound in these words:

co(ck)   bla(ck)   (c)ool   (k)ite
(c)ake   po(ck)et   po(k)e

5. Which words from the box rhyme with each of these?

tossed **cost**   deeper **keeper**

proud **crowd**   all in blue **kangaroo**

COMPLETE YEAR GRADE 3

256

C, K, CK Words: Spelling

The **k** sound can be spelled with a **c**, **k** or **ck** after a short vowel sound.

Use the words from the box to complete the sentences. Use each word only once.

crowd	keeper
cost	pack
kangaroo	thick

1. On sunny days, there is always a **crowd** of people at the zoo.

2. It doesn't **cost** much to get into the zoo.

3. We always get hungry, so we **pack** a picnic lunch.

4. We like to watch the **kangaroo**.

5. Its **thick** tail helps it jump and walk.

6. The **keeper** always makes sure the cages are clean.

COMPLETE YEAR GRADE 3

257

S Words: Spelling

The **s** sound can be spelled with an **s**, **ss**, **c** or **ce**.

Use the words from the box to complete the sentences below. Write each word only once.

| center | pencil | space |
| address | police | darkness |

1. I drew a circle in the **center** of the page.

2. I'll write to you if you tell me your **address**.

3. She pushed too hard and broke the point on her **pencil**.

4. If you hear a noise at night, call the **police**.

5. It was night, and I couldn't see him in the **darkness**.

6. There's not enough **space** for me to sit next to you.

COMPLETE YEAR GRADE 3

258

S Words: Spelling

Write the words from the box that answer the questions.

| center | pencil | space | address | police | darkness |

1. Which words spell the **s** sound with **ss**?
address   darkness

2. Which words spell **s** with a **c**?
center   pencil

3. Which words spell **s** with **ce**?
space   police

4. Write two other words you know that spell **s** with an **s**.
Answers will vary.

5. Circle the letters that spell the **s** sound in these words.

de(c)ide   ki(ss)   carele(ss)   i(ce)
co(s)t   fier(ce)   senten(ce)

6. Put these letters in order to make words from the box.

sdsdera **address**   sdserakn **darkness**
clipoe **police**   clipne **pencil**
capse **space**   retnce **center**

COMPLETE YEAR GRADE 3

259

C Words: Spelling

The letter **c** can make the **k** sound or the **s** sound.

Example: count, city

Write **k** or **s** to show how the **c** in each word sounds.

cave	**k**	copy	**k**	force	**s**
become	**k**	dance	**s**	city	**s**
certain	**s**	contest	**k**	cool	**k**

Use the words from the box to answer these questions.

| center | pencil | space | address | police | darkness |

1. Which word begins with the same sound as **simple** and ends with the same sound as **fur**? **center**

2. Which word begins with the same sound as **average** and ends with the same sound as **circus**? **address**

3. Which word begins with the same sound as **popcorn** and ends with the same sound as **glass**? **police**

4. Which word begins and ends with the same sounds as **pool**? **pencil**

5. Which word begins with the same sound as **city** and ends with the same sound as **kiss**? **space**

6. Which word begins and ends with the same sounds as **delicious**? **darkness**

COMPLETE YEAR GRADE 3

260

Fractions

A **fraction** is a number that names part of a whole, such as $\frac{1}{2}$ or $\frac{1}{3}$.

Write the fraction that tells what parrt of each figure is colored. The first one is done for you.

Example:
2 parts shaded
5 parts in the whole figure

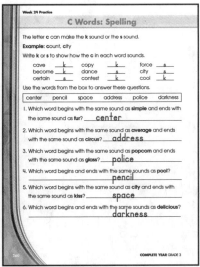

$\frac{1}{3}$ $\frac{1}{2}$ $\frac{3}{4}$

$\frac{5}{9}$ $\frac{2}{4}$ $\frac{3}{6}$

$\frac{1}{4}$ $\frac{4}{8}$ $\frac{3}{6}$

COMPLETE YEAR GRADE 3

261

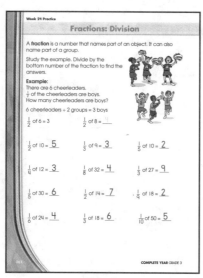

262

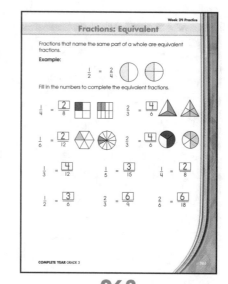

263

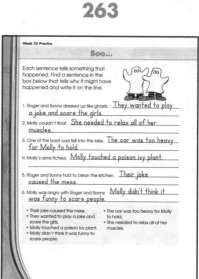

264

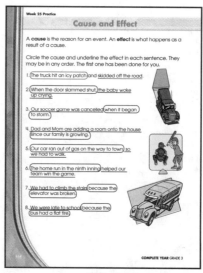

266

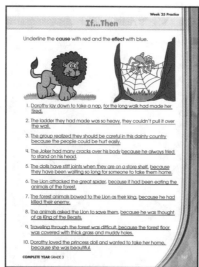

267

268

Week 25 Practice

Cause and Effect

Cause and effect sentences often use clue words to show the relationship between two events. Common clue words are **because, so, when,** and **since.**

Read the sentences on pages 269 and 270. Circle each clue word. The first one has been done for you.

1. I'll help you clean your room, (so) we can go out to play sooner.

2. (Because) of the heavy snowfall, school was closed today.

3. She was not smiling, (so) her mother wanted her school pictures taken again.

4. Mrs. Wilderman came to school with crutches today, (because) she had a skating accident.

5. (When) the team began making too many mistakes at practice, the coach told them to take a break.

COMPLETE YEAR GRADE 3

269

Week 25 Practice

Cause and Effect

6. Our telephone was not working, (so) I called the doctor from next door.

7. The police officer began to direct traffic (since) the traffic signal was not working.

8. The class will go out to recess (when) the room is cleaned up.

9. "I can't see you (because) the room is too dark," said Jordan.

10. He has to wash the dishes alone (because) his sister is sick.

11. (Since) the bus had engine trouble, several children were late to school.

12. Monday was a holiday, (so) Mom and Dad took us to the park.

COMPLETE YEAR GRADE 3

270

Week 25 Practice

Decimals

A **decimal** is a number with one or more numbers to the right of a decimal point. A **decimal point** is a dot placed between the ones place and the tens place of a number, such as 2.5.

Example:

$\frac{3}{10}$ can be written as .3   They are both read as **three-tenths.**

Write the answer as a decimal for the shaded parts.

    .3   .4

Color parts of each object to match the decimals given.

.7   .6   .5

COMPLETE YEAR GRADE 3

271

Week 25 Practice

Decimals

A **decimal** is a number with one or more numbers to the right of a decimal point, such as 6.5 or 2.25. **Equivalent** means numbers that are equal.

Draw a line between the equivalent numbers.

.8	$\frac{5}{10}$
five-tenths	$\frac{8}{10}$
.7	$\frac{6}{10}$
.4	.3
six-tenths	$\frac{2}{10}$
three-tenths	$\frac{7}{10}$
.2	$\frac{9}{10}$
nine-tenths	$\frac{4}{10}$

COMPLETE YEAR GRADE 3

272

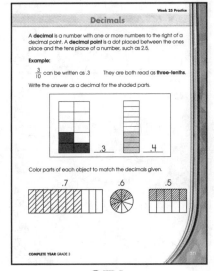

Week 25 Practice

Decimals: Greater Than 1

Write the decimal for the part that is shaded.

Example: $2\frac{4}{10}$

Write: 2.4   Read: two and four-tenths

$1\frac{2}{10}$ = 1.2 $3\frac{6}{10}$ = 3.6

$2\frac{3}{10}$ = 2.3 $2\frac{7}{10}$ = 2.7

Write each number as a decimal.

four and two-tenths = 4.2   seven and one-tenth = 7.1

$3\frac{4}{10}$ = 3.4 $6\frac{9}{10}$ = 6.9 $8\frac{3}{10}$ = 8.3 $7\frac{5}{10}$ = 7.5

COMPLETE YEAR GRADE 3

273

Week 25 Practice

Decimals: Addition and Subtraction

Decimals are added and subtracted in the same way as other numbers. Simply carry down the decimal point to your answer.

Add or subtract.

Examples:

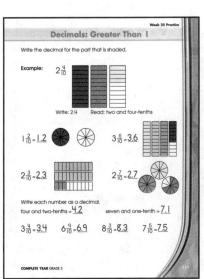

$$1.3 + 2.8 = 4.1$$ $$4.5 - 2.2 = 2.3$$

1.3	4.6	5.1	6.7
+2.2	-3.4	+8.8	-4.3
3.5	1.2	13.9	2.4

7.9	6.4	11.4	0.5
-3.7	+8.7	-9.5	+3.6
4.2	15.1	1.9	4.1

9.3 + 1.2 = 10.5   2.5 - 0.7 = 1.8   1.2 + 5.0 = 6.2

Bob jogs around the school every day. The distance for one time around is .7 of a mile. If he jogs around the school two times, how many miles does he jog every day?   1.4

COMPLETE YEAR GRADE 3

274

Answer Key

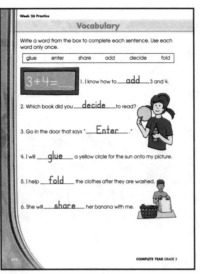

276

Week 26 Practice

Vocabulary

Write a word from the box to complete each sentence. Use each word only once.

| glue | enter | share | add | decide | fold |

1. I know how to **add** 3 and 4.
2. Which book did you **decide** to read?
3. Go in the door that says "**Enter**".
4. I will **glue** a yellow circle for the sun onto my picture.
5. I help **fold** the clothes after they are washed.
6. She will **share** her banana with me.

COMPLETE YEAR GRADE 3

277

Week 26 Practice

Vocabulary

Find the picture that matches each sentence below. Then, complete each sentence with the word under the picture.

list   search
spill   toast
pound   load

1. I will **search** until I find it.
2. Be careful you don't **spill** the paint.
3. Is that **load** too heavy for you?
4. They made **toast** for breakfast.
5. Please go to the store and buy a **pound** of butter.
6. Is my name on the **list**?

COMPLETE YEAR GRADE 3

278

Week 26 Practice

Vocabulary

Find the picture that matches each sentence below. Then, complete the sentence with the word under the picture.

hug   plan   clap
stir   drag   grab

1. She will **plan** where to go on her trip.
2. **Drag** that big box over here, please.
3. My little brother always tries to **grab** my toys.
4. May I help you **stir** the soup?
5. I like to **hug** my dog because he is so soft.
6. After she played, everyone started to **clap**.

COMPLETE YEAR GRADE 3

279

Week 26 Practice

Sentences

Use the words in the box to complete each sentence.

| fast | wish | truck | bread | sun |
| best | stop | track | lunch | block |

Race cars can go very **fast**.

Carol packs a **lunch** for Ted before school.

Throw a penny in the well and make a **wish**.

The **truck** had a flat tire.

My favorite kind of **bread** is whole wheat.

COMPLETE YEAR GRADE 3

280

Week 26 Practice

Sentences

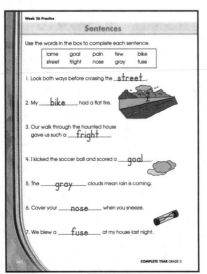

Use the words in the box to complete each sentence.

| lame | goal | pain | few | bike |
| street | fright | nose | gray | fuse |

1. Look both ways before crossing the **street**.
2. My **bike** had a flat tire.
3. Our walk through the haunted house gave us such a **fright**.
4. I kicked the soccer ball and scored a **goal**.
5. The **gray** clouds mean rain is coming.
6. Cover your **nose** when you sneeze.
7. We blew a **fuse** at my house last night.

COMPLETE YEAR GRADE 3

281

Week 26 Practice

Review

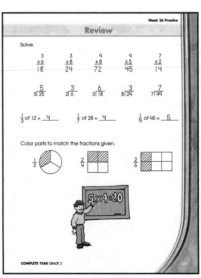

Solve.

$\begin{array}{r} 3 \\ \times 6 \\ \hline 18 \end{array}$ $\begin{array}{r} 3 \\ \times 8 \\ \hline 24 \end{array}$ $\begin{array}{r} 9 \\ \times 8 \\ \hline 72 \end{array}$ $\begin{array}{r} 9 \\ \times 5 \\ \hline 45 \end{array}$ $\begin{array}{r} 7 \\ \times 2 \\ \hline 14 \end{array}$

$5\overline{)25}$ $2\overline{)6}$ $3\overline{)18}$ $8\overline{)24}$ $7\overline{)49}$
5 3 6 3 7

$\frac{1}{3}$ of 12 = **4** $\frac{1}{7}$ of 28 = **4** $\frac{1}{9}$ of 45 = **5**

Color parts to match the fractions given.

$\frac{1}{3}$ $\frac{2}{4}$ $\frac{2}{6}$

COMPLETE YEAR GRADE 3

Answer Key

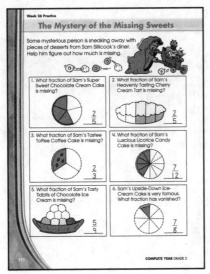

282

283

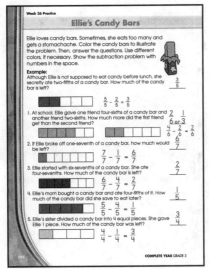

284

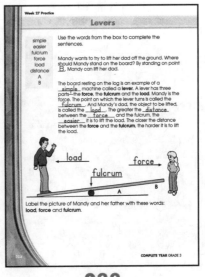

286

287

288

Answer Key

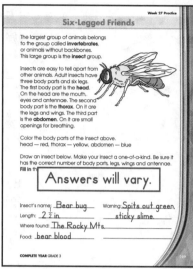

289

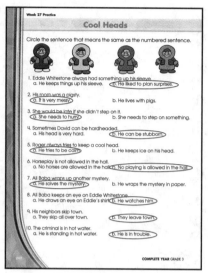

290

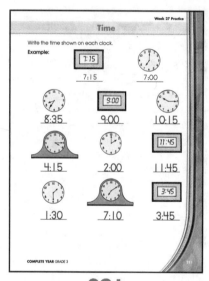

291

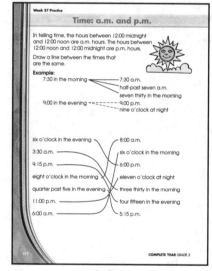

292

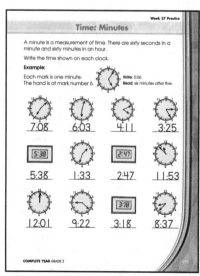

293

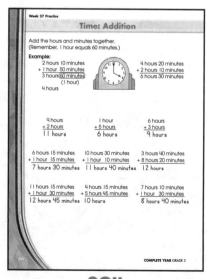

294

Page 300

Sequencing

Read each story. Circle the phrase that tells what happened before.

1. Beth is very happy now that she has someone to play with. She hopes that her new sister will grow up quickly!

   A few days ago . . .
   Beth was sick.
   (Beth's mother had a baby.)
   Beth got a new puppy.

2. Sara tried to mend the tear. She used a needle and thread to sew up the hole.

   While playing, Sara had . . .
   broken her bicycle.
   lost her watch.
   (torn her shirt.)

3. The movers took John's bike off the truck and put it in the garage. Next, they moved his bed into his new bedroom.

   John's family . . .
   (bought a new house.)
   went on vacation.
   bought a new truck.

4. Katie picked out a book about dinosaurs. Jim, who likes sports, chose two books about baseball.

   Katie and Jim . . .
   (went to the library.)
   went to the playground.
   went to the grocery.

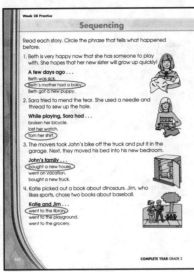

Page 301

Sequencing

Read each story. Circle the sentence that tells what might happen next.

1. Sam and Judy picked up their books and left the house. They walked to the bus stop. They got on a big yellow bus.

   What will Sam and Judy do next?
   (They will go to school.)
   They will visit their grandmother.
   They will go to the store.

2. Maggie and Matt were playing in the snow. They made a snowman with a black hat and scarf. Then, the sun came out.

   What might happen next?
   It will snow again.
   They will play in the sandbox.
   (The snowman will melt.)

3. Megan put on a big floppy hat and funny clothes. She put green make-up on her face.

   What will Megan do next?
   She will go to school.
   (She will go to a costume party.)
   She will go to bed.

4. Mike was eating a hot dog. Suddenly, he smelled smoke. He turned and saw a fire on the stove.

   What will Mike do next?
   He will watch the fire.
   (He will call for help.)
   He will finish his hot dog.

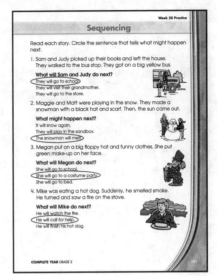

Page 302

Sequencing

Number these sentences from 1 to 5 to show the correct order of the story.

Building a Treehouse

4 They had a beautiful treehouse!
2 They got wood and nails.
1 Jay and Lisa planned to build a treehouse.
5 Now, they like to eat lunch in their treehouse.
3 Lisa and Jay worked in the backyard for three days building the treehouse.

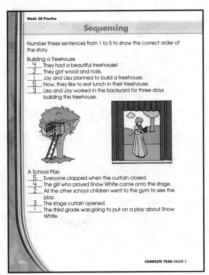

A School Play

5 Everyone clapped when the curtain closed.
4 The girl who played Snow White came onto the stage.
2 All the other school children went to the gym to see the play.
3 The stage curtain opened.
1 The third grade was going to put on a play about Snow White.

Page 303

Sequencing

Number these sentences from 1 to 8 to show the correct order of the story.

4 Jack's father called the family doctor.
8 Jack felt much better as his parents drove him home.
1 Jack woke up in the middle of the night with a terrible pain in his stomach.
5 The doctor told Jack's father to take Jack to the hospital.
2 Jack called his parents to come help him.
7 At the hospital, the doctors examined Jack. They said the problem was not serious. They told Jack's parents that he could go home.
3 Jack's mother took his temperature. He had a fever of 103 degrees.
6 On the way to the hospital, Jack rested in the backseat. He was worried.

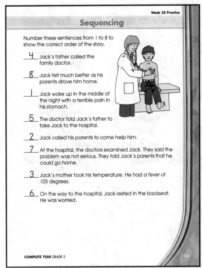

Page 304

Just Swallow It!

Using the diagram, number the sentences in the correct order to show what happens when you swallow a bite of food.

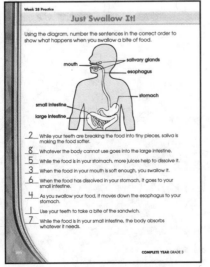

mouth
salivary glands
esophagus
stomach
small intestine
large intestine

2 While your teeth are breaking the food into tiny pieces, saliva is making the food softer.
8 Whatever the body cannot use goes into the large intestine.
5 While the food is in your stomach, more juices help to dissolve it.
3 When the food in your mouth is soft enough, you swallow it.
6 When the food has dissolved in your stomach, it goes to your small intestine.
4 As you swallow your food, it moves down the esophagus to your stomach.
1 Use your teeth to take a bite of the sandwich.
7 While the food is in your small intestine, the body absorbs whatever it needs.

Page 305

Time: Subtraction

Subtract the hours and minutes. (Remember, 1 hour equals 60 minutes.) "Borrow" from the "hours" if you need to.

Example:

```
  5   70
  6 hours 10 minutes
- 2 hours 30 minutes
  3 hours 40 minutes
```

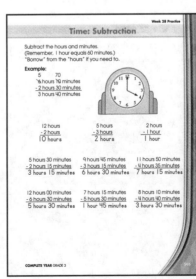

12 hours - 2 hours **10 hours**	5 hours - 3 hours **2 hours**	2 hours - 1 hour **1 hour**
5 hours 30 minutes - 2 hours 15 minutes **3 hours 15 minutes**	9 hours 45 minutes - 3 hours 15 minutes **6 hours 30 minutes**	11 hours 50 minutes - 4 hours 35 minutes **7 hours 15 minutes**
12 hours 00 minutes - 6 hours 30 minutes **5 hours 30 minutes**	7 hours 15 minutes - 5 hours 30 minutes **1 hour 45 minutes**	8 hours 10 minutes - 4 hours 40 minutes **3 hours 30 minutes**

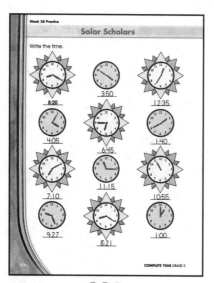

306

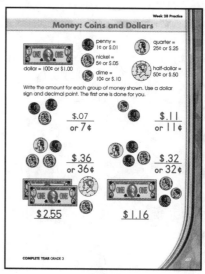

307

308

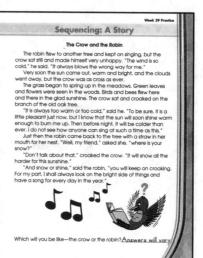

311

312

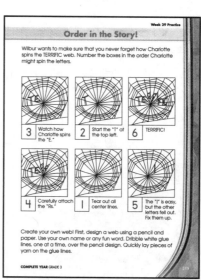

313

Answer Key

Waterworks

Use the diagram to help you number the sentences in the order that tells how water is purified.

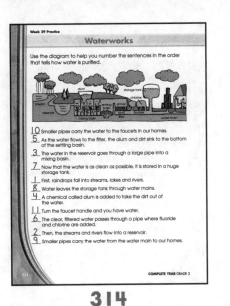

10 Smaller pipes carry the water to the faucets in our homes.

5 As the water flows to the filter, the alum and dirt sink to the bottom of the settling basin.

3 The water in the reservoir goes through a large pipe into a mixing basin.

7 Now that the water is as clean as possible, it is stored in a huge storage tank.

1 First, raindrops fall into streams, lakes and rivers.

8 Water leaves the storage tank through water mains.

4 A chemical called alum is added to take the dirt out of the water.

11 Turn the faucet handle and you have water.

6 The clear, filtered water passes through a pipe where fluoride and chlorine are added.

2 Then, the streams and rivers flow into a reservoir.

9 Smaller pipes carry the water from the water main to our homes.

COMPLETE YEAR GRADE 3

314

Money: Counting Change

Subtract the money using decimals to show how much change a person would receive in each of the following.

Example:
Bill had 3 dollars.
He bought a baseball for $2.83.
How much change did he receive?

$3.00
−$2.83
$0.17

$2.83

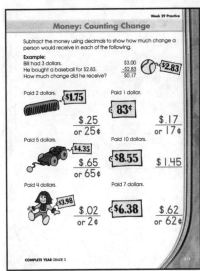

Paid 2 dollars. $1.75 — $.25 or 25¢

Paid 1 dollar. 83¢ — $.17 or 17¢

Paid 5 dollars. $4.35 — $.65 or 65¢

Paid 10 dollars. $8.55 — $1.45

Paid 4 dollars. $3.98 — $.02 or 2¢

Paid 7 dollars. $6.38 — $.62 or 62¢

COMPLETE YEAR GRADE 3

315

Money: Comparing

Compare the amount of money in the left column with the price of the object in the right column. Is the amount of money in the left column enough to purchase the object in the right column? Circle yes or no.

Example:

$1.75

Alice has 2 dollars. She wants to buy a jump rope for $1.75. Does she have enough money? (Yes) No

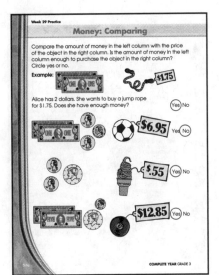

$6.95 Yes (No)

$.55 (Yes) No

$12.85 Yes (No)

COMPLETE YEAR GRADE 3

316

Review

Complete each clock to show the time written below it.

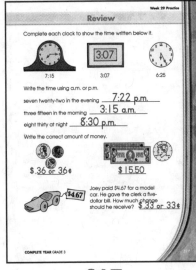

7:15   3:07   6:25

Write the time using a.m. or p.m.

seven twenty-two in the evening 7:22 p.m.

three fifteen in the morning 3:15 a.m.

eight thirty at night 8:30 p.m.

Write the correct amount of money.

$.36 or 36¢ $15.50

Joey paid $4.67 for a model car. He gave the clerk a five-dollar bill. How much change should he receive? $.33 or 33¢

$4.67

COMPLETE YEAR GRADE 3

317

Your Answer's Safe With Me

Find the right "combination" to open each safe. Draw the bills and coins needed to make each amount.

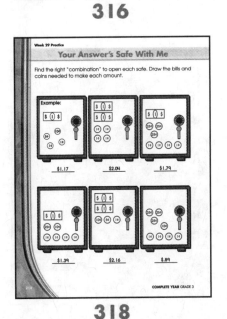

$1.17 $2.04 $1.79

$1.39 $2.16 $.89

COMPLETE YEAR GRADE 3

318

Parts of a Paragraph

A **paragraph** is a group of sentences that all tell about the same thing. Most paragraphs have three parts: a **beginning**, a **middle** and an **end**.

Write **beginning**, **middle** or **end** next to each sentence in the scrambled paragraphs below. There can be more than one middle sentence.

Example:

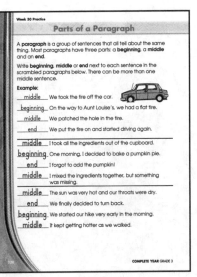

middle   We took the tire off the car.

beginning   On the way to Aunt Louise's, we had a flat tire.

middle   We patched the hole in the tire.

end   We put the tire on and started driving again.

middle   I took all the ingredients out of the cupboard.

beginning   One morning, I decided to bake a pumpkin pie.

end   I forgot to add the pumpkin!

middle   I mixed the ingredients together, but something was missing.

middle   The sun was very hot and our throats were dry.

end   We finally decided to turn back.

beginning   We started our hike very early in the morning.

middle   It kept getting hotter as we walked.

COMPLETE YEAR GRADE 3

320

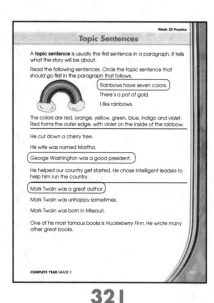

Week 30 Practice

Topic Sentences

A **topic sentence** is usually the first sentence in a paragraph. It tells what the story will be about.

Read the following sentences. Circle the topic sentence that should go first in the paragraph that follows.

(Rainbows have seven colors.)
There's a pot of gold.
I like rainbows.

The colors are red, orange, yellow, green, blue, indigo and violet. Red forms the outer edge, with violet on the inside of the rainbow.

He cut down a cherry tree.
His wife was named Martha.
(George Washington was a good president.)
He helped our country get started. He chose intelligent leaders to help him run the country.

(Mark Twain was a great author.)
Mark Twain was unhappy sometimes.
Mark Twain was born in Missouri.
One of his most famous books is *Huckleberry Finn*. He wrote many other great books.

COMPLETE YEAR GRADE 3

321

Week 30 Practice

Middle Sentences

Middle sentences support the topic sentence. They tell more about it. Underline the middle sentences that support each topic sentence below.

Topic Sentence:
Penguins are birds that cannot fly.
Pelicans can spear fish with their sharp bills.
Many penguins waddle or hop about on land.
Even though they cannot fly, they are excellent swimmers.
Pelicans keep their food in a pouch.

Topic Sentence:
Volleyball is a team sport in which the players hit the ball over the net.
There are two teams with six players on each team.
My friend John would rather play tennis with Lisa.
Players can use their heads or their hands.
I broke my hand once playing handball.

Topic Sentence:
Pikes Peak is the most famous of all the Rocky Mountains.
Some mountains have more trees than other mountains.
Many people like to climb to the top.
Many people like to ski and camp there, too.
The weather is colder at the top of most mountains.

COMPLETE YEAR GRADE 3

322

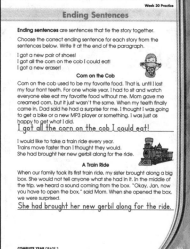

Week 30 Practice

Ending Sentences

Ending sentences are sentences that tie the story together.

Choose the correct ending sentence for each story from the sentences below. Write it at the end of the paragraph.

I got a new pair of shoes!
I got all the corn on the cob I could eat!
I got a new eraser!

Corn on the Cob

Corn on the cob used to be my favorite food. That is, until I lost my four front teeth. For one whole year, I had to sit and watch everyone else eat my favorite food without me. Mom gave me creamed corn, but it just wasn't the same. When my teeth finally came in, Dad said he had a surprise for me. I thought I was going to get a bike or a new MP3 player or something. I was just as happy to get what I did.
I got all the corn on the cob I could eat!

I would like to take a train ride every year.
Trains move faster than I thought they would.
She had brought her new gerbil along for the ride.

A Train Ride

When our family took its first train ride, my sister brought along a big box. She would not tell anyone what she had in it. In the middle of the trip, we heard a sound coming from the box. "Okay, Jan, now you have to open the box," said Mom. When she opened the box, we were surprised.
She had brought her new gerbil along for the ride.

COMPLETE YEAR GRADE 3

323

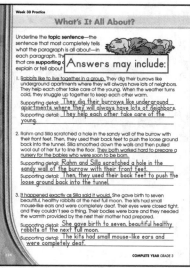

Week 30 Practice

What's It All About?

Underline the **topic sentence**—the sentence that most completely tells what the paragraph is all about—in each paragraph. Th... that are supporting d... explain or tell about...

Answers may include:

1. Rabbits like to live together in a group. They dig their burrows like underground apartments where they will always have lots of neighbors. They help each other take care of the young. When the weather turns cold, they snuggle up together to keep each other warm.
Supporting detail: They dig their burrows like underground apartments where they will always have lots of neighbors.
Supporting detail: They help each other take care of the young.

2. Rahm and Silla scratched a hole in the sandy wall of the burrow with their front feet. Then, they used their back feet to push the loose ground back into the tunnel. Silla smoothed down the walls and then pulled wool out of her fur to line the floor. They both worked hard to prepare a nursery for the babies who were soon to be born.
Supporting detail: Rahm and Silla scratched a hole in the sandy wall of the burrow with their front feet.
Supporting detail: Then, they used their back feet to push the loose ground back into the tunnel.

3. It happened exactly as Silla said it would. She gave birth to seven beautiful, healthy rabbits at the next full moon. The kits had small mouse-like ears and were completely deaf. Their eyes were closed tight, and they couldn't see a thing. Their bodies were bare and they needed the warmth provided by the nest their mother had prepared.
Supporting detail: She gave birth to seven beautiful healthy rabbits at the next full moon.
Supporting detail: The kits had small mouse-like ears and were completely deaf.

COMPLETE YEAR GRADE 3

324

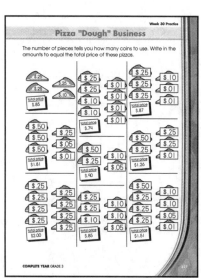

Week 30 Practice

Pizza "Dough" Business

The number of pieces tells you how many coins to use. Write in the amounts to equal the total price of these pizzas.

COMPLETE YEAR GRADE 3

327

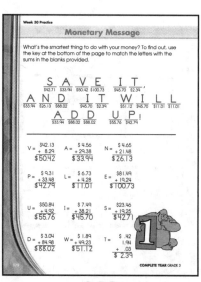

Week 30 Practice

Monetary Message

What's the smartest thing to do with your money? To find out, use the key at the bottom of the page to match the letters with the sums in the blanks provided.

S A V E   I T,
$42.71 $33.94 $50.42 $100.73 $45.70 $2.39

A N D   I T   W I L L
$33.94 $26.13 $88.02 $45.70 $2.34 $51.12 $58.49 $11.01 $11.01

A D D   U P!
$33.94 $88.02 $88.02 $55.76 $42.79

$$V = \begin{array}{r} \$42.13 \\ +\ 8.29 \\ \hline \$50.42 \end{array} \quad A = \begin{array}{r} \$4.56 \\ +\ 29.38 \\ \hline \$33.94 \end{array} \quad N = \begin{array}{r} \$4.65 \\ +\ 21.48 \\ \hline \$26.13 \end{array}$$

$$P = \begin{array}{r} \$9.31 \\ +\ 33.48 \\ \hline \$42.79 \end{array} \quad L = \begin{array}{r} \$6.73 \\ +\ 4.28 \\ \hline \$11.01 \end{array} \quad E = \begin{array}{r} \$81.49 \\ +\ 19.24 \\ \hline \$100.73 \end{array}$$

$$U = \begin{array}{r} \$50.84 \\ +\ 4.92 \\ \hline \$55.76 \end{array} \quad I = \begin{array}{r} \$7.49 \\ +\ 38.21 \\ \hline \$45.70 \end{array} \quad S = \begin{array}{r} \$23.46 \\ +\ 19.25 \\ \hline \$42.71 \end{array}$$

$$D = \begin{array}{r} \$3.04 \\ +\ 84.98 \\ \hline \$88.02 \end{array} \quad W = \begin{array}{r} \$1.89 \\ +\ 49.23 \\ \hline \$51.12 \end{array} \quad T = \begin{array}{r} \$.42 \\ 1.94 \\ +\ .03 \\ \hline \$2.39 \end{array}$$

COMPLETE YEAR GRADE 3

328

Answer Key

Completing a Story

Use verbs to complete the story below. The verbs that tell about things that happened in the past will end in **ed**.

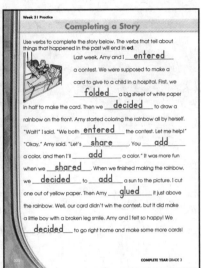

Last week, Amy and I **entered** a contest. We were supposed to make a card to give to a child in a hospital. First, we **folded** a big sheet of white paper in half to make the card. Then we **decided** to draw a rainbow on the front. Amy started coloring the rainbow all by herself. "Wait!" I said. "We both **entered** the contest. Let me help!" "Okay," Amy said. "Let's **share**. You **add** a color, and then I'll **add** a color." It was more fun when we **shared**. When we finished making the rainbow, we **decided** to **add** a sun to the picture. I cut one out of yellow paper. Then Amy **glued** it just above the rainbow. Well, our card didn't win the contest, but it did make a little boy with a broken leg smile. Amy and I felt so happy! We **decided** to go right home and make some more cards!

COMPLETE YEAR GRADE 3

330

It's Major

For each paragraph, circle the sentence that tells the main idea. Underline the sentences with supporting details.

Chapter 1
Just before breakfast one day, Fern saved a pig from being killed and ended up making a new friend. She shouted at her mother and ran outdoors to her father. Though Fern did not understand barnyard life, her father gave her the pig as a pet. She named him Wilbur.

Chapter 2
Fern began caring for Wilbur every day. He would gaze at her with loving eyes as she fed him the bottle. Mr. Arable fixed a special box under an apple tree for Wilbur. Each day Wilbur walked Fern to the bus and stayed in the yard while she was at school.

Chapter 3
Wilbur started to meet other animals in the barnyard. The goose suggested he explore the farm. So he escaped from the barnyard for an afternoon of adventure. He ran, dug up ground and sniffed the afternoon smells. Soon, all the adults on the farm started chasing after Wilbur.

Chapter 5
Charlotte finally introduced herself to Wilbur. She talked to him through his dreams. In the morning, after breakfast, Wilbur located Charlotte. He was eager to know all about her. Wilbur was amazed at how smart Charlotte was.

COMPLETE YEAR GRADE 3

331

Main Idea: Your Lungs

Imagine millions of teeny, tiny balloons joined together. That is what your lungs are like. When you breathe, the air goes to your two lungs. One lung is located on each side of your chest. The heart is located between the two lungs. The lungs are soft, spongy and delicate. That is why there are bones around the lungs. These bones are called the rib cage. The rib cage protects the lungs so they can do their job. The lungs bring oxygen (ox-I-gin) into the body. They also take waste out of the body. This waste is called carbon dioxide. We could not live without our lungs!

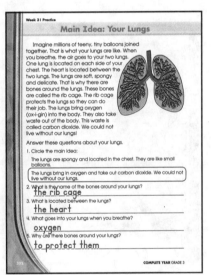

Answer these questions about your lungs.

1. Circle the main idea:
The lungs are spongy and located in the chest. They are like small balloons.
(The lungs bring in oxygen and take out carbon dioxide. We could not live without our lungs.)

2. What is the name of the bones around your lungs?
the rib cage

3. What is located between the lungs?
the heart

4. What goes into your lungs when you breathe?
oxygen

5. Why are there bones around your lungs?
to protect them

COMPLETE YEAR GRADE 3

332

Main Idea: Venus

For many years, no one knew much about Venus. When people looked through telescopes, they could not see past Venus's clouds. Long ago, people thought the clouds covered living things. Spacecraft radar has shown this is not true. Venus is too hot for life as we know it to exist. The temperature on Venus is about 900 degrees! Remember how hot you were the last time it was 90 degrees? Now imagine it being 10 times hotter. Nothing could exist in that heat. It is also very dry on Venus. For life to exist, water must be present. Because of the heat and dryness, we know there are probably no people, plants or other life on Venus.

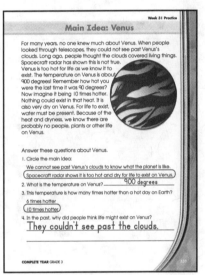

Answer these questions about Venus.

1. Circle the main idea:
We cannot see past Venus's clouds to know what the planet is like.
(Spacecraft radar shows it is too hot and dry for life to exist on Venus.)

2. What is the temperature on Venus? **900 degrees**

3. This temperature is how many times hotter than a hot day on Earth?
6 times hotter
(10 times hotter)

4. In the past, why did people think life might exist on Venus?
They couldn't see past the clouds.

COMPLETE YEAR GRADE 3

333

References — Bat Research

Lucille the bat is always looking up information in reference books because she loves to learn new things. Below is a list of some common references.

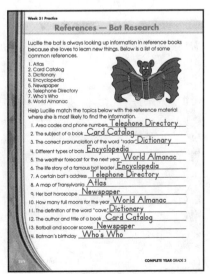

1. Atlas
2. Card Catalog
3. Dictionary
4. Encyclopedia
5. Newspaper
6. Telephone Directory
7. Who's Who
8. World Almanac

Help Lucille match the topics below with the reference material where she is most likely to find the information.

1. Area codes and phone numbers **Telephone Directory**
2. The subject of a book **Card Catalog**
3. The correct pronunciation of the word "radar" **Dictionary**
4. Different types of bats **Encyclopedia**
5. The weather forecast for the next year **World Almanac**
6. The life story of a famous bat leader **Encyclopedia**
7. A certain bat's address **Telephone Directory**
8. A map of Transylvania **Atlas**
9. Her bat horoscope **Newspaper**
10. How many full moons for the year **World Almanac**
11. The definition of the word "cave" **Dictionary**
12. The author and title of a book **Card Catalog**
13. Batball and soccer scores **Newspaper**
14. Batman's birthday **Who's Who**

COMPLETE YEAR GRADE 3

334

Making Change

When you do not have the exact change to buy something at a store, the clerk must give you change. The first amount of money is what you give the clerk. The second amount is what the thing costs. In the box, list the least amount of coins and bills you will receive in change.

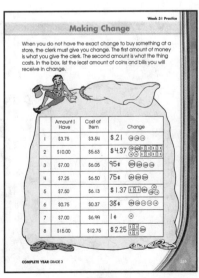

	Amount I Have	Cost of Item	Change
1	$3.75	$3.54	$.21
2	$10.00	$5.63	$4.37
3	$7.00	$6.05	95¢
4	$7.25	$6.50	75¢
5	$7.50	$6.13	$1.37
6	$0.75	$0.37	38¢
7	$7.00	$6.99	1¢
8	$15.00	$12.75	$2.25

COMPLETE YEAR GRADE 3

335

439

Answer Key

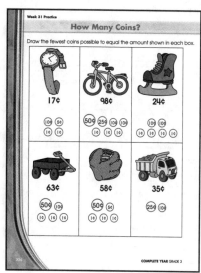

336

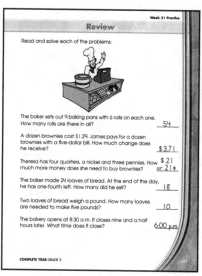

337

338

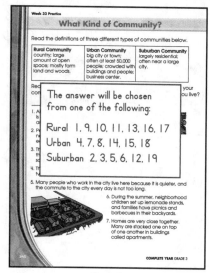

340

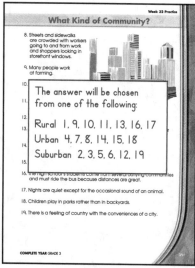

341

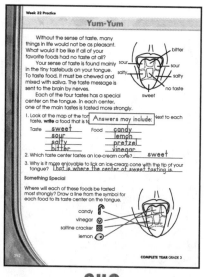

342

Answer Key

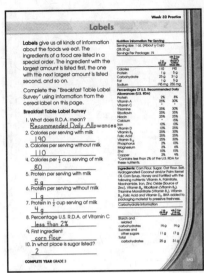

343

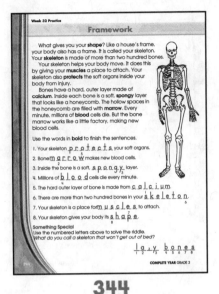

344

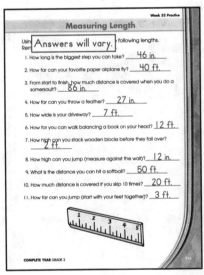

345

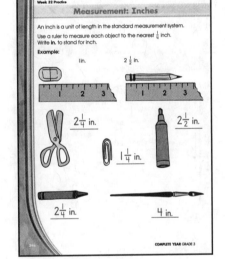

346

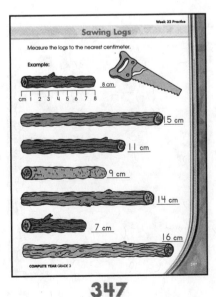

347

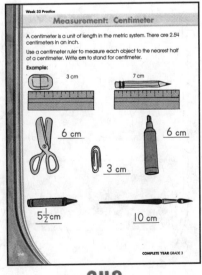

348

Answer Key

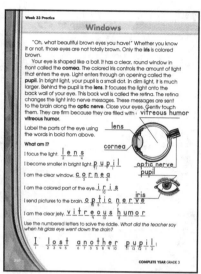

Windows — Week 33 Practice

"Oh, what beautiful brown eyes you have!" Whether you know it or not, those eyes are not totally brown. Only the **iris** is colored brown.

Your eye is shaped like a ball. It has a clear, round window in front called the **cornea**. The colored iris controls the amount of light that enters the eye. Light enters through an opening called the **pupil**. In bright light, your pupil is a small dot. In dim light, it is much larger. Behind the pupil is the **lens**. It focuses the light onto the back wall of your eye. This back wall is called the retina. The retina changes the light into nerve messages. These messages are sent to the brain along the **optic nerve**. Close your eyes. Gently touch them. They are firm because they are filled with **vitreous humor**.

Label the parts of the eye using the words in bold from above.

What am I?

I focus the light. **l e n s**

I become smaller in bright light. **p u p i l**

I am the clear window. **c o r n e a**

I am the colored part of the eye. **i r i s**

I send pictures to the brain. **o p t i c n e r v e**

I am the clear jelly. **v i t r e o u s h u m o r**

Use the numbered letters to solve the riddle. What did the teacher say when his glass eye went down the drain?

I l o s t a n o t h e r p u p i l

Labels: lens, cornea, optic nerve, pupil, iris, vitreous humor

COMPLETE YEAR GRADE 3

350

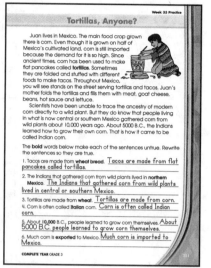

Tortillas, Anyone? — Week 33 Practice

Juan lives in Mexico. The main food crop grown there is corn. Even though it is grown on half of Mexico's cultivated land, corn is still imported because the demand for it is so high. Since ancient times, corn has been used to make flat pancakes called **tortillas**. Sometimes they are folded and stuffed with different foods to make tacos. Throughout Mexico, you will see stands on the street serving tortillas and tacos. Juan's mother folds the tortillas and fills them with meat, goat cheese, beans, hot sauce and lettuce.

Scientists have been unable to trace the ancestry of modern corn directly to a wild plant. But they do know that people living in what is now central or southern Mexico gathered corn from wild plants about 10,000 years ago. About 5000 B.C., the Indians learned how to grow their own corn. That is how it came to be called Indian corn.

The **bold** words below make each of the sentences untrue. Rewrite the sentences so they are true.

1. Tacos are made from **wheat bread**. Tacos are made from flat pancakes called tortillas.

2. The Indians that gathered corn from wild plants lived in **northern Mexico**. The Indians that gathered corn from wild plants lived in central or southern Mexico.

3. Tortillas are made from **wheat**. Tortillas are made from corn.

4. Corn is often called **Italian** corn. Corn is often called Indian corn.

5. About **10,000** B.C., people learned to grow corn themselves. About 5000 B.C. people learned to grow corn themselves.

6. Much corn is **exported** to Mexico. Much corn is imported to Mexico.

COMPLETE YEAR GRADE 3

351

Life in the Village

Juan's house is made of clay. The clay was mixed together with straw and water and shaped into bricks. His roof is made of red tiles that are sloped to let the rain run off easily.

In the back of Juan's house is a shady patio. It has a wall around it to form a courtyard. At night, the cow and burro join the chickens and turkeys there.

The house has a hard-packed dirt floor. Juan's mother or father builds a cooking fire on the floor. It is built near the door so that the smoke can go out the door and windows on either side of the door. That is where Juan's mother makes the tortillas that he loves. It is 10-year-old Maria's job to sweep the floor and bring cool water to drink from the village fountain. She helps her mother wash the family's clothes in the river.

Juan helps his father make the clay animals to sell at the village market during fiestas. Some day Juan wants to be a potter like his father. Juan has already sold some vases at the market.

Draw a picture of Juan's house and yard below. Reread the paragraphs above to include as much detail as possible. When you draw the front door, draw what you can see inside of it.

Answers will vary.

COMPLETE YEAR GRADE 3

352

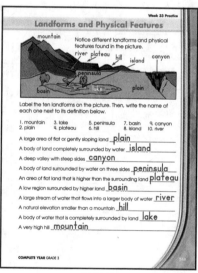

Landforms and Physical Features — Week 33 Practice

Notice different landforms and physical features found in the picture.

Labels: mountain, river, plateau, hill, island, canyon, peninsula, basin, lake, plain

Label the ten landforms on the picture. Then, write the name of each one next to its definition below.

1. mountain   3. lake   5. peninsula   7. basin   9. canyon
2. plain   4. plateau   6. hill   8. island   10. river

A large area of flat or gently sloping land **plain**

A body of land completely surrounded by water **island**

A deep valley with steep sides **canyon**

A body of land surrounded by water on three sides **peninsula**

An area of flat land that is higher than the surrounding land **plateau**

A low region surrounded by higher land **basin**

A large stream of water that flows into a larger body of water **river**

A natural elevation smaller than a mountain **hill**

A body of water that is completely surrounded by land **lake**

A very high hill **mountain**

COMPLETE YEAR GRADE 3

353

Nature's Creations — Week 33 Practice

Match each formation with its definition by writing a number in each blank.

8 river
4 bay
2 island
11 gulf
1 mountain
9 plain
6 lake
3 peninsula
7 valley
5 volcano
10 ocean

1. Land rising high above the land around it.
2. Land surrounded completely by water.
3. Piece of land surrounded by water on all but one side.
4. Inlet of a large body of water that extends into the land; smaller than a gulf.
5. Earth opening that spills lava, rock and gases.
6. Large inland body of water.
7. Lowland between hills or mountains.
8. Long narrow body of water.
9. Large area of flat grasslands.
10. Vast body of salt water.
11. Large area of a sea or ocean partially enclosed by land.

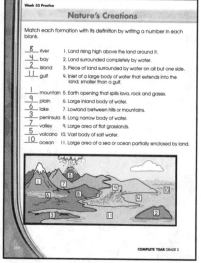

COMPLETE YEAR GRADE 3

354

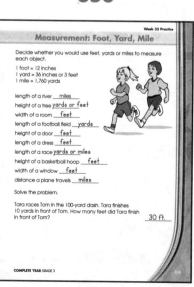

Measurement: Foot, Yard, Mile — Week 33 Practice

Decide whether you would use feet, yards or miles to measure each object.

1 foot = 12 inches
1 yard = 36 inches or 3 feet
1 mile = 1,760 yards

length of a river **miles**

height of a tree **yards or feet**

width of a room **feet**

length of a football field **yards**

height of a door **feet**

length of a dress **feet**

length of a race **yards or miles**

height of a basketball hoop **feet**

width of a window **feet**

distance a plane travels **miles**

Solve the problem.

Tara races Tom in the 100-yard dash. Tara finishes 10 yards in front of Tom. How many feet did Tara finish in front of Tom? **30 ft.**

COMPLETE YEAR GRADE 3

355

Answer Key

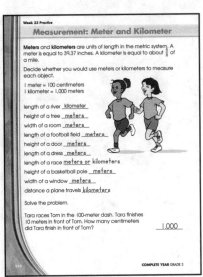

356

Week 33 Practice

Measurement: Meter and Kilometer

Meters and **kilometers** are units of length in the metric system. A meter is equal to 39.37 inches. A kilometer is equal to about ⅝ of a mile.

Decide whether you would use meters or kilometers to measure each object.

1 meter = 100 centimeters
1 kilometer = 1,000 meters

length of a river __kilometer__
height of a tree __meters__
width of a room __meters__
length of a football field __meters__
height of a door __meters__
length of a dress __meters__
length of a race __meters or__ kilometers
height of a basketball pole __meters__
width of a window __meters__
distance a plane travels __kilometers__

Solve the problem.

Tara races Tom in the 100-meter dash. Tara finishes 10 meters in front of Tom. How many centimeters did Tara finish in front of Tom? __1,000__

COMPLETE YEAR GRADE 3

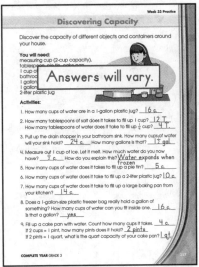

357

Week 33 Practice

Discovering Capacity

Discover the capacity of different objects and containers around your house.

You will need:
measuring cup (2-cup capacity),
tablespoon, pie tin, cake pan
1 cup of water
bathroom sink
1 gallon plastic jug
1 gallon freezer bag
2-liter plastic jug

Answers will vary.

Activities:

1. How many cups of water are in a 1-gallon plastic jug? __16 c__
2. How many tablespoons of salt does it takes to fill up 1 cup? __12 T__
   How many tablespoons of water does it take to fill up ¼ cup? __4 T__
3. Pull up the drain stopper in your bathroom sink. How many cups of water will your sink hold? __24 c__ How many gallons is that? __1½ gal__
4. Measure out 1 cup of ice. Let it melt. How much water do you now have? __⅞ c__ How do you explain this? __Water expands when frozen__
5. How many cups of water does it takes to fill up a pie tin? __5 c__
6. How many cups of water does it take to fill up a 2-liter plastic jug? __10 c__
7. How many cups of water does it take to fill up a large baking pan from your kitchen? __14 c__
8. Does a 1-gallon-size plastic freezer bag really hold a gallon of something? How many cups of water can you fit inside one. __16 c__
   Is that a gallon? __yes__
9. Fill up a cake pan with water. Count how many cups it takes. __4 c__
   If 2 cups = 1 pint, how many pints does it hold? __2 pints__
   If 2 pints = 1 quart, what is the quart capacity of your cake pan? __1 qt__

COMPLETE YEAR GRADE 3

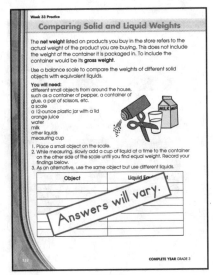

358

Week 33 Practice

Comparing Solid and Liquid Weights

The **net weight** listed on products you buy in the store refers to the actual weight of the product you are buying. This does not include the weight of the container it is packaged in. To include the container would be its **gross weight**.

Use a balance scale to compare the weights of different solid objects with equivalent liquids.

You will need:
different small objects from around the house, such as a container of pepper, a container of glue, a pair of scissors, etc.
a scale
a 12-ounce plastic jar with a lid
orange juice
water
milk
other liquids
measuring cup

1. Place a small object on the scale.
2. While measuring, slowly add a cup of liquid at a time to the container on the other side of the scale until you find equal weight. Record your findings below.
3. As an alternative, use the same object but use different liquids.

Object	Liquid Equivalent

Answers will vary.

COMPLETE YEAR GRADE 3

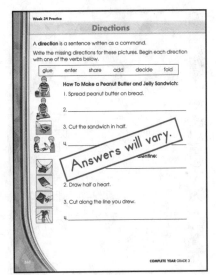

360

Week 34 Practice

Directions

A **direction** is a sentence written as a command.

Write the missing directions for these pictures. Begin each direction with one of the verbs below.

glue	enter	share	add	decide	fold

How To Make a Peanut Butter and Jelly Sandwich:

1. Spread peanut butter on bread.
2. _____
3. Cut the sandwich in half.
4. _____

Answers will vary.

... valentine:

_____

2. Draw half a heart.
3. Cut along the line you drew.
4. _____

COMPLETE YEAR GRADE 3

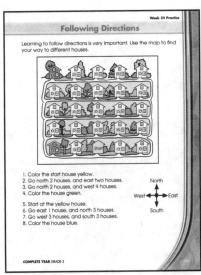

361

Week 34 Practice

Following Directions

Learning to follow directions is very important. Use the map to find your way to different houses.

1. Color the start house yellow.
2. Go north 2 houses, and east two houses.
3. Go north 2 houses, and west 4 houses.
4. Color the house green.

5. Start at the yellow house.
6. Go east 1 house, and north 3 houses.
7. Go west 3 houses, and south 3 houses.
8. Color the house blue.

North
West — East
South

COMPLETE YEAR GRADE 3

362

Week 34 Practice

Following Directions

Read each sentence and do what it says to do.

1. Count the syllables in each word. Write the number on the line by the word.
2. Draw a line between the two words in each compound word.
3. Draw a circle around each name of a month.
4. Draw a box around each food word.
5. Draw an **X** on each noise word.
6. Draw a line under each day of the week.
7. Write the three words from the list you did not mark. Draw a picture of each of those words.

2 April	4 vegetable	3 tablecloth
1 bang	1 June	1 meat
2 sidewalk	3 Saturday	1 crash
3 astronaut	1 March	1 jingle
1 moon	2 cardboard	2 rocket
2 Friday	1 fruit	2 Monday

moon   astronaut   rocket

Drawings will vary.

COMPLETE YEAR GRADE 3

364

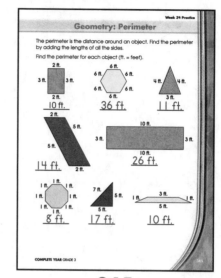

365

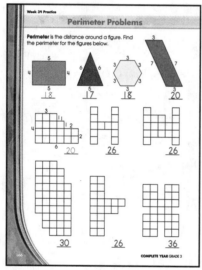

366

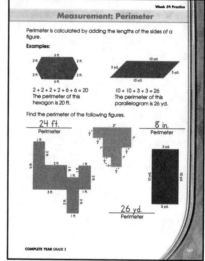

367

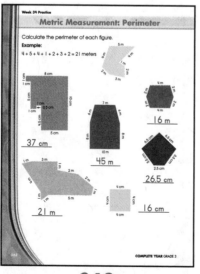

368

370

Answer Key

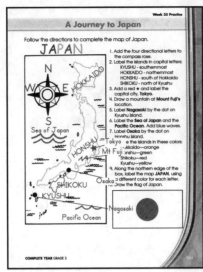

371

372

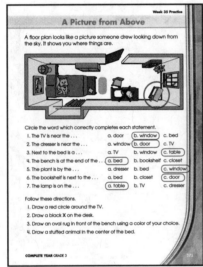

373

A Picture from Above

A floor plan looks like a picture someone drew looking down from the sky. It shows you where things are.

Circle the word which correctly completes each statement.

1. The TV is near the . . .   a. door   **b. window**   c. bed
2. The dresser is near the . . .   a. window   **b. door**   c. TV
3. Next to the bed is a . . .   a. TV   b. window   **c. table**
4. The bench is at the end of the . . .   **a. bed**   b. bookshelf   c. closet
5. The plant is by the . . .   a. dresser   b. bed   **c. window**
6. The bookshelf is next to the . . .   a. bed   b. closet   **c. door**
7. The lamp is on the . . .   **a. table**   b. TV   c. dresser

Follow these directions.
1. Draw a red circle around the TV.
2. Draw a black **X** on the desk.
3. Draw an oval rug in front of the bench using a color of your choice.
4. Draw a stuffed animal in the center of the bed.

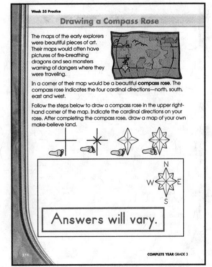

374

A Square Activity

Area is the number of square units contained in a surface. Find the area by counting the square units.

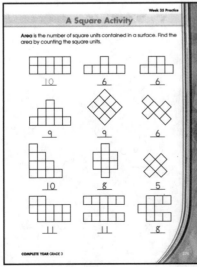

10   6   6

9   9   6

10   8   5

11   11   8

375

Measurement: Perimeter and Area

Perimeter is the distance around a figure. It is found by adding the lengths of the sides. **Area** is the number of square units needed to cover a region. The area is found by adding the number of square units. A unit can be any unit of measure. Most often, inches, feet or yards are used.

Find the perimeter and area for each figure. The first one is done for you.   □ = 1 square unit

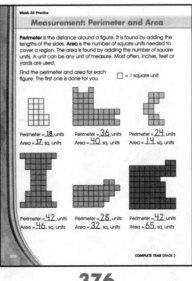

Perimeter = 18 units   Perimeter = 36 units   Perimeter = 24 units
Area = 17 sq. units   Area = 40 sq. units   Area = 14 sq. units

Perimeter = 42 units   Perimeter = 28 units   Perimeter = 42 units
Area = 46 sq. units   Area = 32 sq. units   Area = 65 sq. units

376

Answer Key

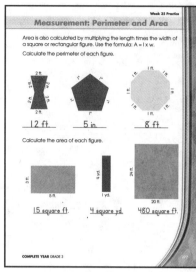

377

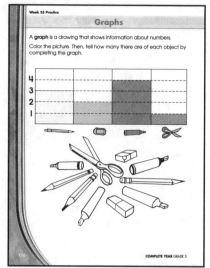

378

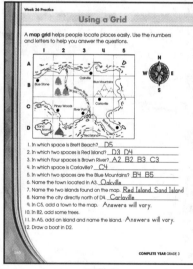

380

Connect-A-Dot

Week 36 Practice

Follow these directions to complete a drawing. Begin at the star. The first two steps are done for you.

Draw a straight line . . .
1. Five spaces west.
2. Two spaces south.
3. Four spaces east.
4. Nine spaces south.
5. Two spaces east.

6. Nine spaces north.
7. Four spaces east.
8. Two spaces north.
9. Five spaces west.
What letter did you draw? T

Begin at the circle to complete another drawing.

Draw a straight line . . .
1. Four spaces south.
2. One space west.
3. Three spaces north.

4. One space west.
5. One space north.
6. Two spaces east.
What number did you draw? 7

COMPLETE YEAR GRADE 3

381

Answer Key

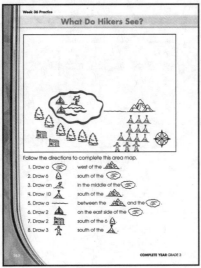

382

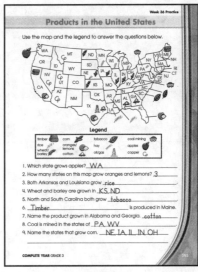

383

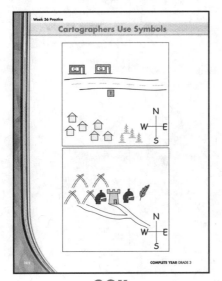

384

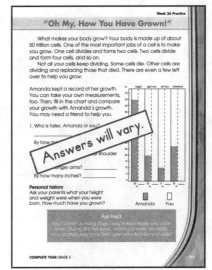

385

Answer Key

386

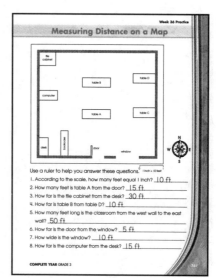

387

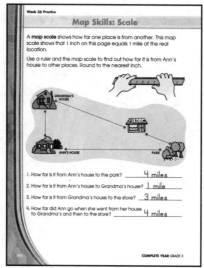

388